Histories of Art And Design Education: Collected Essays

Edited by Mervyn Romans

Series editor: John Steers

intellect™
Bristol, UK
Portland, OR, USA

First Published in the UK in 2005 by
Intellect Books, PO Box 862, Bristol BS99 1DE, UK
First Published in the USA in 2005 by
Intellect Books, ISBS, 920 NE 58th Ave. Suite 300, Portland, Oregon 97213-3786, USA

A catalogue record for this book is available from the British Library

ISBN 1-84150-131-X
ISSN 1747-6208
Cover Design: Gabriel Solomons
Copy Editor: Julie Strudwick

Printed and bound by The Cromwell Press, Trowbridge, Wiltshire

Contents

Section Four: Towards Art Education as a Profession

Section Five: Pivotal Figures in Art and Design Education History

Section Six: British/European Influence in Art and Design Education Abroad

Preface

This book is the second in a planned series of anthologies dealing with a range of issues in art and design education. The first to be published addresses issues surrounding critical and contextual studies: other titles in preparation include assessment and evaluation and postmodernism. The primary – but not exclusive – source of chapters are papers previously published in the [*International*] *Journal of Art & Design Education* and where appropriate these have been updated.

The *National Society for Education in Art and Design* is the leading national authority in the United Kingdom, combining professional association and trade union functions, which represents every facet of art, craft and design in education. Its authority is partly based upon a century-long concern for the subject, established contacts within government and local authority departments, and a breadth of membership drawn from every sector of education from the primary school to universities. More information is available at www.nsead.org or from NSEAD, The Gatehouse, Corsham Court, Corsham, Wiltshire SN13 0BZ (Tel: 01249 714825).

John Steers, Series editor

Notes on Authors

Graeme Chalmers

Graeme Chalmers is Professor of Art Education and Director of the Centre for Cross-Faculty Inquiry in Education at the University of British Columbia. He writes widely on the socio-cultural and historical foundations of art education, with a particular interest in the nineteenth century. Recent work includes a biography of Walter Smith (NAEA, 2000); art education in nineteenth century Canada in a mechanics' institute, elite boys' school, and a convent; the study of nineteenth century father and son drawing masters at Winchester College and Upper Canada College (Toronto); and a chapter 'Learning from Histories of Art Education' in Eisner and Day's (2004) *Handbook of Research and Policy in Art Education*, Erlbaum & NAEA.

Rafael Cardoso

Rafael Cardoso, Ph.D. (Courtauld Institute of Art, 1995) is presently assistant professor at the Pontificia Universidade Catolica, Rio de Janeiro, Brazil. Major publications include *Art and the Academy in the Nineteenth Century* (Manchester UP & Rutgers UP), *O Design Brasileiro antes do Design* (Cosac Naify) and the design history textbook *Uma Introduçao a Historia do Design* (Edgard Blucher), as well as numerous articles on the histories of art and design. He is also the author of two novels in Portuguese and a regular contributor to the Brazilian press.

Ray Haslam

Ray Haslam is Adjunct Professor within the Ruskin Programme at Lancaster University and Honorary Research Fellow at St Martin's College Lancaster where he was formerly Professor of Art Education and Head of the Department of Art, Design, and Technology. His more recent publications include 'Ruskin and the Tradition of Architectural Illustration' in Wheeler, M. and Whiteley, L. (1992) (Eds.), *The Lamp of Memory: Ruskin Tradition and Architecture*, MUP; 'According to the requirements of his scholars': Ruskin, Drawing and Art Education' in Robert Hewison (2000) (Ed.), *Ruskin's Artists: Studies in the Victorian Visual Economy*, Ashgate; and 'The Venetian Notebooks: Some work in Progress' in *The Companion: The Journal of the Guild of St George*, 1: 3, Autumn/Winter 2003. He was Consultant Editor (Annotations) for 'The Ruskin Programme Electronic Edition of John Ruskin's *Modern Painters* Vol. 1'http://www.lancs.ac./users/Ruskin /empi/index.html (2003) and is currently joint editor of an AHRB funded hypertext project entitled, 'Ruskin's Venetian Notebooks: Reconstructing the Research Methods and Compositional Practices for *The Stones of Venice*'.

Bruce Holdsworth

Bruce Holdsworth MA, M.Phil. has had a distinguished career in art education. He taught in schools in Manchester and trained teachers for the University of

Manchester for many years. He has been a regular contributor to the *International Journal of Art and Design Education* and was a member of the Editorial Board. His collection of working books and papers is held at the National Art Education Archive at Leeds University. He is the owner of bruceholdsworthbooks.com, which specialises in books on British Art and Design and related subjects, and is a practicing painter.

Diana Korzenik

Diana Korzenik, Professor Emerita of Massachusetts College of Art, Boston, Massachusetts, USA served more than a decade as Chairperson of its Department of Art Education. She co-authored – with Maurice Brown – Getty-commissioned *Artmaking and Education*, (University of Illinois Press, 1993) and co-edited with Caroline Sloat and Georgia Barnhill *The Cultivation of American Artists in the Nineteenth Century* (Oak Knoll Press with American Antiquarian Society, 1997). Dr Korzenik's research is largely based upon ephemera – original documents, sales publicity, how-to-draw books, and surviving child art from the nineteenth century. Her first book *Drawn to Art* (University Press of New England, Fall 1985) won the 1986 Boston Globe L.L. Winship Literary Award. It documented nineteenth century art education's shift from informal private teaching to institutionalized, government support. Throughout her years of teaching about American art education history Dr Korzenik gathered a collection now donated to The Huntington Library and documented in Korzenik's *The Objects of Art Education,* (Huntington Library Press 2004). She was a founding member of Harvard Project Zero and contributing author to the project book, *Arts and Cognition.* She also founded and served as first president of The Friends of Longfellow House, an advocacy and preservationist group. Dr Korzenik earned her doctorate at Harvard in 1972.

Akio Okazaki

Akio Okazaki is Associate Professor of Art Education at the University of Tsukuba, in Japan. He received his B.Ed. degree from Kochi University in 1975, and his M.Ed. from Osaka Kyoiku University in 1979, and his Ph.D. in art from the University of Tsukuba in 1996. He was a teacher of art at a junior high school in Kobe, 1975–77, and has taught art education in both undergraduate and postgraduate programmes at Utsunomiya University and the University of Tsukuba since 1980. His special scholarly interest is in the History of American and European art education and its influences on the education of the Japanese. His articles have been published in the *Journal of Multi-cultural and Cross-cultural Research in Art Education, Art Education* and *The History of Art Education: Proceedings of the Penn State Conference* (1985, 1992, 1997), The *International Journal of Art and Design Education, Trends in Art Education from Diverse Cultures,* and *Journal of Aesthetic Education.* He has presented papers at the InSEA World Congresses (1999, 2002). He was a world council member of InSEA (1999–2002), one of the keynote speakers at the First Asian–Pacific Art Education

Conference in Hong Kong in 2000, and co-editor of 'Symposium: Aesthetic Education in Japan Today' in the Winter 2003 issue of *Journal of Aesthetic Education*.

Mervyn Romans

Mervyn Romans has worked in secondary and teacher education and then in further and higher education in art and design, and was for a number of years Head of Art and Design at Bedford College of Higher Education. He completed his doctorate in 1998 and currently teaches histories of art and education to Masters students at the Birmingham Institute of Art and Design, University of Central England. In addition he undertakes consultancy projects in art and design education for a number of organisations. A past member of the editorial board of the *International Journal of Art and Design Education* and its Reviews Editor, he is actively engaged in research and publishing in the field of nineteenth century art and design education.

John Steers

John Steers became General Secretary of what is now the NSEAD in 1981 after fourteen years teaching art and design in secondary schools. He was the 1993–96 President of the International Society for Education through Art and has been a member of its executive committee in several capacities. He has served on national committees and as a consultant to government agencies. He completed a Ph.D. at the University of Liverpool in 1994 and has published widely on curriculum, assessment and policy issues. He is a trustee of the Higher Education in Art and Design Trust and the Chair of the National Arts Education Archive Trust: Bretton Hall. He is also a visiting Senior Research Fellow at Roehampton University, London.

John Swift

John Swift is Emeritus Professor of Art Education, University of Central England in Birmingham. Until his retirement from UCE in 2001 he was Professor of Art Education, chief editor of ARTicle Press, Principal Editor of the *International Journal of Art and Design Education* for the National Society for Education in Art and Design, MA Art & Education Course Director and Keeper of the Archives. His interest in the history, theory and practice of art education is evident in many publications and conference presentations both here and abroad, and in his supervision and examination of masters and doctoral students. Since retirement to South West Scotland he has written *An Illustrated History of Moseley School of Art: Art Education in Birmingham 1800-1975*, and with his wife begun a local publishing house, 'an machair press', and opened a gallery showing their respective work.

David Thistlewood

David Thistlewood was Reader in Architecture at the University of Liverpool until his untimely death in 1998. He was a Past President (1990–1992) of the NSEAD and editor of the *International Journal of Art and Design Education* from 1986–1993. His publications on Herbert Read include the critical biography *Herbert Read: Formlessness and Form* (Routledge & Kegan Paul, 1984) and the memorial exhibition catalogue (edited with Benedict Read) commemorating the centenary of Read's birth *A British Vision of Modernism* (Lund Humphries, 1993).

Richard Yeomans

Richard Yeomans studied Fine Art at Newcastle University, took his MA in Art Education at Birmingham Polytechnic and his Doctorate at the Institute of Education, London University. He is a painter and art historian, and author of *The Story of Islamic Architecture* and *The Art and Architecture of Islamic Cairo: 641–1517.* Formerly a Senior Lecturer at the Institute of Education, University of Warwick, he is now retired, painting full-time and working as an independent scholar.

Introduction: Rethinking Art and Design Education Histories

Mervyn Romans

A little over a decade ago the NSEAD in conjunction with the publisher Longman produced a book with a very similar title to this one. *Histories of Art and Design Education: Cole to Coldstream* was a collection of essays by British and North American authors dealing with a highly diverse set of topics and, as the title implies, covering a lengthy time span. There is therefore an element of intention in the similarity of titles, in that this book too has those features; indeed a number of the authors who contributed to the earlier volume also have work included here. Although the authorship in this book is principally British, contributions also come from as far afield as North and South America and Japan. A secondary reason for the similarity is to foster a sense of continuity where, in Britain, books dealing with histories of art and design education remain something of a rarity.

The chapters in this collection are, with two exceptions, drawn from articles previously published in the *International Journal of Art and Design Education (iJADE)* over the last ten years, and they are therefore highly representative of research in the field during that period. The subjects covered are, at first sight, diverse but they are brought together here under section headings that propose a structured division of interests. This has emerged from the progressive maturation of research in the field of art and design education history over the past decade. These headings are intended to help the reader navigate their way through the book, but also to indicate a further evolutionary growth of the discipline evident in journals like *iJADE*.

Whereas 30 years ago it was sufficient, perhaps, to title a publication with some variant of 'the history of art and design education', now historians of the field have generally adopted a more relativist position. Hence, the book that David Thistlewood edited was deliberately titled *Histories of Art and Design Education: Cole to Coldstream*, rather than 'The history of Art and Design Education: Cole to Coldstream'. Here too the emphasis is on 'histories' rather than 'the history'. Rethinking the history of art and design education necessitates an on-going re-evaluation of our historiography. There is nothing new in this statement, it should be emphasised. The case for revisionism has periodically been made over the past twenty years, most significantly at the two Penn State Conferences on the subject in 1985 and 1989. At the 1985 conference Donald Soucy in his 'Approaches to Historical Writing: Their Limits and Potentialities', and Karen Hamblen in her

'Historical Research in Art Education: A Process of Selection and Interpretation' both illuminated the gulf that existed between historical writing in general (where alternative theoretical models had been implicit for much of the previous century), and that of art and design education in particular. In the 1989 conference there were three papers concerned with historiography. Hamblen returned to the subject with her 'Shifting Historical Interpretations', and Soucy also returned to his revisionist theme, observing the determination in art education historians to examine socio-political questions and 'go beyond mere chronological listing of uncontextualised art education ideas'. In the third of these papers, by Elliot Eisner, the readiness of historians of art and design education to engage in this complex of debates had at that time, as he made clear, been disappointingly slight. Indeed Eisner's paper entitled 'The Efflorescence of the History of Art Education – Advance into the Past or Retreat from the Present' made the then position clear. He stated – 'As far as I know we have yet to see a powerful revisionist social history of American art education.' And of Britain he said, 'I know of no such work on the English scene.'

Happily, since these two conferences a number of historians have responded positively to these calls for a rethinking of approaches to writing art and design education history. On both sides of the Atlantic the discipline has developed significantly. This collection of essays represents a further contribution to that response.

The first section 'Drawing from examples' comprises two essays concerned with nineteenth century publications to teach drawing in Britain and America. Rafael Cardoso examines the development of publications to teach drawing in Britain during the middle of the nineteenth century. As printing costs were reduced and literacy rates rose these books were instrumental in democratizing art education in the nineteenth century. Where once only the rich could afford to employ a drawing master, as the century progressed more and more of these 'How-to-do-it' books became available at lower and lower prices, often directed at people of humble means. Cardoso sees in these books a number of common threads including the view that drawing had an important role to play in the moral education of (particularly) the 'lower orders'. That he also notes the perceived importance in these books of hand and eye training, chimes with the second essay in this section. Diana Korzenik looks at these 'How to Draw' books on the other side of the Atlantic. Based upon her impressive collection of some 500 books and a thousand pieces of art education related ephemera (now housed in the Huntingdon Library in Pasadena, California), she seeks to discover why it was that nineteenth century Americans placed so much importance on learning to draw. While their British counterparts emphasized moral imperatives – it was the Reverend St John Tyrwhitt who suggested 'that teaching children good drawing, is practically teaching them to be good children' – for American settlers and their children, Korzenik argues, it involved a more fundamental life or death struggle in successful farming practice and home-building skills. Placing these two essays side by side reinforces the powerful impact that drawing books have had on art and design education, and Cardoso's declaration that his motivation in writing this paper was to 'encourage more extensive research in the field' will hopefully be realised. Certainly, public access to Diana Korzenik's collection represents a real opportunity for researchers.

The second section 'Motives and rationales for public art and design education in Britain' sets out to challenge a number of accepted orthodoxies of art and design education history, and to locate the subject within a wider nineteenth century historical perspective. In a recent essay ('Living in the Past: Some Revisionist Thoughts on the Historiography of Art and Design Education' *iJADE* 23: 3) I have challenged the often-repeated economic rationale for the introduction of art and design education in Britain in 1837. In both of the essays in this section I look afresh at the primary source material for this important event; the Minutes of Evidence and Report from the 1835/6 Select Committee on Arts and Manufactures. In the first essay I foreground 'taste' as the predominant theme of the evidence rather than the economic concerns that have dominated earlier interpretation. 'Taste', and the realisation of a 'national taste' was an endlessly recurring theme in this select committee, which in turn had both a socio-political and a subliminal economic dimension. By looking at the evidence given to the select committee in 1835/6 through this lens I attempt to reveal alternative explanations for the introduction of a system of public art and design education into Britain in the 1830s. In the second essay I am concerned with the issue of social class. In earlier histories of art and design education the relevant social groups are often rather casually ascribed to either the working class or middle class. My concern in this essay is to apply the work on social class conducted in the wider community of social historians to the particular instance of the evidence given to the 1835/6 Select Committee on Arts and Manufactures. I am particularly concerned with the social interactions identified elsewhere between the working class, the artisan and the middle class, and find important parallels in the evidence given to this select committee that illuminates our understanding of these issues.

All of this is brought into sharper focus in section three 'Features of institutional art and design education'. In his former role as Head of the School of Art Education and keeper of the School of Art Archives at the University of Central England, John Swift carried out exhaustive research on art and design education in Birmingham. His recent book *An Illustrated History of Moseley School of Art: Art Education in Birmingham 1800-1975* has added greatly to our historical understanding of art and design education in this key centre. The first of his two essays on the Birmingham School of Art during the nineteenth and early twentieth century that form this section, looks at the evolution of art and design education in Birmingham from 1800–1921. It challenges the accepted wisdom that during this period London totally dominated and controlled a growing number of submissive art education establishments across the country. The presence of an unusually substantial archive at Birmingham provided the evidence to question this interpretation. Swift reveals that despite an organisation in London that was centralist and controlling in its outlook, Birmingham (perhaps alone in this respect – there are too few archives to generalise) was progressively proactive in determining its future. The tensions that existed between the evolving educational philosophies at the Birmingham Art School, the powerful and influential in the city, and government agencies in London are explored here, illustrating how it was that towards the end of the nineteenth century opportunities for autonomy increased, resulting in Birmingham's singular influence on the art and design education of the time. His second essay examines the place of women at the Birmingham Art School in the late nineteenth and early twentieth century. Birmingham's pioneering of arts and crafts educational philosophy and the notion of executed design (where students realised their ideas in the actual material) was entirely novel in Schools of Art. Female students at Birmingham were enthusiastic and successful beneficiaries of this development. For a short time the success that women enjoyed in competitions far exceeded their male counterparts at a time when 'women', 'artist', 'lady' and 'work' had very particular social connotations. Swift shows how it was that despite this success at Birmingham, gender stereotyping proved to be the ultimate stumbling block.

The 40-year period at Birmingham's art school that Swift deals with begins under the headship of Edward R. Taylor. Taylor also features prominently in the opening of the stories told in section four 'Towards art education as a profession'. The two essays that comprise this section look at the national and international 'professionalisation' of art and design education. In the first, by the late David Thistlewood, the early history of the National Society for Education in Art and Design (NSEAD) is traced from its origins in 1888 (this paper was written in 1988, the centenary year of the NSEAD) when Taylor brought together some 60 of his colleagues from around the country to form the Society of Art Masters. The origins of the ongoing battle that public art and design education has been forced to wage to secure recognition of its value to society can be found here, not least in the efforts to secure academic parity with other disciplines. Thistlewood documents the 'highs' and 'lows' of this first professional organisation for art educators and its successor the National Society of Art Masters (NSAM), revealing the often very innovative work it undertook early in the twentieth century. The period leading up to 1944 and the Education Act of that year was one of significant engagement in educational policy and influence for the NSAM in Britain, but at a global level it was also a time to reflect on the failure of the human enterprise to prevent two world wars. In the second essay in this section John Steers reflects on the past, present and future of the International Society for Education through Art (InSEA). The United Nations Educational, Scientific and Cultural Organisation (UNESCO) had been founded as a response to the Second World War, and InSEA grew out of

UNESCO. As Steers makes clear a seminal figure in the establishment of InSEA was Herbert Read whose experience as a soldier in the First World War and horror at a second such war in his lifetime shaped his philosophy of art education. Read's 1943 book *Education through Art* remains arguably the most influential text on art education, and Steers gives due weight to the importance of its contents on the initial direction of the society and for its future. A past president of InSEA himself, Steers is well placed to make this timely analysis of the organisation.

Inevitably, Herbert Read must reappear in section five 'Pivotal figures in the history of art and design education'. There are four essays in this section, demonstrating historians' continuing fascination with the innovative ideas of those people who have made a significant impact on art and design education. The essays are arranged chronologically by their subjects' lifetimes to allow the reader to reflect on the similarities and differences in the philosophical positions of these people over the 150 or so years covered. Ray Haslam is concerned with John Ruskin's period of teaching drawing at the Working Men's College in London. For a large part of the twentieth century Ruskin was an almost 'forgotten' figure, and his voluminous writings ignored. Haslam has been instrumental in re-appraising Ruskin's contribution to art and art education; in this essay showing how surprisingly 'modern' his approach to teaching drawing was by noting the correlation of late twentieth century government documents on the subject to Ruskin's *The Elements of Drawing*, for example. If John Ruskin's intention was to help his students to 'see', Marion Richardson, the second pivotal figure in this section, was concerned to elicit the 'expression of mental images' from her pupils. Bruce Holdsworth looks at the remarkable career of Richardson and her influence on art education in schools during the first half of the twentieth century. An early advocate of the New Education Movement and indelibly associated with New Art Teaching, Holdsworth argues the continuing relevance of Marion Richardson's approach to art education. Unlike Marion Richardson, whose theories were informed by her practice, the subject of the third essay in this section had no practical experience of teaching art. Written in 1993, David Thistlewood's 'Herbert Read: a Critical Appreciation at the Centenary of his Birth' deals with a towering figure on the cultural landscape of the mid-twentieth century, and for art educationalists worldwide, a person of inestimable importance. In this definitive appreciation, Thistlewood explains and contextualises Read's complex intellectual journey that incorporated his championing of the avant-garde linked to a philosophy of political engagement for art, and his very active international engagement with art education. For this reason Thistlewood's essay is an excellent companion to John Steers chapter on InSEA. Thistlewood identifies the scientific philosophy of D'Arcy Wentworth Thompson's book *On Growth and Form* as informing Herbert Read's thinking. It too influenced both the subject of the final chapter in this section and the pivotal figure involved. Richard Yeomans looks at the events of the third quarter of the twentieth century in art and design education in his 'Basic Design and the Pedagogy of Richard Hamilton'. From the end of the Second World War there were significant developments in the structure of art education, the art world, and the cultural life of Britain that in combination gave rise to what became known in art education as the 'Basic Design' movement. By the 1960s it underpinned almost all art and design education in the country becoming the blueprint for the curriculum offered in first Pre-diploma, and then Foundation Courses. The movement involved many of those now considered giants of twentieth century British art – amongst others, Victor Pasmore, Eduardo Paolozzi, William Turnbull, Alan Davie and Richard Hamilton. Yeomans essay focuses on the highly influential Foundation Course Hamilton developed at Newcastle University, showing its intellectual basis and describing the particular character of the work he initiated there. Evaluating its merits, Yeomans interestingly connects the first subject of this section with the last when he says of Richard Hamilton's Foundation Course:

> *Certain features of the course are timeless and link with art educational practice which goes back to the eighteenth and nineteenth centuries. Some of the line exercises could have come straight from Ruskin's* Elements of Drawing.

It is, as this quotation intimates, one of the interesting aspects of editing a collection such as this that their proximity illuminates the interconnections between the content of the essays. For example, Marion Richardson trained at Birmingham; her theories on children's art were lauded by Herbert Read. Ruskin's importance to art education was acknowledged by Read, who attended the now famous conference 'Adolescent Expression in Art and Craft' at Bretton Hall where the case for Basic Design was argued out with advocates of intuition and expression enshrined in the New Art Teaching that Richardson pioneered, and so on.

Section six is concerned with British/European influence in art and design education abroad. The two essays included here look at British art education in nineteenth century Canada, and the influence of European Modernist Art on Japanese art education in the early twentieth century. Graeme Chalmers essay 'Who is to do this Great Work for Canada? South Kensington in Ontario' incorporates a topic that makes a number of appearances in this book. The 'South Kensington' system as Henry Cole and Richard Redgrave's approach to art and design education was popularly known, was exported all over the world in the second half of the nineteenth century. It has been generally accepted that Walter Smith, a former headmaster at Leeds, was singularly responsible for taking the South Kensington system to North America. Graeme Chalmers questions this orthodoxy, suggesting a more textured reading of the situation. Chalmers notes that because very little historical research has been done on art education in Ontario, the reader may need to be introduced to a presently little known figure – the 'Sir Henry Cole of this story' – Samuel Passmore May. Ontario's 'King Cole', Chalmers reveals, had many characteristics of the British model. Indeed, the parallels between the circumstances in which May operated in Canada and Cole in England are interestingly drawn out by Chalmers at a number of levels. In this collection of essays for example, it is useful to relate Chalmers sub-section 'The art education of girls and women' in his essay, with Swift's chapter on women and art education in Birmingham. Coming full circle, as it were, Akio Okazaki's essay 'European Modernist Art into Japanese School Art: the Free Drawing Movement in the 1920s' begins by discussing the translation of the kind of nineteenth century British drawing manuals discussed by Rafael Cardoso, into Japanese. Okazaki shows that the export of the South Kensington system was not confined to British colonies, but was introduced to Japan by Japanese art educators who had travelled to America and Europe experiencing versions of the system first hand. Key elements of the system were incorporated in Japanese art education by the first decade of the twentieth century in the *New Textbooks of Drawing*. The backlash came with the short-lived Free Drawing Movement. Okazaki places the development of the movement in its wider socio-political context in Japan. In a carefully balanced account he shows how it was that European ideas of child-centred art education fused with exposure to European modernist art seemed a much more attractive approach and steadily eroded interest in the official national textbooks.

The fourteen essays included in this collection are a genuine response to the periodic reminders from historians like Soucy and Hamblen during the last twenty years to take on board the effects of 'the new history' (*La nouvelle histoire*) and the methodologies associated with it. But it is important to set this in context. Paradoxically, it could be argued, it was 'the new history' or 'total history' as it has also come to be known, that legitimized the study of art and design education history in the first place. Where once the Rankean parameters of the discipline 'history' were confined to the study of politics, war and the 'great people' who conducted these affairs (with the history of art, science or education, for example, relegated to the margins of 'real' history), 'the new history' spawned a massive growth of sub-headings of the discipline. Hence, economic history broke away from social history, which in turn gave rise to research in labour history, and so on, elevating them all to positions of equal importance. Early historians of art and design education were presumably content to view the subject as one of these discrete sub-divisions. But although this progressive fragmentation of research is the inevitable outcome of 'the new history', in hindsight it is possible to see how it might create problems. For example, Peter Burke in his *New Perspectives on Historical Writing* (1991) noted that these sub-groups tend not to communicate with each other. Clearly, historians of art and design education are not exempt from these problems, and as the discipline grows and creates its own sub-divisions the problem of talking to each other will become more acute. But not only is there a need for historians of art and design education to maintain a dialogue amongst themselves, more importantly there is a need to engage in a dialogue with the wider community of historians if the kind of synthesis of approaches Burke called for is to be achieved. By this means histories of art and design education will remain vital and alive.

Chapter 1: A Preliminary Survey of Drawing Manuals in Britain c.1825–1875

Rafael Cardoso

Among the many sources available for looking at nineteenth-century art and design education, drawing manuals stand out for their exceptional ability to uncover the many nameless procedures and discourses which only rarely filtered through to more formal expressions of theory and policy. Sifting through the great mass of 'useful knowledge' contained in the many hundreds of manuals published throughout the period, they can be found to contain a wealth of contemporary ideas not only on drawing instruction itself but also on art and education as broader social issues, often revealing hidden attitudes or barely articulated ones which, nonetheless, underpinned the nature of instruction at the time. Drawing manuals possess the further advantage of reflecting a wide and eclectic range of practices, often blurring or cutting across otherwise rigid barriers within nineteenth-century education demarcating divisions of age, gender, class or nationality. Despite their potential usefulness, however, surprisingly little has been published on the subject.[1] The aim of the present article is to provide an initial survey of the historical development of drawing manuals during the critical 50-year period spanning the middle part of the nineteenth century, in the hope that this will encourage more extensive research in the field.

Until the 1830s, most treatises on drawing were directed almost exclusively towards well-to-do amateurs interested in sketching landscape and/or figure drawing, in pen and ink, sepia and watercolours. Like all illustrated books of the time, these tended to be fairly expensive items, a fact which necessarily limited their circulation. A series of technological developments throughout the first three decades of the century including the coming of the steam printing press and the increased use of wood pulp as a raw material for paper-making greatly reduced publishing costs, contributing significantly to the expansion of a new reading public among the middle and working classes.[2] These segments of the editorial market were subsequently targeted with a barrage of elementary drawing manuals, a new cheaper range of manuals on landscape and, increasingly after 1850, manuals on technical subjects such as geometrical drawing, mechanical drawing and drawing for specific trades like carpentry or bricklaying. Manuals were often published in conjunction with the manufacture of artistic materials by companies such as Ackermann & Co., Reeves and Sons, Winsor and Newton or George Rowney and Co., the latter two coming to dominate the largely amateur market for one shilling manuals during the late nineteenth century. Publishing houses like John Weale's, Chambers's and Cassell's were responsible for many of the technically oriented manuals, especially the cheaper ones, which found a ready market among the upper reaches of the working-class public. Prices for manuals during the Victorian period began at one penny or sixpence for very simple 'drawing-copies' and ranged as high as several pounds, with most resting in the one shilling to two shillings and sixpence range. Drawing books published in parts proved to be extremely popular, especially in the segment of elementary and technical manuals geared to artisans and mechanics, who might not be able to afford a single large outlay but were willing to invest smaller amounts over an extended period of time. A successful manual easily achieved four or five editions in as many years, and the most popular ones sometimes reached upwards of ten editions in a career spanning as many as 30 years or more in print. By the late 1840s and early 1850s, the supply of drawing manuals was already so great that one especially prolific author, Nathaniel Whittock, felt moved 'to apologize for adding to the number'.[3] Most of his fellow authors, however, saw the overwhelming demand for new editions as justification enough for writing even more manuals.

The impact of cheap engraving and printing was so immediate that the engineer and writer of manuals Robert Scott Burn described this contemporary revolution in mass communication as 'more powerful than the press for printing words'.[4] Independently of purely technological considerations, though, the expansion of the market for manuals cannot be dissociated from the broader drive to popularise instruction in art and design which served as a backdrop for the growth of educational and cultural institutions like those of South Kensington. The Department of Science and Art was itself a powerful agency for the dissemination of manuals – sold, issued and distributed under its authority by the publishers Chapman and Hall. Manuals often came recommended with the sanction of the Department, the Society of Arts, the Committee of Council on Education and other educational or charitable entities. Within a few decades, drawing ceased to be perceived as simply an 'elegant art' contributing to 'a genteel education' – as Whittock described it in 1830 – to become a necessary part of general education, for children of both sexes and all classes, as well as many working-class adults.[5] An 1853 circular from the Committee of Council on Education reinforced this point, stating firmly that drawing 'ought to no longer be regarded as an accomplishment only... but as an essential part of education', and, by 1864, the Schools Inquiry Commission reported that 95 per cent of grammar and other publicly supported schools were teaching drawing to children, while 92 per cent of private schools were doing so.[6] The speed and efficiency with which the new educational establishment succeeded in transforming drawing instruction into a standard commodity must be attributed, in no small degree, to the exceptional power of printed manuals and examples as tools for spreading visual knowledge.

With the initial expansion of the market between about 1825 and 1830, the comparative uniformity of manuals in terms of format and price gave way to more variegated and sophisticated publishing strategies. Whereas an older style of treatise like Dougall's *The Cabinet of the Arts* (1815?) tried to encompass as many aspects of artistic practice as possible – claiming not only to teach drawing but also etching, engraving, perspective and even surveying – the newer manuals began to address particular media, topics of interest and stages of proficiency in a rather more specific manner. Some of the earliest books emphasising the possibility of learning elementary drawing without the aid of a master were published around this time, such as Thomas Smith's *The Art of Drawing in Its Various Branches* or Whittock's *The Oxford Drawing Book,* both dating from 1825.

Although both these books still bore a strong stylistic resemblance to the widely prevalent manuals of amateur sketching authored by noted landscape painters like David Cox, Samuel Prout or John Varley, they made an effort to adapt the tone and content of their lessons to a new audience which might possess neither previous experience of drawing nor ready access to private instruction. The latter book appealed quite unashamedly to the pretensions towards gentility of its eager middle-class public, couching the simplicity of its method in artfully Romantic assertions of the elegance of drawing as a pastime.

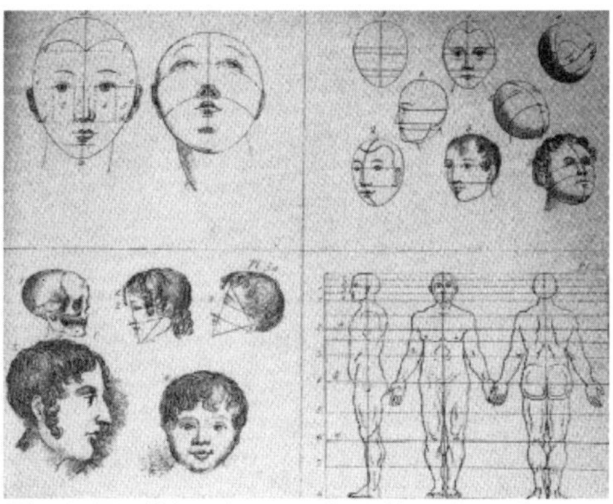

Fig. 1: Traditional examples of heads and figures from Whittock's Oxford Drawing Book.

The 1820s also witnessed the initial publication of one of the earliest truly rudimentary drawing manuals for a mass public. Taking advantage of a format popular at that time for learning all sorts of subjects, *Pinnock's Catechism of Drawing* first appeared around 1821, running into at least two subsequent editions in the 1830s, and followed by Robert Mudie's *A Catechism of Perspective* in 1831. Although the question and answer structure of the catechism left little room for anything substantial in the way of visual instruction, the fact that drawing was considered to be a form of knowledge worthy of inclusion in a popular educational series even at this early date is significant. One final manual worth mentioning in the context of the 1820s is Louis Benjamin Francœur's *Lineal Drawing, and Introduction to Geometry, as Taught in the Lancastrian Schools of France* (1824), the first of two English-language translations of *Le Dessin Linéaire* (1819). Francœur was the author of treatises on mathematics and mechanics, and this simple manual was intended for elementary instruction using the monitorial system.

Nonetheless, the book broke new ground in two ways: firstly, it was specifically directed towards the 'middling and lower classes of society' and, secondly, it attempted to address geometrical drawing as a subject in its own right, apart from the artistic aspects of the study.[7] The tendency thus inaugurated of directing working-class practitioners to a particular kind of low-level, technical drawing is certainly of grave import, but it is a subject too large and complex for the scope of the present discussion.[8]

Despite these early examples, both the number and variety of drawing manuals published in the 1820s and 1830s were still comparatively small. A few truly technical manuals appeared occasionally during the 1830s, like Thomas Sopwith's *A Treatise on Isometrical Drawing* (1834) or *Blunt's Civil Engineer and Practical Machinist* by Charles John Blunt, but these tended to be expensive volumes, directed to very restricted professional groupings like geologists and civil engineers. Growing public and political agitation over education during the 1830s contributed to changing all that, however. The formation of the Committee of Council on Education provided an important incentive by creating an authority interested in bringing out standard classroom texts, particularly in terms of drawing instruction which had not heretofore been perceived to be an integral part of education by any of the sectarian publishing societies. One of the first drawing manuals published under the sanction of the Committee of Council was C. E. Butler Williams's *A Manual for Teaching Model Drawing from Solid Forms* (1843). Butler Williams was a key figure in the history of popular drawing instruction, being among the first to teach drawing on a large-scale basis in his classes at Exeter Hall. His system of teaching drawing from three-dimensional models was based on that of Dupuis, in France, and constituted something of a landmark in the struggle against the widely prevalent practice of copying from the flat, which he dismissed as mere rote-work.[9]

The book was a great success and contributed to the popularity of methods that employed simple models made of wood or wire in learning to draw basic geometrical shapes. Benjamin Waterhouse Hawkins's *The Science of Drawing Simplified* was published that very same year, sold complete with a set of models and a portable cabinet box for a rather pricey £2.2s. Other systems of model drawing continued to be very popular throughout the remainder of the nineteenth century.

Probably the greatest editorial success among drawing manuals of the 1840s was J. D. Harding's *Lessons on Art* (1849). Although the first edition was priced well above the reach of even some middle-class learners, at 21 shillings, the book proved to be enormously popular and went into ten editions over the following three decades. Harding, of course, is better known as a landscape painter; yet his influence as a drawing master was enormous by any standard. *Lessons on Art* typifies the 'progressive method' which became almost standard in the elementary manuals of the latter half of the nineteenth century. The first lessons begin with the freehand

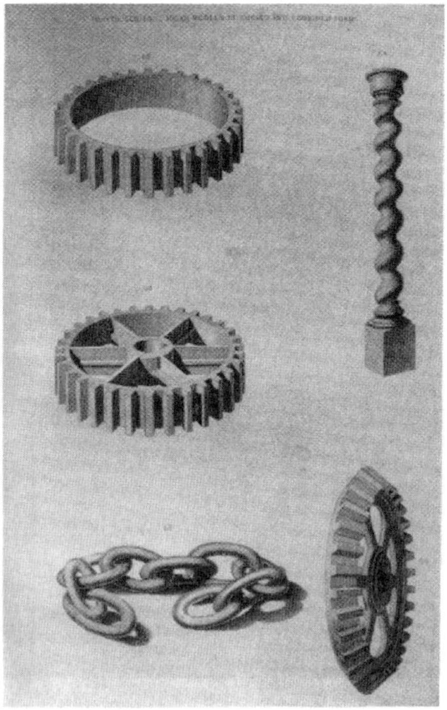

Fig. 2: Solid models used in Butler William's method.

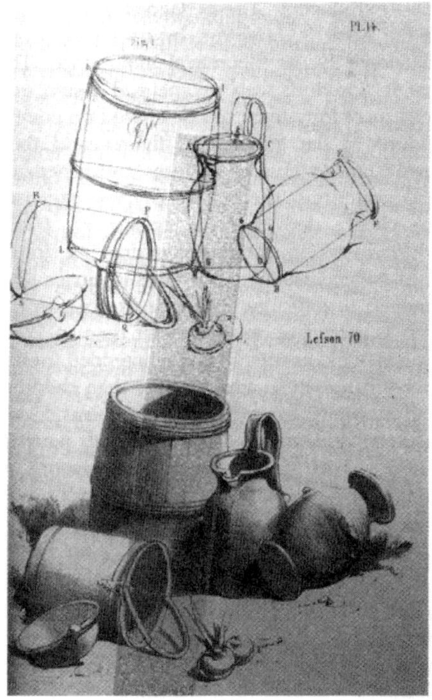

Fig. 3: Harding's method of using auxiliary lines to discover geometric shapes in objects.

drawing of straight lines, angles and rectilinear shapes, moving from there to curves and solid geometrical shapes. The second section of the book involves applying these abstract shapes to simple objects and buildings: drawing a fence from intersecting parallel lines or a bridge from an arc. The third section then moves back to circumscribing solid objects with abstract geometrical shapes, as a simplified means of introducing perspective drawing. More complex objects, larger-scale buildings and whole landscape scenes follow in subsequent sections. The system relies on creating a dynamic tension between abstract shapes and real objects, thus establishing an easy and logical transition from representing two-dimensional surfaces to three-dimensional space. Harding's methods were widely copied by other elementary manuals of the period, but rarely with the same success.

The fact that many elementary manuals employed very similar approaches to drawing is no coincidence, since they were often directed to a fairly homogeneous segment of the public: namely, children and youths of the middle classes, as well as the drawing masters who taught them. Of course, there were those who could not afford drawing masters, and accordingly, self-instruction became an important aspect of the compilation of manuals, many of which emphasised their effectiveness in learning without a master or even as aids for schoolteachers who did not themselves know how to draw. As opposed to supervised work, however, self-instruction posed the risk of students deviating from approved methods and examples. In order to minimise this danger, most manuals stressed the importance of close adherence to the prescribed instructions. In fact, the preoccupation with surveillance was so strong that some authors took the trouble to detail the finer points of how students should sit, hold their chalk, clean their slates or sharpen their pencils. Butler Williams's manual was an extreme example of this disciplinarian attitude, including fourteen pages of minutely itemised directions regarding nearly every aspect of classroom practice.[10]

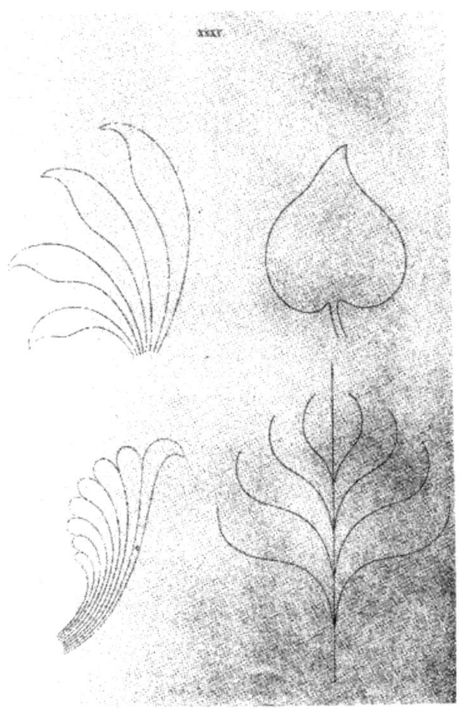

Fig. 4: Some of Dyce's 'tracings'.

Another exceptional manual produced in the 1840s was William Dyce's *The Drawing Book of the Government School of Design; or, Elementary Outlines of Ornament,* which was initially printed for the use of students at Somerset House in 1842–3 but was not made generally available until 1854. Dyce's manual offered a radical departure from previous methods of drawing instruction, not only in the way its exercises were organised but also in the complex theoretical discussion of the nature of design and ornament which constitutes much of its introduction. The pedagogical dimension of the book is, however, by no means overshadowed by its theoretical importance. The first section deals with 'geometrical design' and consists of 45 exercises based on combinations of flat geometrical figures and their application to abstract patterns and schematic botanical forms. The first ten of these exercises are clearly derived from Francœur's *Lineal Drawing,* taking students from drawing simple lines to circumscribing polygons in circles. The increase in difficulty from one exercise to the next is, however, much greater than in Francœur's book, as suits a manual intended for use by adults or young adults, rather than children. The remaining exercises on geometrical design take the student from copying diaper patterns composed of straight lines and polygons to arranging curved lines tangentially around an axis, suggesting abstract representations of leaves, trees and other elementary plant forms. These schematic 'tracings' (as they have sometimes been called) were widely appropriated by later drawing manuals.

Dyce's second section, on 'freehand design', constitutes the real novelty in terms of drawing for ornamental purposes. Unlike Francœur, he does not proceed from flat geometrical figures to solid ones but opts instead for 'a progression... from the conventional form to [the] natural types', sticking mainly to unshaded linear drawing.[11]

Beginning with conventionally treated (i.e., flattened out and symmetrically displayed) plant forms, the exercises in this section take learners through patterns, mouldings and complex ornaments, incorporating natural elements into the schematic design. What was innovative in Dyce's system was his insistence on flat outline as the only correct form of representation in ornamental drawing, rejecting naturalistic representation as incompatible with the purposes of applied design. Contrary to the prevailing attitude of regarding ornamental drawing as a less developed form of imitative drawing, Dyce based his method on the declared assumption that the two procedures are fundamentally opposed in their very conditions of existence. His ideas on the 'abstractive' and 'reproductive' nature of ornamental art, as opposed to the 'imitative' nature of fine art, are at the root of many similar principles later expounded by Richard Redgrave, Owen Jones and Christopher Dresser, thereby constituting what may be one of the first attempts to place design on a separate but equal footing to fine art.[12]

Although Dyce's reflections are fascinating in terms of the subsequent development of artistic theory and practice, they did not manage to achieve much of an immediate impact. On the contrary, even though the plates and exercises of his book were widely circulated and reproduced throughout the mid-Victorian period, they were often sold separately from the text, and the deeper influence of his thinking on the nature of art and design must be traced indirectly through the work of subsequent writers. The other great theoretically inclined manual of the middle part of the century, John Ruskin's *The Elements of Drawing, in Three Letters to Beginners* (1857), managed to achieve a good deal more in the way of shaking up cherished beliefs regarding the nature of artistic instruction. Originally published in response to demands that he make generally available the system of teaching he had been employing at the Working Men's College since 1854, Ruskin's book can be taken as a calculated blow to the practice of copying by rote which Butler Williams and Harding (who taught Ruskin) had already condemned in their manuals of the 1840s. Indeed it was intended as such, directing a good deal of rather inflamed invective against South Kensington's methods and purposes: '[t]ry first to manufacture a Raphael;' Ruskin famously wrote, 'then let Raphael direct your manufacture.'[13] The actual exercises certainly retain a bit of the radical flavour of the politically motivated part of the text, though they fall somewhat short of the boldest experimental methods employed in the Working Men's College.

Perspective is, nonetheless, repudiated as useless to elementary drawing, inaugurating a new tradition of presenting it not as a fundamental study but as a rather unnecessary constraint, outline drawing is castigated as unnatural, a position Ruskin would reverse in his later writings; disciplined work is regretted as a monotonous but indispensable formality, and colouring is presented more freely than in previous texts geared to a popular audience. Such instructions were written off in some quarters as 'amusing absurdities', as *Blackwood's* qualified them, but their influence in art and design education has been enduring.[14]

Steering away from the usual straight lines, Ruskin's manual begins with an exercise on shading, essentially geared towards mastering the manipulation of pen and ink. In order to vary the type of work, the learner then proceeds to an entirely different type of exercise, copying outline and flowers from the flat, using tracings to compare the copy to the original. The third exercise moves back to shading, this time concentrating on producing a perfectly gradated band of shades ranging from white to black. The fourth and fifth exercises introduce the use of the pencil and apply that knowledge to shading in letters of the alphabet and then outlining them, a common type of exercise in the 1850s. The next exercise brings a more original departure, prompting students to look at the bough of a tree against a grey sky and to draw its outline not by examining the branches themselves but by looking at 'the white interstices between them', stressing the appearance of forms and how they are perceived over the actual shape of objects. The following exercises introduce the use of watercolours, repeating the process of moving from abstract shading exercises to leaves and trees. A total of ten exercises constitutes the first of the 'three letters to beginners' and represent the organised core of Ruskin's method of teaching elementary drawing. The second letter, on 'sketching from nature', provides more of a discussion of representing landscape and less of a structured system of instruction. The third letter, on 'colour and composition', offers suggestions on mixing and harmonising colours and arranging composition. Ruskin is at pains to point out that 'so far as it *is* a system', the aim of his system is 'to get rid of systematic rules altogether, and [teach] people to draw as country lads learn to ride, without saddle or stirrups'.[15] Although

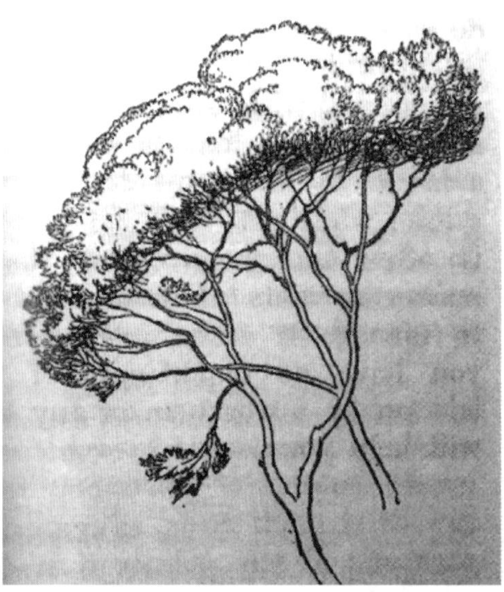

Fig. 5: Outline as a 'bridle' in Ruskin's Elements of Drawing.

it would be disingenuous to take this statement at face value, the most remarkable aspect of *The Elements of Drawing* does reside in its willingness to ignore prevailing pedagogical orthodoxies and to challenge hierarchical notions about what constituted 'elementary' and 'advanced' aspects of artistic instruction.

Neither Dyce nor Ruskin was typical, however, of the manuals dominating the British market at mid-century. The 1850s gave rise to a new force in the realm of art and design education in the shape of the Department of Science and Art; and, appropriately, those manuals corresponding to the system of instruction at South Kensington came into their own at around this time. Depressingly representative of these are a pair of books covering 'Rudimentary Art Instruction for Artizans and Others, and for Schools' prepared by the sculptor John Bell at the request of the Society of Arts, of which he was a prominent member. Bell's, *Outline from Outline, or from the Flat* and *Outline from Objects, or from the Round* appeared in 1852 and 1854, respectively, focusing on what were described as the 'less ambitious but generally more useful requirements of the artizan and art-workman', purportedly at the expense of 'the highest representative art'.[16] Despite claiming applicability to the purposes of work, the method espoused in these books was fairly rudimentary and the exercises quite shoddy, consisting largely of mere copying with occasional tips on the use of guiding lines and other simple timesaving techniques. They were, however, relatively affordable at three to four shillings and were only slightly worse than most of the other manuals being published at around the same time. Hannah Bolton's *Drawing from Objects* (1850), prepared for the Home and Colonial Training Schools, attempted to provide a little more in the way of theory and repudiated copying from the flat, opting for the Dupuis models instead; but it still offered a fairly dull and repressive system of learning drawing, despite the higher price of seven shillings. Another widely employed manual of the time was *Drawing for Elementary Schools* (1857), authored by Ellis A. Davidson, headmaster of the Chester School of Art, who went on to achieve great editorial success through the 1860s and 1870s writing cheaper manuals geared to a working-class audience for the firm of Cassell, Petter and Galpin. His 1857 manual provided a typically composite method of elementary drawing, moving from lines, angles and curves on to Dyce's 'tracings', on through the use of guiding lines and culminating in a process of copying outlines of tools and implements of domestic, agricultural and industrial labour. Like many authors of the time, both Davidson and Bolton believed wholeheartedly in the virtues of teaching working-class children to study and admire the articles of their future trades.

The number of drawing manuals published after 1850 rose so steeply that the output of any single decade of the latter half of the nineteenth century would probably surpass the entire production of the first 50 years. Authors like Richard Burchett, Horace Grant, Walter Smith, Charles H. Weigall, P. H. Delamotte, F. Edward Hulme and others already mentioned, like Whittock, Harding and

Davidson, managed to stay in print almost continually for periods of up to four decades; and, as the market expanded, manuals grew cheaper and more accessible. The publishing firm of William and Robert Chambers, of Edinburgh, was among the first to forge ahead with the publication of a complete course of *Drawing and Perspective in a Series of Progressive Lessons,* published between 1851–55 in a series of 26 booklets costing from one shilling and sixpence to two shillings each. Each book covered a different subject, beginning with elementary lessons in book one and moving on to figures, animals, landscape and perspective as well as mechanical and architectural drawing in the most advanced books. By the late

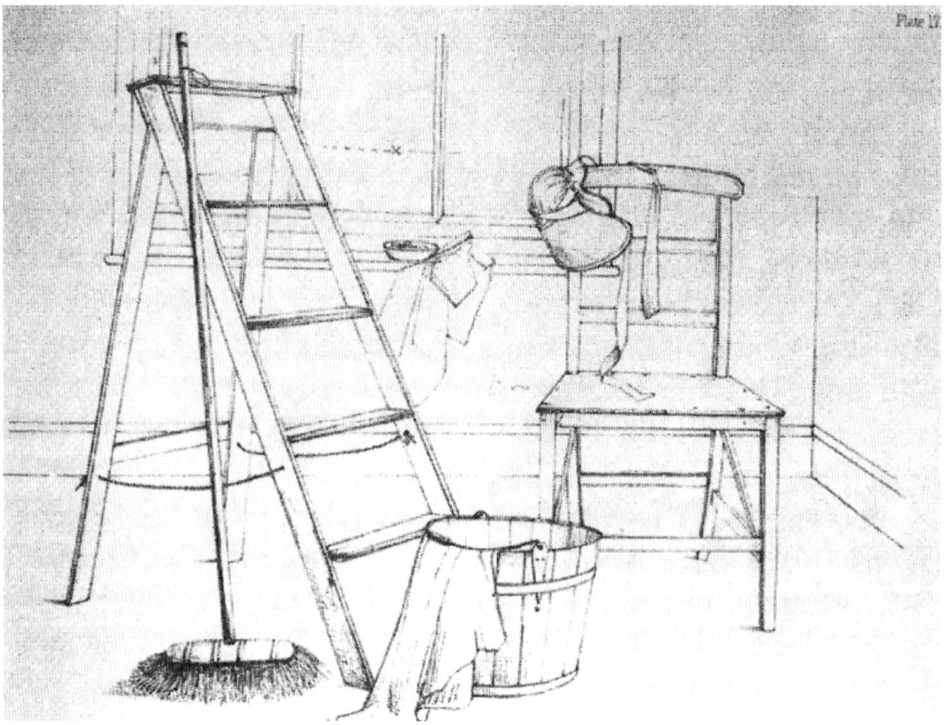

Fig. 6: Models of gender and class in Hannah Bolton's First Drawing Book

1860s, *Vere Foster's Drawing-Copy Books* were published at the even lower price of 3d. each; and, in 1871, *Cassell's Penny Drawing-Copy Books* brought prices down as low as they would go. The quality of such materials was, of course, negligible, consisting of cheap examples to be copied from the flat; but many higher priced manuals were often only marginally better. This great growth in the supply and availability of manuals brought not only an increase in quantity but also in variety. Manuals geared to technical drawing and engineering became very prevalent after the 1850s, for instance, whereas they had been conspicuously scarce earlier in the century.

Perhaps the most influential of these technical manuals was not British at all, but French. Armengaud, Armengaud and Amouroux's *Nouveau cours raisonné de dessin industriel (1848)* was first published in English in 1853 as *The Practical Draughtsman's Book of Industrial Design* and later re-published in part as *The Engineer and Machinist's Drawing Book* (1855). These books were the progenitors of a whole range of manuals on geometrical drawing, engineering drawing, orthographic projection, mechanical and machine drawing which proved to be highly successful throughout the latter half of the nineteenth century. Their special appeal resided in the scale drawings of working machines and machine parts which were thus made available to a much wider audience than ever before. Two of the most popular authors of such manuals were William S. Binns, who was employed as master of mechanical drawing at Marlborough House and the Government School of Mines, and the engineer Robert Scott Burn, whose

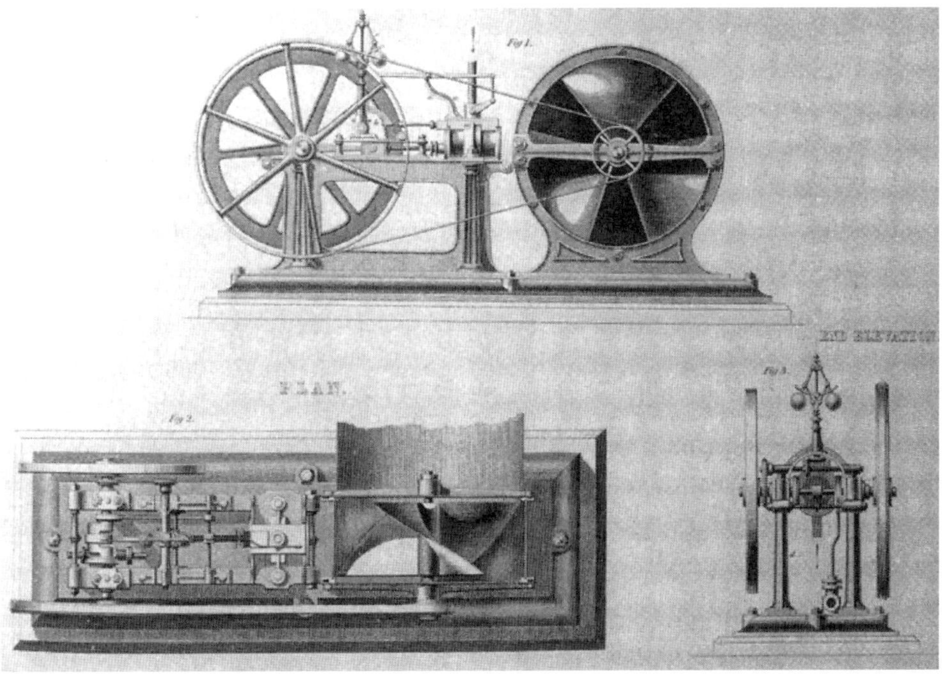

Fig. 7: Orthographic projection of a steam engine from Chamber's Drawing and Projective in a series of Progressive lessons.

numerous works include *The Illustrated London Drawing-Book* and *Mechanics and Mechanism,* both of which managed to stay in print for about 40 years after their initial appearance in 1853. The increased demand for technical manuals reflects a fundamental shift in the way instruction in drawing was already moving away from being strictly the preserve of artists, towards a wider role in scientific and vocational education as well.

The rise of technical manuals did not imply a corresponding decline in the supply of drawing books geared to landscape. With increased leisure for a larger segment of the middle classes, a new market for amateur sketching blossomed after the 1830s, and the number of landscape manuals tended to grow continuously. Significantly, though, the amateur manuals of the 1850s and 1860s were no longer the expensive, elegant tomes of the early part of the century but often no more than cheap paperback editions costing as little as one shilling. Thomas Rowbotham's *The Art of Sketching from Nature* published by Winsor & Newton in 1850, went through eighteen editions in just five years, making it one of the most unqualified editorial successes of that or any other time. Landscape sketching seems to have survived the demise of the traditional eighteenth-century 'amateur' precisely by recasting the class-specific appeal of that identity along more popular lines, thereby transposing the ideal of gentility to an ascending middle-class public. This sort of social cross-over in terms of the specificity of particular educational practices became increasingly common as the century wore on. By the 1870s, the market had become so fragmented and complex that drawing manuals of every type were available in every price range: in other words, it was no longer possible to assume that landscape was up-market or that elementary self-instruction was strictly for those who could not afford lessons. Even technical manuals, which had traditionally been associated with a working-class public, began to appear in luxury editions by the late 1860s and 1870s, as wealthy and successful mechanical engineers formed their libraries.

Despite this increasing fragmentation of the market during the period under investigation, nineteenth-century manuals possess a striking homogeneity in their terms of discourse; and certain recurring themes can be singled out as underpinning the conceptual framework within which drawing instruction tended to operate. Even though a proper discussion of the significance of these discourses is beyond the scope of the present article, it may be useful to point out their existence as a means of concluding this brief historical introduction. Five propositions seem to recur with extraordinary regularity: firstly, that drawing is important as a source of useful knowledge and moral edification, especially for the lower classes of society; secondly, that the exercise of drawing is particularly suited to training eye and hand, thereby perfecting their mutual operation; thirdly, that drawing and writing are fundamentally related as forms of visual and manual expression, making it advantageous to learn them in tandem; fourthly, that drawing is a universal language, comprehensible to people of all races and nationalities, and therefore of great utility in commerce and industry; and, lastly, that drawing provides a means of intellectual and moral refinement, exercising an elevating influence capable of raising the mind above sensual or material pursuits. The bearing of these pedagogical assumptions upon even larger issues involving the associations between work and leisure, mind and body, individual and society, science and art, is indeed portentous and deserves to be explored in a much deeper and more systematic manner than has heretofore been the case. A heightened attention to the significance of manuals as constituent elements in the construction of nineteenth century educational agendas will make the task of unravelling the complex meanings of such intriguing discourses a more fruitful one.

Originally published in the Journal of Art & Design Education, *Volume 15: 3, 1996*

All photographs are published by courtesy of the Board of Trustees of the Victoria and Albert Museum.

Notes and References

1. The Fitzwilliam Museum's exhibition catalogue (1988), *Gilpin to Ruskin: Drawing Masters and Their Manuals, 1800-1860*, provides a good introduction to the early part of the century, focusing mainly on books geared to amateur sketching. David Jeremiah has done useful research on the Society of Art's role in publishing manuals; see (1968–69), 'The Society of Arts and the National Drawing Education Campaign' *Journal of the Royal Society of Arts*, 117, esp. pp. 440–2. Some further writings are available on drawing manuals in the USA; see Marzio, P. C. (1976), *The Art Crusade: an Analysis of American Drawing Manuals, 1820-1860*; and Korzenik, D. (1985), 'How to Draw' Books as Sources for Understanding Art Education of the Nineteenth Century' *Journal of Art & Design Education*, 4, pp. 169–77 (see Chapter 2 of this book). The development of engineering drawing has been usefully surveyed in Baynes, K. & Pugh, F. (1981), *The Art of the Engineer*. For an insightful discussion of late-C19 drawing instruction in the context of its influence on Modernism, see Nesbitt, M. (1986), 'Ready-Made Originals: the Duchamp Model' *October*, 37, pp. 53–64. The same subject is taken up in greater detail in Nesbitt, M. (1991), 'The Language of Industry' in de Duve, T. (Ed.), *The Definitively Unfinished Marcel Duchamp*, pp. 351–84. Finally, the National Art Library is currently compiling an inventory of nineteenth century drawing manuals: for more on this project, contact Rebecca Coombes at the NAL/Victoria & Albert Museum, Cromwell Road, London SW7 2RL.
2. For more on the technological aspects, see Clair, C. (1976), *A History of European Printing*, esp. pp. 355–83. On the expansion of the editorial market and the fragmentation of the reading public, see Goldman, P. (1994), *Victorian Illustrated Books 1850-1870*, pp. 33–76; Landon, R. G. (Ed.) (1978), *Book Selling and Book Buying: Aspects of the Nineteenth-century British and North American Book Trade*, esp. pp. 45–50; and Altick, R., (1957), *The English Common Reader, passim.*
3. Whittock, N. (1849), *A New Manual of Perspective*, p. 5.
4. Burn, R. S. (1853a), *The Illustrated London Drawing-Book*, pp. 129, 144–5.
5. Whittock, N. (1830), *The Oxford Drawing Book*, p. iii. Among the numerous affirmations of the importance of drawing in general education, see Clark. J. (1837), *Elements of Drawing and Perspective*, p. i; Burn, (1853a), *op. cit.* pp. i–ii; Davidson, E. A. (1857), *Drawing for Elementary Schools*, p. v; Ryan. C. (1868), *Systematic Drawing and Shading,* p. 9; Hulme below (1882), pp. 1, 24.
6. CCE circular cited in *Art-Journal,* 1853, p. 98; Schools Inquiry Commission report cited in F. Edward Hulme, E. F. (1882), *Art Instruction in England*, p. 71.
7. Francœur, L. B. (1824), *Lineal Drawing, and Introduction to Geometry*, pp. 7, 69, 82. An even earlier example of a book geared to technical drawing is Blunt, C. (1811), *An Essay on Mechanical Drawing* which appears to have been much the standard reference on the subject during the early part of the century. It was, however, quite expensive at £3.16s. and certainly never reached a popular audience.
8. For a full analysis of this subject and other aspects of mid-Victorian drawing instruction, see my 'The Educated Eye and the Industrial Hand: Art and Design Instruction for the Working Classes in Mid- Victorian Britain,' unpublished Ph.D. dissertation, Courtauld Institute of Art/U. London, 1995, Ch. 1.
9. Acland, T. D. (1858), *Some Account of the Origins and Objects of the New Oxford Examinations*

for the Title of Associate in Arts and Certificates, p. 7n. Butler Williams was also professor of geodesy in the College for Civil Engineers; for more on his teaching, see Macdonald, S. (1970), *The History and Philosophy of Art Education*, p.34.

10. Butler Williams, C. E. (1843), *A Manual for Teaching Model-Drawing from Solid Forms, the Models Founded on Those of M. Dupuis*, pp. 237–51.

11. Dyce, W. (1842–43), *Drawing Book of the Government School of Design*, section II, preceding Exercise 46.

12. *Ibid.,* p. i.

13. Cook, E. T. and Wedderburn, A. (Eds.) (1903–12), *The Works of John Ruskin*, v. 15, p. 12.

14. *Blackwood's Edinburgh Magazine*, 87 (1860), p. 32; for more on the influence of Ruskin's ideas, see Carline, R. (1968), *Draw They Must*, Ch. 8–12; Haslam, R. (1988), 'Looking, Drawing and Learning with John Ruskin at the Working Men's College' *Journal of Art & Design Education*, 7, p. 69 (See Chapter 9 of this book); and Efland, A. D. (1990), *A History of Art Education: Intellectual and Social Currents in Teaching the Visual Arts*, pp. 133–9.

15. Cook, E. T. and Wedderburn, A. (Eds.), *op. cit.,* v. 15, pp. 15–6.

16. Bell, J. (1852), *Outline from Outline*, pp. iii–iv.

Chapter 2: 'How to Draw' Books as Sources for Understanding Art Education of the Nineteenth Century

Diana Korzenik

Art education has much to gain from researching its own history. Art teaching is long, slow, daily work that escapes the eye that seeks sudden news. In America almost everyone alive has been a consumer of art instruction and as such, holds a bit of data on how art was taught. Everyone was once a child and once spent many hours drawing, and perhaps even painting, building, and sculpting. In each individual's history and in fact in every era, adults reacted to what children drew and directed what young people would do. Clues to changing attitudes of instruction appear in circulars, newspapers, old magazines, art material catalogues, invitations to art exhibition openings, and public school art events. Such ephemera offers incontestable evidence that certain events took place and reminds people of what may have been more convenient to forget. Events considered ordinary in their time may be documented with dates, names, places, and even the entrepreneur's aspirations for the event.

The premise of my research is that circulated images and documents convey actual practices and commitments of people, revealing attitudes of which users themselves were largely unaware. Though historical treatises may have described what people did or ought to do, ephemera are evidence of what people actually did and believed.

The Task

Ferreting in flea markets and old bookshops, I observed something amazing. How-to-draw books, kits, political treatises, and school circulars revealed nineteenth century Americans as obsessed, perhaps pre-occupied, with learning to draw. I wanted to find out *why* this was the case.

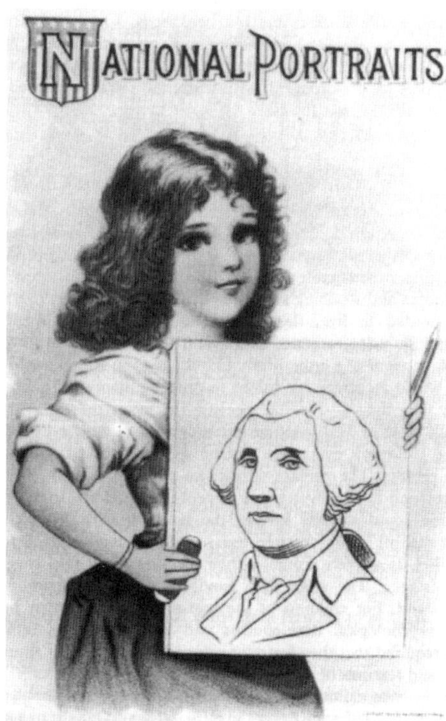

Fig. 1: Cover of late 19th century drawing manual Korzenik Collection.

Background

The descendents of Europeans who boarded ships to become farmers on North American soil had to become astute observers of the earth and the climate's effect on it. They contended with steep hills, innumerable unwanted rocks and marshes, through icy winters and steaming summers. Since they grew part of what they needed to live, they became attentive to the smallest changes in colour, texture, and shape that could indicate the health or vigour of a crop. Many like them, even if they couldn't read, would recognize conditions in growing plants and animals. What they judged as edible became the meals they ate. They literally lived or died based on the judgement of their eyes.

The children's eyes were trained as they worked alongside their parents. The parents taught the children to look, notice, and respond to whatever would improve their efforts, so that the children could actually further the family's work. Today, we know that all young children learn through their senses. Whatever they do actively promotes their learning about size, weight, and distance. The more they handle and do, the more they understand. For children of the mid-nineteenth century, both their psychological development and the agricultural society itself required that they learn by responding to different appearances and textures of objects.

These same children, who could recognize conditions of the soil, of plants and animals on the farm, were also taught to adapt that skill to working with cloth. Even when at mid-century, textiles were largely imported from England, children learned to cut and sew the cloth to form shirts and skirts. As they grew older, and their clothes wore out, those same good eyes transformed the worn garments into subtly calculated visual patterns to adorn beds as quilts, or floors as rugs. By the time the youngsters had grown to adulthood, they had an intimate acquaintance with colour, shape, texture, line, and pattern.

Americans had developed good eyes through observing their plants and their livestock, through cutting and sewing their own clothes, quilts, and rugs. Only some instruction was needed to redirect their observational skills from farming to pictures.

School Work

Farm families aspired to get from education something quite different than the subtle work they already could accomplish with their eyes and their hands. People who went to schools wanted skills they didn't already have; they wanted to learn to write, do sums, and read.

Education was a privilege and a problem. The schools were to feel every change and every strain in the community. People wrote articles, held meetings and talked among themselves: something had to be done to meet the pressing needs in the schools. If a way could be found to help the 'vicious non-producers' to become self-supporting wage earners, it was agreed the schools would be providing a great service to the community.

The school leaders struggled to find an answer. Perhaps new skills should be taught in addition to those of reading, writing and ciphering. Drawing might help, Horace Mann suggested in the *Common School Journal,* which he edited. Drawing could release the tension that otherwise might be directed toward shooting spitballs, and might teach obedience and work skills that could be useful to future labourers. Drawing could prove useful to all students, even the most unwilling.

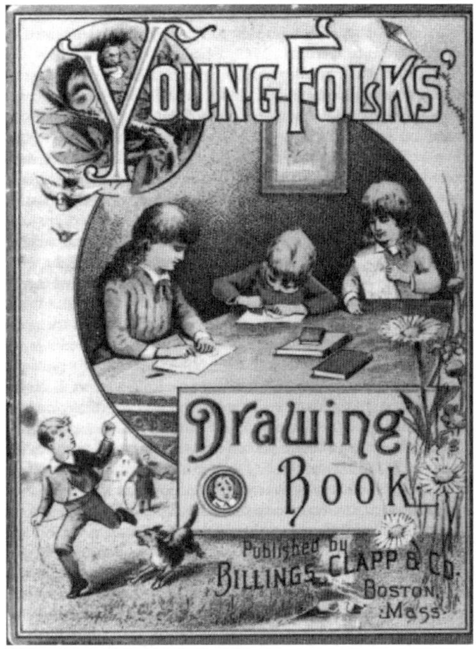

Fig. 2: Cover of late 19th century drawing manual Korzenik Collection.

School systems learned about new curricula via publications advertised and distributed through commercial catalogues, as well as through the *Common School Journal.* Growing demand for school curricula made companies vie with one another for products. In 1855, the E. P. Dutton and Company Catalogue advertised a book, which, though first printed back in 1827, had been reprinted in many editions, and taught just the sort of drawing that suited the public schools. The book, William Bentley Fowle's *The Eye and the Hand: Linear Drawing,* claimed 'to provide practical lessons for training those important organs,' and proved more suitable to schools than the host of available amateur drawing manuals. In this book, drawing looked like geometry. Dutton announced:

> *The object of this little volume is to furnish regular and systematic lessons such as teachers unacquainted with drawing may use with advantage and such as all children may and ought to learn. The work is devoted to that portion of the art which is subject to fixed rules and which lies at the foundation of drawing, considered as a science.*[1]

This advertisement signalled all the concerns of the public schools. School committees wanted order. Any kind of system and sequence was better than none. Teaching could not depend on teachers who were assumed to be without intelligence, interests, and abilities. Lessons with 'fixed rules' were insurance against variations in abilities of both teachers and students.

Fowle's book, an adaptation of an earlier French drawing manual, was ideally suited to the aims of the developing public schools. The introduction explains that the French manual by M. Francoeur resulted from Napoleon's request for a curriculum from his Bureau of Instruction:

> *When Napoleon was Emperor of France, he established a national system of education and one of the earliest studies was Drawing; not fancy drawing, which is hardly subject to any fixed rules... but that portion of the art which is subject to rules.*[2]

Fowle, a teacher in Boston's Monitorial School, anticipated what was appropriate. He had large numbers of students to be educated at little expense, so he had to simplify his curriculum to such a degree that 'monitors' who were themselves still students, could teach it. Fowle used his experience as his guide and stayed safely with simple, measurable rules of geometrical drawing, using only circles, triangles, cylinders, and pyramids as the bases of his instruction.

Fowle's books first appeared, leather-bound, with many steel engravings. Though they were later issued in a less costly hardback format, schools needed cheaper books that every child could hold, see up close, and even copy. Here, enter William Bartholemew, watercolour artist from Grafton, Vermont, and a drawing teacher for the Boston Public Schools, whose instructional drawing materials were adopted well beyond the borders of Massachusetts. Bartholemew's first drawing lessons appeared in 1853, followed by a series of numbered workbooks, in which a child viewed an image on one page and then drew his best replica of that image on the page opposite. Bartholemew's examples were an amalgam of romantic, rather English bits of landscape from the early amateur drawing books, combined with the purely geometrical drawing that appeared in Fowle's book. When Bartholemew pictured the side of a house, he showed just one single plane, which was textured with boards so it looked more like a house than a mere geometrical shape. He acknowledged:

> *With young pupils the pleasure of drawing is so great, that they are inclined to give little attention to truthfulness of form, the basis of art. To correct this error, the teacher should insist on their making a complete and careful drawing.*[3]

The pleasure of drawing was indeed so great that many children found it impossible merely to render the form correctly. Pages in students' surviving sketchbooks ornament a house, for example, with trees, animals, and people, though only a plain geometrical house was printed as an example on the opposite page.

In 1859, Bartholemew produced *Linear Perspective Explained,* followed in 1860 by five sets of *Progressive Drawing Cards.* Now drawing cards, old family home amusements, were adapted to schools, so that children could hold their own cards and make their own copies on a paper or slate before them. Bartholemew's twelve

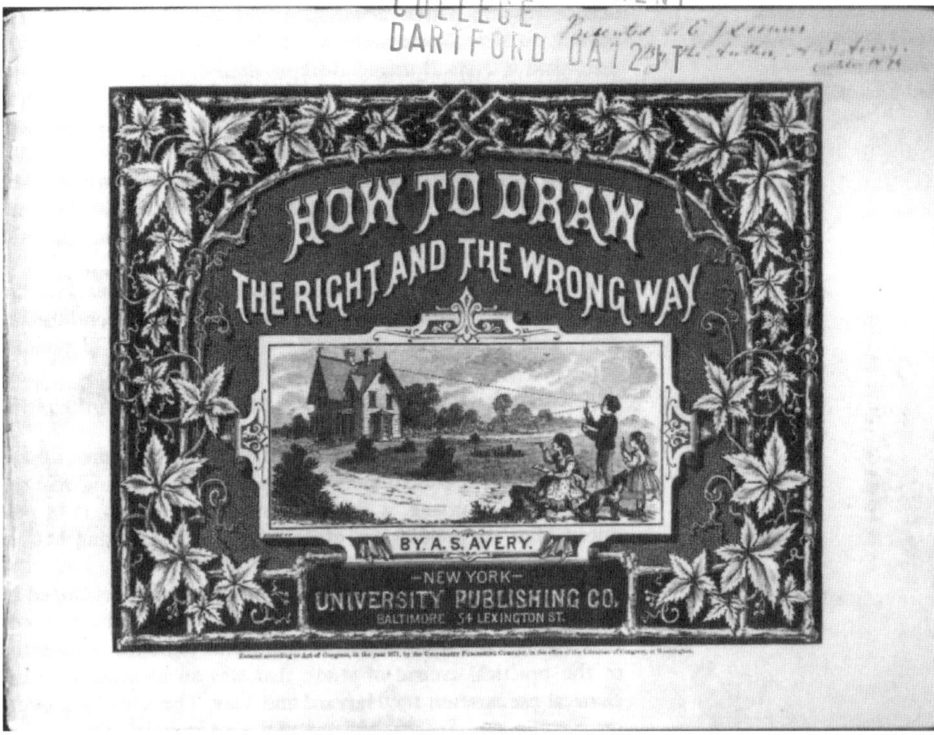

Fig. 3: Cover of How to draw: the right and wrong way *by A.S Avery, 1871* Korzenik Collection.

card set had assignments pertaining to each particular image, mixing elements of landscape drawing with the elements of geometrical drawing. A student perfected straight lines by drawing a straight picket stuck into the ground or improved his triangles by drawing a triangular unit of fencing. Bartholemew's instructions stressed giving the drawings 'character,' by which he meant preserving the qualities of, for example, brick, stone, or boards without having to render every detail. Bartholemew's manuals and copy cards, published in Boston, enjoyed prestige across the states, where all Massachusetts's educational ideas were admired. The schools adopted the geometrical, straightforward exercises prescribed by Bartholemew.

The great New York Exhibition of Industry of All Nations of 1852 had shown how artistic skill enhances industrial production. Drawing that looked like preliminary drafting proved useful for developing the skilled labour needed by the industrial mills. Bartholemew's copy cards promised to reverse the shocking statistics of American dollars flowing out of the country to foreign skilled art labourers. Now everyone agreed that drawing should start in childhood and that government should apply art training to America's young so that education could serve the nations own best interests.

Self-instruction

Schools didn't serve all the needs. In the effort to avoid curriculum that would reveal any individual differences, particularly any individual excellence, the school system, in fact, catered to the lowest human expectations. School policy aimed low. Neither the capacities of the teachers nor of the students were believed capable of inspiration. As people debated about what the schools should provide, the best-intentioned public leaders found themselves trapped. The aspirations and needs of different social classes no longer could be ignored. Families with means, after a brief time, continued to educate their children at academies and seminaries at their own expense. As people acknowledge that different types of schools taught students in different ways, it became obvious that many of the things you wanted to learn, you had to teach yourself outside of school. The book market eagerly expanded to provide self-instruction, how-to manuals.

Though students sought the skills taught in the schools, it was not clear how these meagre achievements would ever enable ordinary Americans to realize the aspirations of which they dreamed. The skills of ciphering, reading, and writing were a long way, it must have seemed, from what Americans imagined to be the polish and eloquence of European culture.

The more people learned of reading and writing, the more they must have craved learning to draw. With drawing, at least one could describe one's own house, or horse, or plan the planting of one's garden. A young person could feel more powerful drawing from observation than when copying 'Procrastination is the thief of time.'

The burgeoning world of illustrated books and the pictorial press, the plethora of instructional drawing manuals, and the hunger for education and self-improvement all conspired to persuade a young person of the value of learning to draw.

As people noticed and saved the images that surrounded them, they found they could not just look at pictures, they developed an appetite for learning to make them. Publishers responded to this interest. Today, looking back, we can see how the proliferation of manuals, cards, and books for drawing instruction paralleled the growth of popular illustrated books and periodicals. Through the first half of the nineteenth century, English drawing manuals were imported, but American variants of these were also printed in vast numbers. Many of the 109 various American manuals published between 1830 and 1860 assured the aspiring draftsman that drawing was just like farming; both required that a person know how to draw a straight line. Drawing manuals were designed to teach diligent students how to draw the forms that they observed in nature. Drawing skills, it was argued, were essential to the carpenter, the shipbuilder, and the mechanic. Every effort was made to distinguish this work from the schoolgirl's flower drawing manuals like those imported from England. Whatever the many attractions to drawing may have been, its utility served to conceal the pleasure people found in it.

As the quality of printing improved, the quality of the drawing manuals improved, and ever more beautiful images enticed the student to persist. Benjamin H. Coe, the Hartford art teacher who gave Frederick Church his early art lessons, also provided lessons for the nation at large. At the time Frederick Church moved to New York State to study with Thomas Cole, Coe published a *New Drawing Book of American Scenery.* At about that time, he also published *First Lessons in Perspective.* Throughout the early 1840s, various editions of *Easy Lessons in Landscape Drawing* appeared. The many editions of his hard covered, full-paged, illustrated lithographed volumes indicate Americans' hunger for visual instruction. Coe's books continued to be published into the 1850s, feeding the increasing appetite for learning to draw.

No single artist-author could satisfy this booming market. The 1840s saw the publication of Drawing Cards for children to copy, published under the name of Jacob Abbott, a popular children's storybook author. Also from Hartford came a small drawing book, *Self-Instructor No.1, Child's First Book*, by Josiah Holbrook.

New York publisher J. S. Redfield produced Chapman's book, but Boston also contributed its share to this growing market. Benjamin F. Nutting, a Boston drawing teacher, in 1848 produced his own popular set of drawing cards, depicting houses, gates, and trees bordering rivers.

Most manuals were for home use, but some were developed by teachers in schools. In Boston's first comprehensive high school, Boston English High School, drawing was regarded as essential to the practical course of study that was an alternative to the classical preparation for Harvard and Yale. The school's drawing teacher, Edward Seager, was one of the many artist-teachers who contributed to the outpouring of popular drawing manuals. Seager's *Progressive Studies of Landscape Drawing* (1847), of course, would not have been expected to make great profits on sales to the English High School students alone. Seager and all the other producers of instructional drawing books knew the surge of out-of-school interest in these books. Well into the 1860s, they knew that masses of publications of art instruction books would be purchased by learners of all ages who craved personal self-improvement.

Conclusion

From studying the bits and pieces of surviving old drawing manuals, we realize their creators had their fingers on the pulse. They spent most of their days in their studios teaching drawing classes to students who eagerly sought them out. They understood and exploited the growing sophistication in American printing. They may even have realized that the invention of printable pictures was of even greater importance than that of movable type, revolutionizing people's notion of information, and what they, themselves, were capable of conveying.

The various drawing manuals designed for home use retained their popularity up to the Civil War years. Perhaps because, of all skills, drawing could be seen most visibly to improve with practice and one stage of study could be compared to another, drawing skills became a metaphor for other types of learning and self-improvement. Parents applauded their children's progress in drawing. Drawing had become one of those useful things children could learn. A belief in drawing, so contrary to our own, only emerged by careful scrutiny of ephemera, discards of child's play and old school exercise books.

Originally published in the Journal of Art & Design Education, *Volume 4: 2, 1985.*

Footnote

Since this article was first published, Diana Korzenik has donated the art education collection that inspired it to the Huntington Library in Pasadena California. The collection contains roughly 500 books and a thousand pieces of art education related ephemera. Thanks to the National Endowment for the Humanities, researchers now have access to the multitude of actual How-to-do-it books, paint-boxes, kits, stencils and other devices used for accomplishing drawing skills. The Huntingdon Library has housed, catalogued, and produced a searchable CD-Rom of the Korzenik Collection that is also accessible on the RLG website. Many of the objects in the collection are pictured in full digitised colour in Korzenik, D. (2004), *The Objects of Art Education*, Huntingdon Library Press and the University of California Press, Berkeley.

Notes and References

1. Dutton, E. P. (1855), *A Descriptive Catalogue of Books, Maps and Charts and School Apparatus*, Boston, pp. 63–64.
2. Fowle, William B. (1866), *Principles of Linear ad Perspective Drawing for the Training of the Eye and Hand*, New York, p. 3.
3. Bartholemew, William. (1855), *Drawing Book No. 3* (inside cover).

Chapter 3: A Question of 'Taste': Re-examining the Rationale for the Introduction of Public Art and Design Education to Britain in the Early Nineteenth Century

Mervyn Romans

Introduction

Early historians of the subject have insisted that in 1837 public art and design education was started in Britain 'as an economic necessity'.[1] This is an explanation that has been challenged elsewhere[2] and does not need to be re-rehearsed here. Rather, the intention is to suggest other explanations for the introduction in Britain of a system of art and design education.

Central to any discussion of this topic is the 1835/36 Select Committee on Arts and Manufactures, since this is where the debate about art and design education took place. For a story that apparently hinges on parliamentary political action, early historians like Quentin Bell and Stuart Macdonald give little attention to parliament and politics. Their attention to the proceedings of the 1835/6 Select Committee that, they claim, instituted its proposed object is summary.[3] With only brief references to the wider political landscape, these historians allow, to a great extent, a politically disembodied art and design education to begin in 1837. And yet a close examination of the minutes of this select committee reveal that any concerns with the economy were far outweighed by other matters. The committee returned again and again to question witnesses about 'taste'.

The following two examples graphically illustrate the wide-ranging influence of the notion of 'taste' in the nineteenth century. First: In the eighteenth century Joseph Addison had made substantial social and political claims for the power of 'taste'. He suggested that 'as soon as Taste was established, vice and ignorance would be banished.'[4] Elsewhere he went further saying that a beautiful distant vista was 'an image of liberty'. A series of exchanges during the 1835/6 Select Committee on Arts and Manufactures in which the chairman, William Ewart, asked a number of witnesses about access to art galleries and museums demonstrates that such beliefs were still current in the early nineteenth century. Typically, the committee asked Messrs. Philip and Robert Barnes about the connection between the opening of galleries of art and the improvement of public taste. 'Do not you think that the institution of such places of instruction and of such galleries of art would have the effect not only of improving manufactures, but the moral and social conditions of the people? Unquestionably it would to a very great degree' replied the witnesses. In a series of similar exchanges between the committee and its witnesses there is a desire to harness, through forms of education, the powerful force that 'taste' appeared to represent for social and political gains.

Second: In an 1849 edition of the *Edinburgh Review* Stafford Northcote, writing about manufacturers, said that they were 'in general no judge of beauty.' Northcote went on to say 'he (the manufacturer) learns the taste of his customers, and he strives to produce what will please them, or in other words, what will sell. The ultimate control is, therefore, with the public; and here we come to our chief difficulty; for the public itself stands in need of the schoolmaster, as much as either the manufacturer or the designer.' The subject of this article was the School of Design, and if Northcote was right, by 1849 art and design education in one form or another needed to be extended to the entire population, to educate the 'taste' of Britons.

In this essay I intend to do four things. First, I want to discuss the almost obsessive nineteenth century concern with 'taste', exploring its origins and tenets, the notion of a 'national taste', and its diffusion amongst the population of Britain. Next, I want to consider how the 'language of taste' adopted in the early nineteenth century, having a politicised dimension, might connect with social issues in this period. Then I want to examine the role of 'taste' in a rapidly expanding consumer society that still had much to come to terms with where capitalist practice was concerned. Notions such as 'fashion' proved to be particularly troublesome in this select committee, for example. Finally, I would like to draw these threads together to reveal some explanation of the network of thinking about these issues that finally gave rise to public art and design education.

The Nineteenth Century Concern with 'Taste'–what Constituted 'Taste'?

Defining the word 'taste' has been endlessly problematic. Spinoza and Leibniz and Locke's influence on the eighteenth century British school of aesthetics in Addison, Kames, Hume and Burke formed the cocktail of meaning stretching from the mid-seventeenth century to the early nineteenth century. It was articulated in the Romanticist language of the 'sublime' the 'beautiful' and the 'picturesque', and influentially formulated in Kant's *Critique of Judgement* (1788). In the early nineteenth century these philosophical debates were overlaid by other concerns. In the 1830s and 1840s, and in the context of commerce, the escalating importance of the relationship between taste, fashion and consumerism is discernable. This triplet existed in tandem with 'taste' in relation to moral and behavioural imperatives. Often these themes are not distinguished one from another. The use of the word 'taste' in its eighteenth century guise often connects beauty to morality. But the extension of the beauty/morality couplet to commerce and morality, often in seemingly quite illogical ways in the nineteenth century, is more problematic and requires closer analysis. That it then impinges on the debate about art and design education is a major factor in the creation of the difficulties that beset the development of the discipline over the course of the first half of the nineteenth century. The legacy of these problems is still felt today.

The concern with 'taste' in the nineteenth century was not new. The trite Latin phrase saying 'There is no disputing about Taste' is primal evidence that the business of taste has (always) involved the matter of choice, whether individual or collective'.[5] The idea of taste as a measure of good judgement was based on neo-classical rules, and it was this meaning and canon of 'taste' that came to England by the early eighteenth century. In *A Philosophical Inquiry into the Origins of Our Ideas of the Sublime and Beautiful* (1757) Edmund Burke laid emphasis on the inherent effect that certain objects have on our senses. The physical sensations generated being either pleasing or not, he suggested, gave rise to ideas of beauty or sublimity. Burke distinguished the sublime from the beautiful, and in the second half of the eighteenth century the Reverend William Gilpin became concerned with an experience not sufficiently stirring to be called sublime, but it was an experience that left an aesthetic satisfaction in him which was not the same as that of definitions of the beautiful. Gilpin therefore gave shape to the idea of the 'picturesque' in a number of published works.

The qualities of the 'sublime', the 'beautiful' and the 'picturesque' were clearly not the same thing as 'taste', but they were inextricably linked in the sense that without taste none of these qualities would be recognisable. Equally, they were agents in an account of the nature of taste. Most importantly for this discussion, they were located within a moral framework.

Burke believed that if there is a standard of taste it is fixed by the majority agreeing on the quality of a work of art. During the last decade of the eighteenth century and the first of the nineteenth century the debate about the nature of taste, in opposition to Burke, can be very clearly seen in two books. The first of these is Archibald Allison's *Essays on the Nature and Principles of Taste* (1790). The second, *An Analytical Inquiry into the Principles of Taste* (1805) was written by Richard Payne Knight. Allison's book is an exposition of Scottish Associationism, an aesthetic doctrine derived from David Hume, who argued an external object triggers an association of ideas formed by past experience. Payne Knight's book attacks Burkean ideas, but also questions the comprehensiveness of Alison's (and therefore Hume's) associationist arguments. For Hume 'reason' was to be distinguished from 'taste'. Hume, like Leibniz before him, believed that its principles could be understood and taught. 'This insistence that the right taste be taught is characteristic of the whole (eighteenth century British) school (of aesthetics)'[6], and connects directly with the thinking of the 1835/6 Select Committee on Arts and Manufactures.

However, there were objections raised to Associationism and they are important to the argument ventured here. Uvedale Price argued that not only did Associationism fail to explain the true nature of taste, 'but (it) would also militate against the possibility of establishing any fixed standard of taste.' In this context Burke's theory was preferable since 'the sensationalist theory which Burke advance(d)... allowed that there were certain fixed standards.'[7]

That 'taste' should be taken out of the realm of 'individual' choice and made a 'collective' issue of civic importance was a feature of late eighteenth century politics. This 'collective' aspect of taste was evidenced in the circumstances that led to Lord Castlereagh's decision to appoint a 'committee of taste'. In fact the influence of this debate on a wide range of policy makers at the time was considerable. The wish to determine a 'fixed' standard was certainly apparent in the 1835/6 Select Committee. But what constituted taste, and how did this feed into the thinking of this committee?

There was an overwhelming desire to, as it were, 'pin taste down'. In brief, this involved connecting it with what was perceived to be the perennial values of antiquity. Wincklemann's claim that 'For us, the only way to become great... is by imitation of the ancients',[8] was not exclusively a clarion call for its time. Its echo can be heard throughout the 1835/6 select committee report and minutes.

The driving force was that all people should recognise, and adopt this paradigm of classical truth and many witnesses to the committee alluded to it. Charles Harriott Smith was of the opinion 'that the public, as a body, (was) not yet sufficiently educated in the arts to discriminate between pure classical elegance and meretricious finery.'[9] William Wyon claimed that 'the finest bronzes in existence are derived from the ancient Greeks'[10]; and Henry Sass required little prompting to encourage him to corroborate this view. The question was put to Sass; 'Are not the perceptive powers awakened, by the opportunity of seeing those things which should be seen by persons among whom art is to be encouraged?' Sass replied that having taught its people how to look at art, every town should have a museum housing 'those archetypes of art which have passed through the approbation of ages – the Greek statues as a foundation of pure and elegant taste.'[11] So certain were the committee that classical art was the embodiment of their aspirations, they ordered examples of Greek vases to be printed in the Minutes of Evidence.

In his evidence James Skene felt that the study of art should be 'founded upon unvarying principles of art'.[12] The reification of these 'unvarying principles' was ventured by some witnesses who set out in practical terms how to achieve the ideals of classical taste with pencil and paper. Edward Cowper related a lengthy anecdote to the committee. It concerned some terracotta garden pottery that he had embellished with Etruscan decoration inspired by a visit to the British Museum.

Cowper had given the idea of decorating the pots in this way to the Lowesby terracotta works, from which he had originally bought the pots. From this action a problem had emerged. Illustrating the issue with examples of pottery he said, 'I will now point out the difficulty attending the introduction of art into manufacture.' Cowper told the committee:

> *...this arises from the men; the difficulty is owing to the ignorance of the men. The men have been accustomed to make a straight line flower pot, and therefore they cannot think there is more taste in making it curved. This (producing another one) is a little more bent than the ordinary one, but the difficulty is to get the men out of those rigid forms and into the forms of taste.*

Cowper went on to show more and more examples of pots, finishing with the observation that 'If once the workman had the idea of an oval in his mind he would never make a bad vase'.[13]

Brought down to a practical course of action in this way, the lofty ideals of neo-classical theory seem somewhat banal. Moreover, they clearly illustrate the kind of thinking that ultimately fed into the design of the curriculum of the first school of design.

A 'National Taste' and its 'Diffusion Amongst all Classes of Society'

'Why should we attempt to cultivate a national taste', *The Art Union* asked its readers in 1842.[14] In the 1830s the question appeared to be even more pertinent. Then, all the evidence suggests it was a commonly held belief that a 'national taste' was absent in Britain, and the consequences were, in a variety of ways, highly detrimental. The 'true' and 'unvarying principles' of classical art, were at the centre of a strong desire to establish a 'national taste', and the 1835/6 Select Committee reflected that wish continually.

The discussion of a 'national taste' was always couched in comparative terms. France and Italy were most often singled out as exemplars of countries that had a 'national taste', and populations where taste was not confined to the upper social echelons, but extended throughout all classes of society. In Britain, this was seen to be a highly desirable objective. It was seemingly no longer acceptable that the rich should continue exclusively (as they always had), to display superior taste in their clothing and households, as a sign of their power. Now, 'taste' needed to be democratised, but the problem was not to be underestimated.

Samuel Wiley, of Betteridge & Jennings in Birmingham was asked whether he could offer suggestions 'which would increase (his) trade and encourage artists?' He replied 'By improving the public taste; the public taste is bad; I could sell them the worst things, the most unmeaning, in preference to the most splendid designs and the best executions.'[15] For Wiley, his market was seemingly not in jeopardy so long as he continued to supply the taste of his public.

Seeking the agreement of witnesses that a 'national taste' *was* important, and should be built on reference to the 'ancients' and 'old masters', by committee members was relentless. The 'national taste', the committee was convinced, would be achieved through exposure to classical works, on display in public galleries and museums.

While the wish to establish a 'national taste' was endlessly rehearsed by committee members and witnesses, two questions were never specifically asked. First, what was meant by a 'national taste', and second, why was the acquisition of a 'national taste' so essential? Superficially, the answer to the first question might be that a 'national taste' would involve all citizens subscribing to the same idea of what was 'good', namely neo-classicism. To the second, the degree of taste that continental populations were believed to enjoy, had supposedly brought them social, political and economic benefits. Hence, emulation would bring similar benefits to Britain. But neither of these answers can be left at that, because they mask more important underlying issues.

What the committee was seeking in raising the issue of a 'national taste' was most often discussed in the context of the arts and manufactures, but it was certainly not confined to the arts. In the following statement, posing as a question, put to William Wyon, a great deal is revealed. It was put to Wyon that 'the supply of art would create a demand for art, and the demand for art would in turn create a supply of art?' The capitalist theory embedded in the question has relevance far beyond 'art'. It looks to the realisation of a society based on the expansion of consumerism. But Wyon's answer to this is even more fascinating. He said, as though answering an entirely different question, 'Yes, and the morals of the country would be greatly improved by creating a new taste.'[16] Encapsulated within this exchange are the ingredients that require explanation in relation to art and design education. The rationale for the committee's ambition to foster a public sensitized to a prescribed art, and to institute methods of instruction in the subject might at first appear vague, but it was clearly not without intent. At root, there are two major themes that can be identified here; 'taste' to guide and promote consumerism in the interests of an expanding capitalist economy, and 'taste' to influence behaviour. These were part and parcel of an ambitious capitalism that valued social and political stability as prerequisites for its success.

The Social Dimension of Taste

It could be argued that political stability was as central to the relationship of 'taste' and morality as it was to 'taste' and capitalism. In this connection, the fact that the antique, personified in Greek and Roman art, was seen to be the ideal is relevant. The ideals of Greek and Roman civilisation vested as they were in political order, it could be suggested, were a powerful attraction to politicians. Hence, the desire to connect it to all things. With this historical perspective 'taste' acquired an increasingly concrete social dimension in the early to mid-nineteenth century.

By the time of the 1835/6 Select Committee 'taste' was allied to the full range of moral and social class terminology. The language of 'taste' was used at different points during the hearings, and in connection with all social classes. It was most vociferously employed however, when discussing the poor. This group was singled out as being in particular need of the benefits of 'taste'.

When referring to 'the lower orders' (or one of the large number of other epithets applied) the discussion was most often centred around access to exhibitions of 'high art' in galleries, and the provision of museums and libraries. These were the primary means by which the 'taste' of this amorphous group of people would be raised, and the context in which moral imperatives were invariably invoked. Messrs. Wilkins and Woodburn were asked whether opening the National Exhibitions on a Sunday had been beneficial. The reply came, 'I should think any rational amusement that you could give to the lower order of people would be very desirable', and was added to later with the statement that 'any pleasurable excitement that you can give to the mind (of the lower orders) to draw it from vicious pursuits is doing good.'[17] Vicious pursuits covered a multitude of perceived evils but, as in this instance, the target was most often alcohol.

Many were convinced that the diffusion of knowledge among the lower classes would promote temperance. The 'encourage(ment) (of) places of meeting for the labouring population, for the enjoyment of athletic games, of lectures, and discourses upon entertaining topics, and drawings and sculpture, and museums and natural curiosities'[18] would counter drunkeness they claimed. With barely disguised self interest, James Nasmyth was of the opinion that a small selection of 'graceful forms of antique designs' exhibited in the factory would be an antidote to drink resulting in enjoyment for his workers, and ultimately national prosperity through improved manufactures. Messrs. Wilkins and Woodburn were convinced that the absence of 'sufficient amusement' drove the 'lower order of people' to the 'gin shop',[19] and similar words concerning the 'pot houses' of Sheffield, Birmingham and Glasgow were used elsewhere in the 1835/6 Select Committee on Arts and Manufactures.

So there was an ongoing obsession with these connections both inside and outside of the debate about schools of design. The recurrent connection that is made between the perceived problem of immorality, and the redemptive effect of exposure to exemplars of 'taste', is focused principally on the 'labouring poor'. This was so in the 1830s and remained the case for the rest of the century and beyond.

Taste, Consumerism and Fashion

The morally irreproachable aspiration for consumerism by those involved in the committee is contained in this quotation from the Minutes – 'A taste more refined would of course create a production more elevated.'[20] However, its compatibility with the demands of capitalism are debatable. The 'niceties' it expresses are at variance with the aggressive capitalism that as a social and economic system, gained an ever more secure hold in Britain from the early nineteenth century, not only economically but also semiotically. Indeed, from the late eighteenth century, it had become increasingly difficult to imagine alternatives. For different sections of society, the consequences were obviously not the same. But, some historians argue, for the population as a whole capitalism was beneficial, since over time it positively increased stability in the system. Others have gone even further, emphasizing the improving opportunities for employment and income in a period of unprecedented growth in prosperity.

Levels of disposable income correlate closely with the capacity for a commodity culture to flourish. In the late eighteenth and early nineteenth century, the foundation for this kind of prosperity was being laid via the expanding manufacturing base in Britain and slowly improving conditions of work and leisure. Relatively more leisure time and the fact that increased prosperity created more disposable income, stimulated consumerism. Along with increased consumption came greater interest in commodities.

Some historians suggest that 'more men and women than ever before in human history enjoyed the experience of acquiring material possessions' in the eighteenth century.

> *The result of these changes for those engaged in making and selling objects for the person and for the home were revolutionary. And those making and selling such consumer goods had not only responded to these changes; they had, as a result of their earnest commercial endeavours, played a substantial and a positive role in bringing them about. They had helped to release and to satisfy a consumer boom of major proportions.*[21]

However basic a human need material consumption might be, the ability to do so remained the pastime of the few until the eighteenth century. What distinguishes developments in consumerism then from its predecessors was 'the sharp break in trend between Stuart England and Georgian England.'[22] It was the watershed that increasingly enabled the gap between the desire, and the ability to consume, to be closed.

It is true to say that against this background of commercialisation the 1835/6 Select Committee showed a slim understanding of the mechanisms of consumerism.

They discussed it at length, but their grasp of the issues was repeatedly demonstrated to be rather weak. These discussions invariably connected 'taste' to consumerism.

Noel St Leon and Joseph Clinton Robertson were two of a tiny band of witnesses whose evidence to the committee showed insight into the relationship between fashion, taste and consumerism. Both men's evidence was greeted with similar hostility. The committee asked Robertson, a great believer in the purely vocational uses of art education, 'Do you think, that if they (the manufacturers) exercised a greater degree of taste upon the same material of manufacture there would be a greater demand for that manufacture?' Robertson thought not, rather 'the taste, such as it is, does not seem to be any drawback on the demand. You must improve the public taste greatly before you can expect to witness any material improvement in the productions of those who minister it.' The committee speculated on how public taste could be improved. Perhaps, it was ventured, 'by the sight of works of good design?' The question was then put to Robertson, 'Do you suppose, if works of good design went into the market with works of bad design, that in the end the works of good design would not be preferred?' To which Robertson replied, 'I am not sure of that; I think the public eye requires to be educated in matters of taste, in the same way that the understanding requires to be enlightened by reading and study'. A little later in his evidence the committee put it to Robertson, perhaps with a degree of irritation in their tone, 'Then you lay down this principle, that it is in vain to offer the great mass of consumers works which combine, with perfect manufacture, elegance of design, because they would not be appreciated by them?' Robertson replied, 'I think, considering the existing state of taste among the great mass of consumers, you might produce patterns so elegant that they would not sell.'[23] This simple truth was obviously not what the committee wanted to hear, but it represents a kind of socio-economic realism that was most often absent in the hearings of the committee.

It is clear that the challenge presented to the committee by the couplet 'taste' and 'consumerism' was daunting. But one of the most interesting things about the committee is the attitude that virtually all participants had toward the additional notion of 'fashion'. Like 'taste' the history of 'fashion' is long. But here, the key difference between its legion appearance in pre-eighteenth century history and that of the late eighteenth and nineteenth century, is that its former usage usually refers to attitudes, whilst the latter very definitely embraces commodities that can be made and sold.

When Josiah Wedgewood said in the late eighteenth century, 'Fashion is infinitely superior to merit', he may well have been divulging a key factor in his commercial success, but such a view would not have been generally endorsed, and it would have been heresy to the 1835/6 Select Committee. If there was one enemy to be overcome by those discussing the progress of arts and manufactures in this committee, it is that of fashion. Fashion is perceived as a problem, an uncontrollable and insidious variant that, if only it could be eradicated, would allow the 'taste' of universal principle to reign supreme. Hence, it attracted much attention. The fact that fashion was an integral element in the progress of consumerism that all desired went generally unrecognised (with the notable exception of Noel St Leon).[24] For the population at large, where once domestic objects, furniture and so on, had been bought once in a lifetime and clothes were replaced only as a necessity, from the eighteenth century onwards fashion stimulated the economy. The 'acceleration' of fashion change can be noted in Elizabeth Gaskell's first novel, *Mary Barton*, published in 1848, when one of her characters says 'I left 'em my fashion book (though it were two months old).'[25]

Hindsight allows the thought that far from being a problem, fashion might have been seen as having an important role to play in validating the need for art and design education. But this was far from the case in this committee. Taste was always to be defended against fashion. The concern was constantly raised that the 'people' were often selecting foreign articles, of whatever description, which were inferior 'in point of art'; although for the moment they were attractive 'in point of fashion'.

The dismissiveness with which fashion is often treated in the committee raises a number of questions. It is of course plausible that someone like Robertson, and the other witnesses called, were simply unaware of the importance of understanding movements of fashion in securing markets. Although it would have been theoretically possible to assemble a significant number of witnesses with expertise in those areas, and manufacturers who already understood the mechanisms of successful consumerism, this was not done. Indeed, the entire list of witnesses could have been very different, maybe producing a very different Report. It would be easy to pass these questions off by saying that in the early stages of consumerism few understood the import of such connections. But the point has already been made that by the early nineteenth century consumerism was well developed in Britain. It is reasonable therefore to draw the conclusion that the degree of economic understanding of how consumer societies work amongst the participants in the 1835/6 Select Committee was still rather slim.

But this is not the whole story. Perhaps one of the most important undercurrents in the Minutes of evidence and the Report is that it reveals the peculiar mixture of rectitude and guilt that permeated nineteenth century feelings about consumerism. It was a guilt that was assuaged by an unfettered optimism in the possibility of 'improvement'. It might be argued that these feelings of guilt about consumerism play a key role in understanding aspects of the 1835/6 Select Committee on Arts and Manufactures. How can this be explained?

A particular interplay of guilt and consumerism dates back to the eighteenth century and the publication of Bernard Mandeville's *Fable of the Bees-Private Vices, Publick Virtues* (1724). It caused enormous offence in arguing 'the national, social and economic benefits that could (and in his view did), spring from luxury, avarice, prodigality, pride, envy and vanity'.[26] Mandeville's economic message, or 'moral', was very simple. But for the enjoyment of luxury, he argued, those with money would not spend it, and hence craftsmen and tradesmen would soon go out of business. Hence, these 'private vices' are actually 'public virtues'. This was not however, a message that was readily acceptable in the eighteenth century.

> *The ideas that 'consumption was the logical end of production', that the 'latent consuming capacity of the public at large might become an engine for sustained growth', that 'society was an aggregation of self-interested individuals tied to one another by the tenuous bonds of envy, exploitation and competition' were new and, to many alarming.*[27]

Such deeply held reservations about the morality of consumption had not been allayed by the early decades of the nineteenth century. Indeed, they were growing alongside religious revivalism that, in the 1830s, saw 'Anglican champions of social reform appear(ing) side by side with Chartists and radicals.'[28] This alliance was an uneasy companion to capitalism. The kinds of reservations created by this circumstance may be clearly detected in the committee's discussions of taste. The moral relationship between taste and consumerism is repeatedly mentioned. Whilst at times the committee was patently exploring the possible economic link between a population largely unaware of something called 'taste' (or, as was continually evidenced by reference to the continent, the desirability of acquiring it), and accelerating patterns of consumerism at home, it could not be done with a kind of capitalist abandon. The committee felt bound to seek a moral justification for consumerism, freed from Mandeville's abhorrent and guilt inducing economic realities.

What was Art and Design Education Intended to Achieve?

In the light of themes that have been explored here, what can be said about the committees intentions for art and design education? There were, of course many instances in the committee when witnesses thought that art and design education was a route to raising the public taste. Equally, there were many instances of art and design education being allied to the improvement of manufactures.

I have suggested that the issues being discussed in this select committee often converge. It was insisted that a 'national taste' was to be achieved in part through access to museums and exhibitions, and also through the instruction of 'young men' in the principles of 'correct' drawing from the antique. Throughout the whole of the hearings the connection between art and design education (in the wider sense of schools of design, museums and exhibitions) and taste was clearly established in the minds of the committee, as was taste and consumerism, taste and morality, and taste and manufacturing, leaving aside that of protection of copyright and so on. It is possible to trace the progress of any of these couplets through the minutes of evidence of the committee and beyond. By doing so, evidence can be found for the primacy of any of them.

The reality is that the evidence suggests that the project was never *solely* or arguably *primarily* about art and design education, but an agglomeration of things that the word 'taste' stood in for. Taste was an all-embracing term that took in moral imperatives, civic behaviour, good judgement in consumer choices, and the promotion of economic interests. 'Taste' was, in a sense, the word that brought together two of the most important themes of the early to mid-nineteenth century. It allowed Victorians to be able to overcome the legacy of guilt that Mandeville had bequeathed them and, in a period of religious revival, indulge a growing passion for consumerism. It was in effect the word that gave moral justification to consumerism, with art and design education being harnessed as a vehicle for its implementation.

Notes and References

1. See Bell, Q. (1963), *The Schools of Design,* Routledge and Kegan Paul; Macdonald, S. (1970), *The History and Philosophy of Art Education*, London University Press.
2. See Cunningham, P. (1979), 'The formation of the Schools of Design: 1830–1850 with special reference to Manchester, Birmingham and Leeds' Unpublished Ph.D. thesis, University of Leeds. Romans, M. (1998), 'Political, Economic, Social and Cultural Determinants in the History of Early to Mid–nineteenth Century Art and Design Education in Britain' Unpublished Ph.D. thesis, University of Central England. Romans, M. 'Politics, Economics and Art Education: Problematising a Nineteenth Century Panacea' in Swift, J. (1998), *Art Education Discourses*, Volume 1, ARTicle Press; and Romans, M. (2004), 'Living in the Past: Some Revisionist Thoughts on the Historiography of Art and Design Education' *International Journal of Art & Design Education*, 23: 3.
3. In their respective (and both very short) chapters 'Haydon and the Radicals' and 'The Petitioner and the politicians' Bell and Macdonald are casual in their description of nineteenth century political history.
4. Addison, J. (1854), *Works Volume 2*, New York, p. 138.
5. Bayley, S. (1983), Catalogue of 'Taste – an exhibition about values in design' Boilerhouse Project – Victoria and Albert Museum, p. 12.
6. Everett Gilbert, K. & Kuhn, H. (1972), *A History of Esthetics*, Dover Publications, p. 246.
7. Clarke, M. & Penny, N. (Eds.), *The Arrogant Connoisseur: Richard Payne Knigh*t *1751-1824,* Manchester University Press, p. 84.
8. in Honour, H. (1991), *Neo-Classicism*, Penguin, p. 61.
9. Report from Select Committee on Arts and Manufactures: together with the Minutes of Evidence, and Appendix (1835), (Question 670) p. 51.
10. Report from Select Committee on Arts and Manufactures: together with the Minutes of Evidence, and Appendix (1835), (Question 1731) p. 137.
11. Report from Select Committee on Arts and Manufactures: together with the Minutes of Evidence, and Appendix (1836), (Question 230) p. 23.
12. Report from Select Committee on Arts and Manufactures: together with the Minutes of Evidence, and Appendix (1835), (Question 1134) p. 88.

13. Report from Select Committee on Arts and Manufactures: together with the Minutes of Evidence, and Appendix (1836), (Question 586) p. 49.

14. *The Art-Union,* 1 January 1842, p. 14.

15. Report from Select Committee on Arts and Manufactures: together with the Minutes of Evidence, and Appendix (1835), (Question 766) p. 58.

16. Report from Select Committee on Arts and Manufactures: together with the Minutes of Evidence, and Appendix (1835), (Question 1727) p. 137.

17. Report from Select Committee on Arts and Manufactures: together with the Minutes of Evidence, and Appendix (1836), (Question 1750) p. 141.

18. Report from Select Committee into Drunkeness among Labouring Classes of UK, together with Minutes of Evidence and Appendix (1834), (Question 3548) p. 298.

19. Report from Select Committee on Arts and Manufactures: together with the Minutes of Evidence, and Appendix (1836), (Question 1751) p. 141.

20. Report from Select Committee on Arts and Manufactures: together with the Minutes of Evidence, and Appendix (1835), (Question 672) p. 52.

21. Mckendrick, N., Brewer, J. & Plumb, J. H. (1982), *The Birth of a Consumer Society: the commercialisation of eighteenth-century England*, Europa Publications, p. 1.

22. Mckendrick, N., Brewer, J. & Plumb, J. H., *Ibid.* p. 5.

23. Report from Select Committee on Arts and Manufactures: together with the Minutes of Evidence, and Appendix (1835), (Question 1617) p. 129.

24. Noel St Leon's evidence to the 1835/6 Select Committee on Arts and Manufactures was the shortest of all the witnesses, and yet it was one of the most insightful. St Leon clearly understood the relationship between fashion and consumerism and voiced it, much to the apparent chagrin of the committee.

25. Gaskell, E. (1994), *Mary Barton*, Penguin, p. 42.

26. in Mckendrick, N., Brewer, J. & Plumb, J. H., *Op. Cit.* p. 16.

27. Mckendrick, N., Brewer, J. & Plumb, J. H., *Ibid.* p. 18/19.

28. Harrison, J. F. C. (1979), *Early Victorian Britain, 1832-51*, Fontana, p. 125.

Chapter 4: Social Class and the Origin of Public Art and Design Education in Britain: In Search of a Target Group

Mervyn Romans

Introduction

The first school of design had opened in London in 1837. Between then and 1852, when Henry Cole and Richard Redgrave took charge of the system, a further 21 had opened around the country. But who were these schools of design for? Who was to benefit from an art and/or design education in post 1837 Britain? If an answer to this question is to be found anywhere it should be in the report of the 1835/6 Select Committee on Arts and Manufactures, where the firm proposal for public art and design education was made. Referring to social groups, the word 'artisan' is frequently used here, but 'the people' and 'the manufacturing population' are also terms commonly applied in the minutes. 'Mechanics', 'workmen', 'operatives' and 'journeymen' are intermingled with more convoluted terminology. 'Manufacturing classes', 'classes of operatives', 'intelligent labourers', 'the labouring classes', 'active classes of the community' and 'men devoted to productive industry' are but a further sample of the various descriptions used over the course of the hearings. And if this plethora of terms suggests a degree of uncertainty about social class among the members of the select committee, it is an uncertainty that is mirrored in the historiography of art and design education. A distinct lack of clarity about social class pervades much writing on this period of public art and design education in Britain, leading writers to ignore the terminological intricacies in favour of broad categorizations of social class. In pursuit of an answer to the questions posed above, most of these historians have been content to amalgamate the terminology used in the select committee to discuss the issue from within an unmediated 'working class' discourse (Macdonald 1970 *et al.*).[1] But can the matter be left at that?

In 'The Language of "Class" in Early Nineteenth Century England' Asa Briggs rehearses three major points that were made about 'class' that suggest historians of art and design education have some rethinking to do in this arena.

> *First, England was a country where there was a marked degree of individual mobility and this made class distinctions tolerable. Second, the dividing lines between classes were extremely difficult to draw. Third, there were significant divisions* inside *what were conventionally regarded as classes, and these divisions were often more significant than divisions* between *the classes.*[2]

Hence, in concerning itself with the interrelationship of social class and its representation, with art and design education in the early to mid-nineteenth century, this essay argues it is not possible to discuss the subject solely from within a single set of class discourses. It suggests that recognition of the subtle and complex nature of social class is a necessary prerequisite of addressing the issues raised by its juxtaposition with art and design education. In order to begin the process of getting closer to determining whom the schools of design were for, a context needs to be established in which social class is being discussed.

An Overview: The Representation of Social Class, and Social Relations in the Early to Mid-nineteenth Century

Historians give considerable significance to the mid-nineteenth century in relation to a dual turning point in social organisation in Britain. This is seen in both the evolution of the working class and the middle class. The latter first: Dror Wahrman (1995) has suggested in his *Imagining the Middle Class - The Political Representation of Class in Britain, c.1780-1840* that by the early nineteenth century 'an extensive array of British commentators seemed no longer able to describe the world or understand it without a middle class'.[3] There are three main 'middle class' narratives to be introduced here. The first two of them, although presented here separately, can be viewed as an amalgam of historiographical variants forming their individual 'grand' narratives. Central to this story is the issue of whether there was disruption or continuity in the progress of the social and economic history of nineteenth century Britain.

So far as the 'disruption' model is concerned it is suggested that the people concerned were a new social group created by the specific conditions of late eighteenth and early nineteenth century circumstance who emerged as a result of the Industrial Revolution and, in a 'linear progression, inexorably (rode) forth on the crest of social change.'[4] The 'grand' narrative that suggests disruption as the catalyst for this new middle class, bifurcates at the mid-century period. The 'classic Marxian' view sees the new industrial bourgeoisie as British society's masters after 1850, with the aristocracy fulfilling a ceremonial, but essentially powerless role. Political and economic power were already in their hands as, in the second half of the century, they also established their cultural hegemony. Set against this interpretation of 'success' is that which argues for the 'failure of the middle class. Here, the 'grand' narrative is also followed to the mid-nineteenth century, whereby the middle classes secured reform in 1832, but suggests that this was achieved against a backdrop of both fear of the English proletariat's revolutionary potential to replicate 'the terror' in France, and an insurmountable deference to the authority of the landed class with whom they settled for an alliance. Thus, this argument goes, the aristocracy, regenerated by late nineteenth century imperialism, maintained its hold on power for the rest of the century.

Second, is the narrative that rejects the sudden emergence of the middle class in the nineteenth century, in favour of a longer continuous evolution of this social group. In place of destabilisation there is continuity, resulting in a more benign 'new order' of 'aristocratic landlords/financiers' and 'independent skilled workers'.[5] This oppositional version of 'middle class' history, argues that there was a middle class from at least the beginning of the eighteenth century. Equally those who argue for the 'long eighteenth century' suggest that there was no marked disruption of an 'Industrial Revolution' between the period 1790–1850. Rather, historians such as N. F. R. Crafts (1983, 1985, 1987), F. M. L. Thompson (1988)[6] and A. E. Wrigley (1989) claim that there was a slow and steady economic development, and whilst Maxine Berg (1994) argues for a 'low tech' revolution, it is still one that emerged slowly rather than in disruptive fashion. In terms of social history this evolution was one in which the 'middling ranks' were integrated rather than emerging as a distinct and novel class.

The third way challenges the socio-economic historical premise on which these arguments are based, in favour of a political representation of the middle class. Here, Dror Wahrman suggests that the changing 'political configurations' are the determinants in how the British people came to see themselves as living in a society where the middle class was its centre. Wahrman traces the political origins of middle class language in England, in the events of the French Revolution, where it was by turns applauded and reviled.

Just as the mid-century has a particular resonance for middle class discourses, so too the history of the working classes sees the mid-century as crucial to its development. Here, the mid-century is important in relation to the 'artisan'. A parallel discourse has explored the emergence of a 'labour aristocracy' from the 1850s, whose occupational distinction, economic status, social and cultural aspirations sharply separated them from the great mass of the working classes. As with middle class discourses, the 'labour aristocracy' theme has its supporters and detractors, who argue alternative positions.

In place of this middle class industrial bourgeoisie, a working class representation would present ruthless new capitalists who made fortunes in 'cottonopolis'. This perception is essential to create the conflict fundamental to labour historians view of the working class in a capitalist society. This is the now familiar narrative suggesting that the process of industrialization created an exploited group of people Marx identified as a 'subordinate factory proletariat'. These were a new class of people who had been largely de-skilled by the Industrial Revolution, and who were without property, forced together in vast numbers by the factory system, to live in congested urban poverty. This proposition of suppressed economic conflict creating the conditions of potential revolutionary activity, had as its natural corollary the political supremacy of a ruling class committed to the containment of those revolutionary tendencies. The powerful influence of Marxist historians' reading of nineteenth and twentieth century social history in the 1960s has, ever since, had both its more dogmatic opponents[7] and those who, viewing class formation from other perspectives, have challenged with more reasoned zeal.[8] So that the claim that the Industrial Revolution de-skilled and destroyed the artisan class in British society, and thus created the conditions for its subordination, is seen to overstate and perhaps even misrepresent the case.

An important subdivision of this history of labour for this essay has been research into the 'artisan' by a number of historians.[9] Collectively they ask questions about the identity of the 'artisan' as a social group that can be applied to the art and design education issues under discussion here.

Gareth Steadman Jones (1975) warned of the ambiguities in the use of the term 'artisan', suggesting that 'Indicative of its lack of precision is the elasticity of the stratum of the working-class referred to.'[10] A corollary of this is the uncertainty in the lexicon surrounding 'the artisan'. In addition to the term 'artisan', which Hobsbawm suggested 'belongs largely to the world of nineteenth-century social and political discourse'[11] further apparent classifications such as 'superior artisans', the 'aristocracy of labour', 'intelligent artisans' and 'the elite of the working classes'[12] are also frequently applied. The presence of these terms in a wide variety of contemporary nineteenth century texts has instigated an ongoing debate.[13]

In 1954 in a refinement of the Marxist reading of social history, Eric Hobsbawm argued for the existence from the mid-century period of a small percentage of the nineteenth century working class who, by virtue of their higher and relatively stable earnings, and their organisations into trade unions, could be separated off from the rest of the working class into a 'labour aristocracy.' Having influentially proposed the concept of a 'labour aristocracy', 30 years later, and following other important contributions to the field, in his 'Artisan or Labour Aristocrat?' (1984) Hobsbawm again offers a definition of the 'artisan', saying that 'In most European languages the word *artisan* or its equivalent, used without qualification, is automatically taken to mean something like an independent craftsman or small master, or someone who hopes to become one.'[14] When he says 'artisan or its equivalent', it might be assumed he is including the terms 'superior artisans', the 'aristocracy of labour', and 'the elite of the working classes.' But, symptomatic of the problem of nomenclature, he then says, 'used without qualification', suggesting that '*superior* artisans' etc. are in some way different from 'artisans'. In fact, he makes clear in this essay he is not referring to 'intelligent artisans' when he is discussing the 'artisan'. Significantly, Hobsbawm calls upon the authority of Thomas Wright, the nineteenth century working class commentator,[15] to distinguish between this further small minority of artisans who might or might not be also titled 'superior artisans' and so on. In any event the 'intelligent artisans' are the people whose intellectual interests had led them to develop a reading habit, and who are usually drawn into the mid-Victorian parliamentary reform debate. They are a separate group from the remainder of the artisans whose interests, Hobsbawm claims, remained identical to those of the proletariat. So that arguably there are not only fundamental distinctions to be drawn between the terms 'artisan', and 'labourer' as sub groups of the working class, but also within the artisan group, where there may be further distinctions. Contributors to the discussion have adopted different positions and offered various supportive explanations for the notion of the 'aristocracy of labour', along with those who have argued for its denial. Building on Hobsbawm's criteria, those who argued for the existence of such a group have tended to return to particular themes. The most important of these have concerned occupational skill, respectability and independence in a social setting, and political and cultural imperatives. Although conclusive arguments are absent, there remains a desire to demonstrate the social differences between the artisan and the labourer, and also in some instances, the differences between the artisan and the middle class. These other indicators of 'artisan' identity have been seen in such areas as housing and the social identities of marriage partners for example.

The theoretical analysis of the connection between the artisan and the middle classes is also important here. One such analysis is that an important ingredient in the 'age of equipoise' was middle class efforts to come to terms with the lessons of Chartist agitation, rather than suppress it. The moderating influence of the labour aristocracy theme is closely associated with the failure of Chartism to develop beyond the mid-century in Britain (at the same time as socialism grew on the continent). Both Gray (1981) and Thompson (1988) express serious reservations about such arguments but Thompson concedes that many of the middle classes did actively foster the kind of superior aspirations in the artisans that would bolster the middle classes claims to hegemony. Whether they were successful in doing so or not is debatable, but less so is the idea that at the same time as engendering notions of 'improvement' in the artisan, the middle classes were encouraging them to turn their faces away from the residuum.

If these summaries of middle class and artisan discourses suggest a 'state of play' that is complex and volatile, then they have served their purpose of opening up the field for a more complicated and textured interpretation of the place of social class in the history of art and design education than has hitherto been ventured.

Art and Design Education, Social Class, and Social Relations in the Early to Mid-Nineteenth Century

Many histories of art and design education conflate 'the labouring poor' with 'the artisan' into one class of people to whom art and design education was directed. The working class discourses reviewed here suggest that this should be queried, and opens up considerable room for debate about some historians cursory representation of the social status of the group for whom, apparently, art and design education had been established. Although the wider historical debate about the 'artisan' and the 'labour aristocrat' outlined in the previous section, overlooked the recurrence of such terminology in the 1835/6 Select Committee on Arts and Manufactures, its high profile there does explain the emphasis placed on the 'artisan' in most early histories of art and design education.

In the 1835/6 select committee there is a strong temptation to reduce its complex social language to a simple division of 'lower' and 'middle' class issues. But whatever the difficulties it presents, perhaps the most noticeable characteristic of the Report and Minutes so far as class is concerned is the jumble of terminology used, and its apparently chaotic application. Clearly, the confusion about social class in this committee is not an isolated incident. Rather, it is symptomatic of wider social uncertainties. In one sense these uncertainties are given a public voice in the remit of the select committee. The attention of the committee was seemingly rather vaguely directed towards 'the people (especially the manufacturing population)'. At first sight this might be interpreted as rather casual drafting of the order. Who were 'the people' – the whole population of working, middle and upper class people, only the working class, or perhaps some sections of the working class? The answer to this question can be narrowed, but beyond that can only be speculative. In reality the choice of words is probably a revealing reflection of the very limited degree of understanding of social class and its movements by those charged with phrasing the remit. Given this beginning it is unsurprising that an analysis of the minutes for the contexts in which class terms are used often shows the committee desperately attempting to come to terms with social groups that are occupationally more complex than the members of the select committee could have imagined, and whose structure and identity was rapidly changing and fragmenting. Far from being an uncomplicated class question, requiring a simple consideration of whether the artisan should receive an art education or not, the minutes persistently demonstrate that the committee had serious difficulties in working out who they were addressing.

When Charles Harriott Smith was asked by the committee whether wages increased with the complexity of the task undertaken by his workforce, he replied that this was so, and such work was done by 'ingenious common workmen, if I may so term them.'[16] At other times the cautious elaboration in Smith's attempt to identify a specific group, is rejected in favour of broad bands of class description. In stark contrast to Smith, Willliam Ewart (the chairman of the committee), in a question to James Morrison uses the terms 'the lower and the middling classes', and 'the upper classes'. Similarly another witness, Robert Butt talked about 'the middle class of France, as compared with the same class in England', and went on to refer to 'the upper classes', and in another response to an 'ignorant workman'.[17] Where the artisan is to be positioned in these instances is uncertain. An easy assumption would be that they were to be subsumed into the 'lower class', but this would be mistaken, given the social contexts in which the 'lower class' is often discussed. Numerically, the kind of graded class description offered by Smith outweighs those of Ewart and Butt. Closer examination reveals that this shifting use of terminology about the artisan in the early nineteenth century may appear to be arbitrarily applied, and to a degree possibly was so, but it is not without meaning. At one extreme, there is a profusion of terminology which can be characterised as descriptions of the 'lower orders'. This moves on a decreasing scale of frequency and variety to terminology that might be characterised by 'highly skilled artisans' at the other extreme. Where the latter is applied however, as in James Crabb's reference to 'intelligent journeymen'[18] it is more often to bemoan the absence of such people in England than to affirm their presence. But given this range and weighting of language, it is difficult to believe that in the minds of the select committee and its witnesses, there was real conviction in these descriptions being of one group of people – the artisan. Indeed, the level of uncertainty in the minds of those struggling to define the group to whom they were referring is amply demonstrated in this linguistic plurality.

The recurrence of the term 'artisan' is not a demonstration of familiarity with the social group. Rather, it is apparent that the committee, and often its witnesses, had very little insight into this group, and that their grip on the social and occupational changes that surrounded the artisan in the early nineteenth century was tenuous indeed. The uncertainties being revealed by middle class committee members about the artisan were a mirror image of their own class uncertainties. The pressures on middle class identity were equally great. The circumstance was not then, one that was conducive to a clear articulation of problems and solutions.

But that social class was in a state of flux was noticed by witnesses. When Ewart asked Charles Harriott Smith, 'Are the habits of the workmen in your branch of art improved of late years?', he thought they were. But he attributed this specifically to:

> *...the change that has taken place of late years, by dividing those workmen who are fond of malt and spiritous liquors, from those who attend coffee-houses and coffee-shops; the establishment of those shops seems to have separated the two classes, which has, in my establishment, the effect, that men who attend the coffee-shops seem to consider themselves belonging to a more respected class of society, and will not associate with those who go into public houses.*[19]

Sadly, Smith makes no observation on whether this division was also drawn along specific occupational lines, but as a sculptor for architectural ornament, it is possible to surmise that his workmen spanned a skill range that might have correlated with these choices. Whether Smith was actually observing the consequences, or the causes of this social division of the working classes, is another debate, but there are important points to be made here. Plainly, the notions of 'improvement' and 'respectability' were active within the working class at this time, and form part of a complex network of social practice. What is very clear from this statement is that, despite the confusion about social class evident in so many of the select committee's deliberations, Smith and some other witnesses acknowledged that social mobility within the working class was emerging, and that distinctly different sub groups were being established. Smith was distinguishing the group that came to be viewed as the 'residuum', or 'the labouring poor' who frequented the 'pot houses', from another sub group who were clearly seen, and wished to be associated with 'respectable' society. The parallels with some of the discourses of social class introduced above are obvious.

A second example can be found in the evidence given by Thomas Jones Howell, an inspector under the Factory Regulations Act. At Worcester, Howell had visited a society called The Literary and Scientific Institution where instruction in drawing was offered to members. They also held a number of lectures and John Constable had delivered one of these earlier. Howell wished to determine the effect it had had on the 'operatives', as he termed them, and so he talked to some of them about the lecture. In a relatively rare example of the use of 'the highly skilled artisan' language being applied to a member of the English working class in these minutes, the spokesman for the group impressed Howell as 'an extremely intelligent person'.[20] The final report reinterpreted this description as 'the enterprizing and laborious classes.' But Howell's terminology is much more significant, since it is closer to the language of Thomas Wright who, later in the century, talked about the 'intelligent artisan' as being a distinct group of 'respectable' people. Whereas the committee often missed the importance of such observations, Howell perhaps, recognised in his discussion a forerunner of the members of the working classes that Wright later described.

Making the point that the distinctions between the 'the labouring poor' and the 'artisan' were being made in the 1830s however, is rather to affirm the fluidity of social class than to imply that they originated there. The antecedents in the language of social class that Hobsbawm described suggest a much longer history. He stressed that the language and institutions of pre-industrial craft organisation were bequeathed to the working class in the Victorian period, and also argued that Victorian class distinctions within the working class derived from these craft traditions and are 'deeply rooted in the vocabulary, and hence the congealed memories, of the pre-industrialised craft world.'[21] So that it is suggested that the working classes themselves had formulated a division of their class into 'artisan'/'mechanic' and 'labourer' long before the middle classes were able to recognise it. Though now seen to be probably too simplistic, the 'working classes' generally accepted this division at the time. It was a division that was being observed with interest by some members of the middle classes in the 1830s, as is demonstrated in the select committee minutes, but the implications of its progress were not fully understood. Indeed, it could be argued that when the select committee talked about 'the artisan' they were looking back to an earlier age, with more romance than insight. Nevertheless, Smith and Howell could be seen as testifying to the fact that the germ of the 'labour aristocracy' theme was being voiced as early as the 1830s, and in an art and design arena.

Conclusion

At the beginning of this essay it was claimed that it was not possible to discuss the history of art and design education from within a single set of class discourses. There are some final points to emphasize. It can be seen at this point that the generalized use of the term 'artisan' in previous histories as a catch-all term to apply to those for whom art and design education was intended is inadequate. A differentiated use of the language of class with reference to sub-groups of the working class in the 1830s is apparent in the primary sources and must be acknowledged. Whether or not it is justifiable to argue forcefully for the emergence of an artisan 'elite' that precisely corresponds to Hobsbawm's mid to late nineteenth century model, must remain an open question. It is however, reasonable to argue that the language that would come to more accurately represent this social group was being rehearsed and to a degree formulated, in the hearings of the 1835/6 Select Committee on Arts and Manufactures, albeit in a rather unscientific manner.

In the context of a language of class infused with recent political history, the middle classes were, as Thompson has said, searching for their social, and indeed cultural identity in the period leading up to the mid-nineteenth century. For people such as the women who entered the schools of design, the problems were multiplied. Insofar as they sought to earn a living as designers they were entering a social vacuum. Had they become designers they may, or may not, have remained in the middle class that so many of them came from. It is apparent therefore that the debate on social class in relation to art and design education must take place in the interface between the artisan and the middle class discourses that have been introduced. The issues that have been raised suggest a more complicated set of social relationships and interdependence than is described elsewhere. There is no simple correlation between social class and art, and design. The schools of design might, post 1849, have successfully introduced the occupation of designer. Undoubtedly, had this happened, as in post revolutionary France, designers would have bridged the rigid lines implied by the terms 'working class' and 'middle class' and would have existed according to their success in sub groups across these classes.

Notes and References

1. Peter Cunningham's (1979), 'The formation of the Schools of Design: 1830–1850 with special reference to Manchester, Birmingham and Leeds' Unpublished Ph.D. thesis, University of Leeds, was the first revisionist history of early to mid-nineteenth century art and design education in Britain. Cunningham proposed that far from being introduced for the working classes, art education was introduced by the middle class, and for the middle class.

2. Briggs, A. (1974), 'The Language of "Class" in Early Nineteenth Century England' in Flinn, M. W. and Smout, T. C. (Eds.), *Essays in Social History*, Clarendon Press, p. 170.

3. Wahrman, D. (1995), *Imagining the Middle Class - The Political Representation of Class in Britain, c.1780-1840*, Cambridge University Press, p. 371.

4. Wahrman, D. *Ibid.* p. 411.

   By the time this narrative reaches the mid-century however, there are alternative interpretations within the same middle class hegemonic discourse. For some, the mid-century is seen to be the point at which the middle classes could confidently claim to have achieved their historic destiny. Other historians see the mid-nineteenth century as the point at which the 'failure' of the Victorian middle class to achieve this position is apparent ('failure' here refers to Simon Gunn's essay 'The "failure" of the Victorian middle class: a critique' in Wolff, J. and Seed, J. (Eds.) (1988), *The Culture of Capital: art, power and the nineteenth century middle class* where he argues against proponents of the 'failure' theory, such as Martin Wiener and W. D. Rubinstein).

5. Reid, A. J. (1995), *Social classes and social relations in Britain, 1850-1914*, Cambridge University Press, p. 30.

6. F. M. L. Thompson, for example says in his *The Rise of Respectable Society* that 'not only was this development of more sophisticated and specialised machinery – turret lathes, milling machines, grinding machines – a long drawn out and continuing affair, of American rather than British origin, but also it had scarcely begun to produce automatic machinery before the beginning of the twentieth century. In effect workers acquired power tools in place of hand tools, files, saws, drills, or hammers, and they had vastly greater speed, capacity, and accuracy. But the operation of these power tools continued to depend on the skill and experience of the operator, while the actual construction of the machine tools themselves continued to rely on the craftsmanship of individual workers and a great deal of skilled handwork in fitting together the components, p. 40. Gray also invokes Melling's argument saying 'The impact of capitalist development, especially in the nineteenth century, was not simply to destroy skills, but to create the basis for new forms of skilled labour, within which craft methods and traditions could assert themselves,' p. 32.

7. W. L. Burn, for example, said of Marxist history 'To divide such a society into millionaires and wage-slaves and to speak of a complete divorce of property from labour makes nonsense,' p. 93.

8. For example, Morris, R. J. (1979), *Class and Class Consciousness in the Industrial Revolution 1780-1850*.

9. For example Eric Hobsbawm (1954 and 1984), Gareth Steadman Jones (1975), Geoffrey Crossick (1978), Robert Gray (1981), Alastair Reid (1983) and F. M. L. Thompson (1988).

10. Steadman Jones, G. (1975), 'Class Struggle and the Industrial Revolution' *New Left Review*, 90, p. 61.

11. Hobsbawm, E. (1984), 'Artisan or Labour Aristocrat?' *Economic History Review*, Vol. 2. Series Vol. XXVII, p. 356/357.

    Hobsbawm discusses the relationship of the word 'artisan' to 'trade' and 'tradesman' in a nineteenth century context, suggesting that the latter had more common currency within the working class. He also traces these terms in a pre-industrial craft system, describing 'A craft (as consisting) of all those who had acquired the peculiar skills of a more or less difficult trade, by means of a specific process of education, completed by tests and assessments guaranteeing adequate knowledge and performance of the trade. In return such persons expected the right to conduct their trade and to make what they considered a decent living corresponding to its value to society and to their social status,' p. 359.

12. This is the term Asa Briggs uses in his influential essay 'The Language of "Class" in Early Nineteenth Century England.' He also notes that this phrase was employed in the Poor Man's Guardian 'plain but intelligent workmen... the very elite of the working classes', and was often used with reference to the London Working Men's Association.

13. Robert Gray opens his book *The Aristocracy of Labour in Nineteenth-century Britain c.1850-1914* with a representative quotation from *The Reformer* 5 November 1870, which begins – 'The working man belonging to the upper class of his order is a member of the aristocracy of the working classes.' References surface regularly. Typically, in a footnote of 'The Language of "Class" in Early Nineteenth Century England' Briggs, for example, made use of a quotation

from Thomas Wright's essay 'Our New Masters' – 'Between the artisan and the unskilled a gulf is fixed. While the former resents the spirit in which he believes the followers of "genteel occupations" look down upon him, he in turn looks down upon the labourers.'

14. Hobsbawm, E. *Op Cit.* p. 356.

15. Thomas Wright was employed as a skilled metal worker whilst he was writing the collected essays that were published in three books as *The Journeyman Engineer* (1860s–1870s). Intended as a corrective to misapprehensions about the working class, they represent a unique commentary on the period. Hence, labour historians in the late twentieth century have made use of Wright's essays in one way or another as the authentic voice of the contemporary artisan.

16. Report from Select Committee on Arts and Manufactures: together with the Minutes of Evidence, and Appendix (1835), (Question 652) p. 50.

17. Report from Select Committee on Arts and Manufactures: together with the Minutes of Evidence, and Appendix (1835), (Questions 567, 575) p. 45.

18. Report from Select Committee on Arts and Manufactures: together with the Minutes of Evidence, and Appendix (1835), (Question 999) p. 76.

    Or Mr D. R. Hay who expressed similar sentiments in his phrase 'they are generally respectable my workmen,' (1836), (Question 483) p. 42.

19. Report from Select Committee on Arts and Manufactures: together with the Minutes of Evidence, and Appendix (1835), (Questions 654–5) p. 50.

20. Report from Select Committee on Arts and Manufactures: together with the Minutes of Evidence, and Appendix (1836), (Questions 77) p. 11.

    Similarly, George Morant, a later witness said, 'I find that among many workmen of intelligence there is a great desire to acquire a knowledge of art and taste,' (1836), (Question 554) p. 47.

21. Hobsbawm, E. *Op Cit.* p. 357.

Chapter 5: Birmingham and its Art School: Changing Views 1800–1921

John Swift

Introduction

The beginning and development of nationally organised art and design education in nineteenth century Britain has been recorded by Bell, Macdonald, Sutton, Carline and Ashwin amongst others.[1] Generally this has been pursued through the documents of the centrally responsible bodies, be that the Committee of the Government School of Design, the Department of Science and Art or the Board of Education. Irrespective of the title of the managing body, a national curriculum was followed in all Schools of Design, renamed Schools of Practical or Ornamental Art in the 1850s, and in elementary education both prior to and after the 1870 Education Act.

A pattern of thought has developed which tends to identify this history as being centrally dominated in all aspects from London, with occasional but sporadic rebellions from the provinces. This emphasis I believe is due to two related facts: one, the lack of detailed archives in individual colleges and schools of art, and two: the subsequent reliance on printed material (inevitably produced by the Government or its subsidiaries). Thus historians of the area have furthered the theory of a vice-like grip of central control in all matters from the content of courses, to the methods of learning and teaching, the training of teachers, the appointment of teachers and the spaces and facilities necessary for the task. Whilst there is some truth in the centralist view, it is not the whole story. This view portrays the provincial schools as only reactive rather than proactive and is a view I wish to examine in this article.

I intend to elaborate the local pressures and influence on Birmingham School of Design/Art from its foundation to 1921. In so doing I will make use of the extensive archive that the University of Central England in Birmingham retains in the School of Art and Design Education. I shall not attempt to claim that Birmingham is necessarily typical of all provincial art schools, but I do hope to show that the means could be found to subvert, avoid or extend both the contents and the teaching style of a system which fully intended to dominate. The interest and help of local industrialists, philanthropists and educators was essential and this factor may account for Birmingham being partially distinctive rather than typical. I shall therefore look particularly for signs of local independence under the three distinctly titled periods of the Birmingham School, namely (a) The Birmingham

Government School of Design (1843–1851); (b) The Birmingham Government School of (Ornamental/Practical) Art (1852–1883), and (c) The Birmingham Municipal School of Arts and Crafts (1884 onwards). It is quite instructive to regard Birmingham's increasingly successful struggle against central control as a parable for modern times.[2]

Local and National Prelude to the Schools of Design

The growth of art and design education in Birmingham has to be seen within the context of Birmingham as village, town and city. From a nondescript ancestry, it developed into one of the largest, richest industrial centres in England. Due to its variety of charters and regulations considerable freedom of citizenship was possible; there were no restrictive guilds, corporations or religious denominations to curtail immigrant workers and this appears to have been important in the varied and rapid growth of the area. The proliferation of small workshops rather than large factories typified the landscape where skilled artisans produced an enormous variety of wares. Birmingham was unlike many parallel-growing towns in that its workforce was predominantly skilled and that it was not adversely affected by mechanisation as many other industries with large factory bases were. However, Birmingham's manufactures[3] in common with other towns benefited from: (a) well-designed products, and (b) the ability of the artisan both to produce and understand drawings.

It had been customary in Britain to either train appropriate young workpeople to draw and design within the workshop or to buy, derive or 'borrow' designs from other firms both here and abroad. Some large industries even imported French designers to work for them. It was recognised by many types of manufacturer that design mattered. Before the Government awoke to the fact that well-designed objects created larger markets and more wealth, provincial firms around the country were attempting in a variety of ways to improve their wares by developing their designed function and appearance. Central to the concept of designing was the practice of drawing.

This raised its own problems of what and how to draw. In the eighteenth century, intending professional artists had one school, the Royal Academy where the types of drawing skills were arguably appropriate for their future career. Drawing for leisure was the province of the private drawing master and thus afforded by the wealthy alone. The only drawing being taught for more practical reasons was in military academies where the ability accurately to outline terrain had obvious advantages for warfare. Thus the artisans learned as best they could from copying and adapting earlier examples possibly under the tutelage of persons responsible for designing. That such a situation could lead to stasis was apparent when the Government set up a Select Committee in 1835 to report to the Board of Trade on the increasingly poor financial figures for the export of designed goods. The Report of the Committee concluded that a School of Design should be formed on the basis of European schools.

Well before this time, Birmingham was aware of the need to find more effective ways of training designers. Two men, Joseph Barber and Samuel Lines set up their own schools of drawing in 1801 and 1807 respectively. Both schools tended to perpetuate the private drawing master ethos although Lines's curriculum was more extensive.[4] However, the success of both schools may be seen directly and indirectly. Lines's ex-students became prominent Birmingham designers and were successful at the Great Exhibition in 1851; both schools produced skilled artist-engravers perhaps due to the emphasis on drawing skills,[5] and from Lines's school developed an atelier system and the Society of Birmingham Artists.[6] The potential split between the teaching of fine art and design was present but not identified. The aims of the Birmingham Academy of Arts formed in 1814 encompassed 'the embellishment of manufactures'.[7] Birmingham was creating a climate of artistic and designing endeavour and showing initiative in meeting the appropriate needs. This culminated in 1821 in the formation of the Birmingham Society of Arts through local generosity and support.[8] The new Society was troubled from its inception by a split between the practising artists and the more museum-oriented members.[9] Thus in 1828 two rival exhibitions, one of contemporary art, the other of 'ancient masters' were held. A truce between the two factions was uneasily maintained over the next ten years.

However, although artists were exhibiting and selling to local manufacturers and collectors, the quality of designing throughout Birmingham had not noticeably improved. Although the general public were encouraged to, and did, visit art exhibitions in large numbers, this seemed to have little effect on the design of what they bought – design in Birmingham was according to Pugin, who lived there throughout the 1840s, in a deplorable state.

Arguably the increased speed of mechanisation had outstripped design's capacity to maintain its quality. Perhaps too the implied transfer of taste through contact with fine art examples (coupled with some drawing) had not succeeded in materially elevating standards of production or purchase. Above and beyond this, there were different views of what constituted good design which were to surface more openly just before and after the Great Exhibition.

Birmingham's problem was one the Government had just acknowledged – that the provision for design education was insufficient in both amount and method. The Government had set up a Select Committee to recommend improvements and although its findings were clear, the implementation of them seemed almost perverse. Although the French system with early figure drawing and designing actually produced the more imaginative designers, the Prussian system of 'logical' additions of discrete learning skills coupled with highly imitative objectives appealed more to William Dyce R. A. who coordinated the findings.

The problem faced by the first Government School of Design, and subsequently the others in its footsteps, was what should be taught, by whom and to whom. The most obviously able and qualified people to teach drawing were Royal Academicians although they had studied drawing for quite different purposes. The Royal Academy also had vested reasons in differentiating between teaching methods of its own School and those of the Design School.[10] Dyce as the first director of the Government School erected a system where a simplified, rather geometric series of exercises was linked with lectures on pictorial ornament. The course lacked any practical experience with actual materials, a point that was crushingly made by Pugin.[11] Dyce was not averse to practical learning where designs could be applied to or realised with real materials, but finance, management and staff prevented any extended experiment.

This lack of contact with the materials for which the designs were intended was a frequent feature of most nineteenth century art and design education. However, the London School was seen as the first example of a new flowering, and carefully drawn up regulations were made to control the growth and placement of provincial design schools to serve the needs of local manufacturers whilst following a prescribed national syllabus.

The Birmingham Society of Artists was quick to realise that such a Government supported School of Design could build upon and extend the beginnings already made locally. They approached the Committee of the Government School of Design in 1842 and received the usual reply that offered financial aid if local support was at least equal to that given by the Council of the Schools of Design, if it could be guaranteed for three years, and if the local school would conform to the regulations and syllabus laid down by London. Thus encouraged, a section of the Society accepted the regulations and requirements of Somerset House and the Birmingham School of Design opened in October of 1843.[12]

The Birmingham Government School of Design 1843–1851

Birmingham, as one of the earliest provincial schools of design suffered a similar fate to other contemporary schools. Teachers who had previously been considered expert could no longer be employed unless they retrained within the new system, and their replacements were appointed in London and sent to the provincial schools. Many were young and totally inexperienced in any actual designing capacity. Birmingham received W. Dobson, a young painter in his mid-twenties who had briefly trained under Dyce. It must be remembered that such a person would have had to convince the designers in workshops and the manufacturers that he could train good designers, irrespective of their trades, more efficiently than the extant in-house method, despite having no knowledge of the actual materials of the various trades and little if any experience of teaching. It is hardly surprising that the method ran into problems from an early date.

Classes were divided into elementary drawing and 'others', each occupying distinct rooms or room spaces. All students began by 'drawing in outline' to encourage correctness, moving to 'shading with chalks' initially from flat examples and them from a cast, eventually attaining some study of colour from others' painted works and nature. For those who required it, figure drawing and the study of perspective could follow. After satisfactory standards had been achieved in all areas studied, the student could move to the 'history, principles and practice of Ornamental Design'. This actually meant copying examples, studying various designs in different materials and being lectured on the 'practical application of Design to particular manufacturers'.[13] Initially drawing from life was not taught, in the belief that it raised students' aspirations beyond design to fine art: an ambition that was literally prohibited in the early Schools.[14]

The Birmingham School published its *Rules and Regulations* separately for day and evening students.[15] The reason for differences was probably that of the social class of day and evening students. This became an important factor for many provincial design schools and art schools later; the large number of fee-paying middle-class students enabled the schools to remain financially solvent. This in turn affected the direction of much of the teaching towards a fine art/leisure emphasis to satisfy the needs of the cash customer. The subsidised artisans' needs tended to remain a thinner version of the same thing. Students recommended by financial subscribers to the School were admitted free of charge for any type or level of class; others paid anything from one pound to twelve shillings for one year's study.

All provincial schools' progress was overseen by the Inspector, initially Dyce, who had been ousted as Director of the London School and now had to examine the system which Heath Wilson had installed in place of his own. All requirements had to be met on pain of closure. After three years in which four headmasters rapidly succeeded each other, some degree of stability was achieved with the appointment of Thomas Clark in April 1846. Clark enlarged the number of staff and students, extended the teaching to neighbouring towns and criticised the lack of local financial support. Although a contentious character, under his headship the Birmingham School Committee began to be critical of the London presumption to know better than themselves.[16]

In fact much of the argument with Somerset House was over financial support rather than educational policy. Birmingham was recruiting large numbers of students, but the fees were insufficient, even when coupled with the equal contribution of Somerset House and the Birmingham subscribers, to afford more staff and improved facilities. Birmingham also resented its lack of autonomy and London's apparently high-handed treatment. By the end of 1848, Birmingham was threatening to close the School unless more funds were forthcoming from London.[17] By mid 1849 there were three staff including the headmaster to deal with 491 students.

Birmingham was not alone in this early period, before Cole and Redgrave's reign over the Department of Science and Art, in feeling aggrieved at its lack of autonomy. In 1851 the Birmingham Committee received a letter from the Committee of the Sheffield School of Design arguing for self-control of examinations and inviting Birmingham to support the move. The Birmingham Committee declined the challenge, replying rather feebly that the present system seemed to work well. The School of Design seemed to be settling into a growing, consolidated institution albeit with some financial problems, nevertheless, whenever problems arose the central authority was requested to adjudicate. This was probably politically wise, but it also reveals a dependency out of line with its request for autonomy.

On Clark's removal to Nottingham under dubious circumstances,[18] his eventual replacement by George Wallis from Manchester was not smooth.[19] Wallis's early days were problematic; he closed the School briefly, but by the end of 1851 he seemed to have settled in and made an extensive list of improvements needed for the efficient running of the School.[20] Meanwhile other events were to overshadow the Birmingham School's internal squabbles. In 1849 a Select Committee of Enquiry into the Schools of Design reported that they were ineffectively run and not increasing design skills in a way that the Board of Trade would recognise. Henry Cole had begun his *Journal of Design* in the same year, as both a means of necessary and incisive criticism of design and its training in the country, and as a way of furthering his own prospects in the area. Also in 1849, Birmingham celebrated the second visit of the British Association for the Advancement of Science with an exhibition of industrial design.

This exhibition, often considered the model for the Great Exhibition two years later, was well attended and displayed a large variety of British goods with Birmingham's skills well to the fore.[21] The Great Exhibition itself was understood to reveal that whilst a great variety of manufacture in Britain took place, its overall design quality was not high. The 'failings' of design education were held responsible, and few appeared to question the role of the designer in industry, marketing and production. Instead a new design education system was proposed and Cole cleverly placed himself in a position where total control would be offered to him.

Cole created a separate department of the Board of Trade entitled the Department of Practical Art, (eventually to become the Department of Science and Art) and appointed Richard Redgrave R. A. as his Art Superintendent. He ceased publishing the *Journal of Design* and began a massive reorganisation of art and design education in Britain. Despite Wallis's favourable relationship with Cole, the Birmingham School Committee's complaints over the degree of central control (concerning policy and management decisions and financial control rather than educational content and method) were not upheld.

Birmingham Government School of (Ornamental/Practical) Art 1852–1883

Whilst planning the extensive changes necessary, Cole was also aware that many other types of art training had developed since 1800, e.g., feeder schools for the Royal Academy, geometric and model drawing schools and life-drawing schools.[22] Three strands of art and design education were current – the Academy system, the scientific/design methods and the view that related figure to ornament. All three had in common the belief that drawing as the basis for all art or design could be divided into simple and complex problems; put briefly, that outline was simpler than shading which in turn was simpler than colouring. Thus a sequence of growing complexity could be planned on the same laws – first draw from a flat example, then from geometrical models, small relief casts of details, larger casts, casts of whole figures, and eventually from actual objects culminating in the nude human figure.

Underlying these systems was a division of views over the best material to be studied. Cole and Redgrave, following Dyce and Heath Wilson, favoured drawing from earlier art examples where the vagaries of Nature had been selected and conventionalised by established masters in order to *demonstrate* geometry, order and pattern; the alternative view, espoused by John Ruskin, was that Nature herself should be studied in order to *discover* any governing laws of her physiognomy. The mid nineteenth century views neatly reflect the conflicting arguments of the Humanist and Empiricist traditions in art and design education – in the former working from an *a priori* stance, in the latter learning through doing via sense experience.

Cole first re-organised the London School as the Central School, with the provincial schools serving as nurseries. His plan was to centrally control and define the whole syllabus of art and design, the training and retraining of teachers, the examination system, the prize system, the teaching of drawing in Elementary Schools to enable children to take better advantage of the schools of art, and the improvement of public taste by the provision of exhibitions, museums and art galleries. Whilst every feature of the above tasks had implications for the independence of provincial schools of art, the National Course of Instruction as the syllabus was known, was sufficiently detailed in its order, methods and standards to impose a congruency of style and approach on all subscribing schools.

Stages 1–10 consisted of Drawing; Stages 11–17, Painting; Stages 18–21, Modelling; and Stages 22 and 23, Elementary and Advanced Design. Whilst one did not have to proceed through all the stages to attain the design course, some of the elementary stages were compulsory and many stages could be examined in groups.[23] Many students never progressed beyond geometrical outline study, perspective drawing, freehand drawing from ornament and perhaps some shading from casts. The minority studied the figure from life and painting, unless they were private fee-paying students with no intention of training for artisan work. All teachers had to pass specified sections in order to be qualified to teach them. The works were examined in London where firm definitions of what constituted 'good' work were promulgated by directives, exhibitions and reproductions of previous medal winners' work. Thus within a short time, power had been wrested from the original Design School's Committee and augmented by the considerable organisational skills of Henry Cole. The effect of this in the provincial schools of design was immediate.

In May 1852 all School headmasters were invited to an exhibition at Marlborough House to ascertain the correct criteria and standards for students' work.[24] Cole visited the Birmingham School in December to discuss finance and staffing. By 1853, Birmingham's School of Design was renamed the Birmingham Government School of Ornamental Art, which by 1854 had been abbreviated to The Birmingham Government School of Art. Within the next few years staff numbers increased, but they were all subject to a new payment scheme – 'Payment by Results'; a system whereby part of the salary was fixed but other parts were dependent upon the numbers of students enrolled and the number of examinations passed.

In order to standardise its approach to an increasing amount of elementary drawing, Birmingham planned Branch Schools and a sort of basic course at the central institution. Wallis produced *The Birmingham School of Art Drawing Book* consisting of 24 lessons with detailed instructions. Many of the engravings were taken from earlier publications. His purpose was not to challenge the London publications, but to systematise and make more uniform a given sequence of study. The increasing number of students had made accommodation difficult and eventually plans for a new building to combine with a Scientific and Literary Institute were realised. The new School had six studios, shared use of a lecture theatre and a range of classrooms and plans to develop both libraries and an art gallery on site. On Wallis's retirement the new Head, David Raimbach, from Cork School of Art was appointed, and in July 1858 the School of Art moved to its new buildings and re-opened the following month. The increasing number of students had made the move desirable, but the new building was still insufficient to meet demands in general[25] or from local trades.[26]

Raimbach in his 1859 Report to the Schools Committee was quick to praise the good qualities of the School, but equally wanted to improve it. He blamed poor British design on the poor provision of art schools, lack of access to art collections and the elitist system furthered by the Department of Science and Art at South Kensington. In his view manufacturing needs should dictate locality, and the individual school dictate quality.[27]

Birmingham was beginning to be known as a centre of Pre Raphaelite interest by the late 1850s. The Birmingham Society of Artists invited works from the Brotherhood and these were reviewed in local journals. In fact a whole series of contemporary English and French painting exhibitions could be seen in Birmingham during 1856 and 1857. Groups of individuals were becoming patrons aided by Birmingham's commercial success.

As early as 1838 Birmingham had become a municipal borough and in 1851 the Corporation took over responsibility for all civic and environmental matters. There were obvious needs in the areas of housing, hygiene and education, but cultural aspects were not overlooked. A variety of people with different political and religious beliefs combined their energies towards what became known as the 'Civic Gospel' – an utopian vision of moral, intellectual and social balance.[28] During the 1860s debating societies were formed where these ideas gained new adherents, and from these relatively small but powerful coteries arose many individuals who were to gain positions of influence both nationally and locally.[29] What concerned them as well as physical, social, health and moral issues were the cultural and pleasure amenities necessary for the rapidly expanding town; they wished to develop the citizens' pleasure in the cultural delights of gardens, music, art, literature, the sciences and history, and in so doing create a cultural climate the equal of the Italian Renaissance. Thus civic resources and philanthropic generosity combined to reform Birmingham life.

The School of Art had already outgrown its larger premises and this was affecting its ability to offer training that would extend much beyond elementary drawing. Perhaps this explains the poor proportion of School subscribers from Birmingham's leading art manufacturers – fractionally over two per cent.[30] Certainly there seemed to be a lack of confidence in the School's ability to help Birmingham trades. One person who did believe in the School's potential usefulness was John Bragg whose firm had offered prizes for designs in jewellery from 1865 and who was elected onto the School Committee in January 1868.[31] The following month the Committee formed a sub-committee headed by Bragg to:

'confer with manufacturers and obtain their views of what is required, and to report on the best method of effecting changes in the system of instruction'.[32]

The Report was offered to the Committee the following month. Bragg stipulated that more staff were needed, less emphasis on 'finish' and more on educated vision, a better understanding of design styles by memorising salient features, a more conscious awareness of teaching and learning in staff and students, a systematic course on the 'elements of art applied or manufactured – the elements of design', exhibitions of good and bad taste and a course of lectures to assist in the production of original designs. Finally he suggested that craft and trade areas combined their resources to help realise these ideas in Birmingham.[33] None of these suggestions offered any really radical change – they were more like modifications or slight alterations of emphasis on the current course; nevertheless, the Committee agreed '...to support the School of Design [sic] in any measures calculated to adapt its instruction more specifically at the manufactures of the town'.[34] One year later the Committee resolved to build a new School of Art.

Meanwhile Raimbach had acted on the Committee's advice.[35] At the Annual Meeting of the Birmingham School in 1871, Digby Wyatt's address reinforced the idea of intelligent learning, i.e. understanding causes and principles, discussing reasons for praise and criticism, and, whilst not denying the value of imitation at early stages, stressing that real learning was the result of thought and consideration.[36] Nevertheless, he did not suggest that designing could be anything more than the intellectual understanding and appreciation of its principles and styles clarified through lectures and drawing. The only noticeable change was away from excessive historicist sources towards design and mechanical drawing.[37]

Birmingham School's attempts to move outside the Department of Science and Art schemes were tolerated to some degree, but in the same year the Inspector's Report criticised Birmingham's emphasis on serving the locality despite the fact that its National Competition results were the best in the country.[38] Birmingham vacillated over the degree of independence it desired: on one hand it added extra non-examination classes which were not listed in the National Course of Instruction to assist a more locally aligned provision of design education, whilst on the other hand it was simultaneously training students to achieve the highest grades in the examinations of the very body it wished to challenge.

This situation did not alter immediately when a new Headmaster was appointed in 1877; E. R. Taylor. Taylor, a painter, had considerable sympathy for new ideas at all levels of education. He rapidly developed drawing from memory as a substantial part of all students' studies, believing like Digby Wyatt that what is truly remembered influences the formation of taste and the designing facility. His persistence, growing student numbers and excellent examination results helped persuade the Birmingham Committee to sponsor a new art school. The new building was designed by John Chamberlain and erected in the town centre in Margaret Street. An elaborate Venetian Gothic invention, the building's internal and external decoration reflected Ruskinian ideas on the variety of Nature as the fount of all art. The new School opened in 1884 and became the first municipal school in the country one year later.

The Birmingham Municipal School of Art 1884

The Birmingham Municipal School of Art immediately began a policy of appointing new staff whose persuasion was that of the emerging Arts and Crafts Movement. Birmingham's non-sectarian concentration of manufacturing and professional families was instrumental in assisting this emphasis.[39] They had helped to form Birmingham's non-sectarian education system, and within their concept of a liberal, cultured civic gospel were to plan and implement many institutions. Whereas their philanthropic ideas were not unique in Victorian England, their particular artistic tastes were unusual. Most were believers in Ruskin's idealistic plans for the future of art, craft and design, most admired Pre Raphaelite works and most were or became sponsors and purchasers of Arts and Crafts work. This municipal elite created an environment where practitioners of an arts and crafts persuasion could practise, where some Birmingham industries could follow a parallel path, and where a School of Art could involve its students in suitable and practical skills.[40]

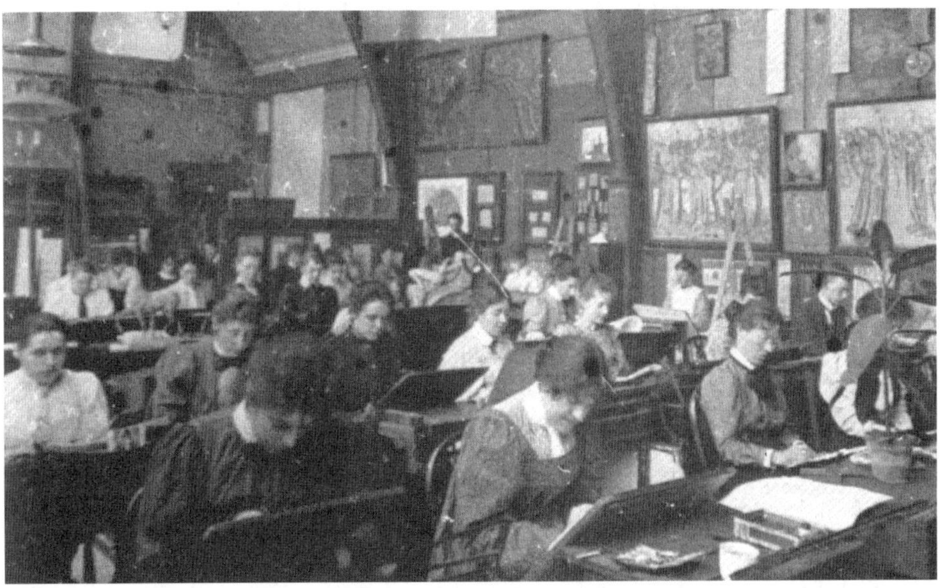

Fig. 1: The Design Room, 'Figure Composition class' Birmingham School of Art c. *1900.*

The emergence of the Art Workers Guild and other features of the arts and crafts groups mostly coincided with the increase in staff and change of purpose in the Birmingham Art School. Within ten years, at least six members of the 'Birmingham Group' or 'Birmingham School' (enthusiasts of Ruskin, Morris and Burne-Jones) had joined the staff, some being ex-students. In the previous buildings no practical design in materials had been achieved.[41] Their remedy at this point was another series of lectures and better examples of applied arts. However, in 1889 Walter Crane's Report on the Art School stated that they:

> *...put the designer in direct relation with tools and materials... to counteract... the mechanical repetition of worn-out ideas and bad trade traditions in design.*[42]

The Technical Instruction Act of the same year had been rather traditional and reactionary from Birmingham's emerging viewpoint, stating:

> *Technical Instruction shall mean instruction in the principles of science and art applicable to industries... not to the practice of any trade or industry or employment.*[43]

While the School still treated the Principles of Ornament and Design as 'copying the demonstration drawn on the blackboard or canvas...' – a particular belief of Taylor's,[44] this could be seen as being due to the term 'principles'. Four years earlier Taylor had introduced design into the elementary courses, in 1887–8 some metalwork skills were physically practised, and by 1891, 'designs (were) executed in the materials for which they were intended'. Unfortunately the materials are not specified.[45]

When the School of Art extension opened in 1892 the traditional titling of the studio's purposes completely altered.[46] Instead of Life Studios and Drawing from the Antique rooms, directions were issued to make more space available for modelling, casting and machine drawing, and to install the proper facilities for *carrying out designs.*[47]

The new 'art laboratories' opened in 1893, and staffing was increased by more Arts and Crafts members. By the late 1890s a wide variety of practical lessons were in progress and in common with the Arts and Crafts philosophy there were frequent staff/student combined works for private houses, churches and public institutions. The range of works could span murals, woven and embroidered wall hangings, furniture, decorative metal fittings and stained glass to prints, jewellery, caskets, vases, bookbindings, paintings and sculpture. The School's staff and students became an unofficial Guild, which partly explains the lack of any substantial independent Birmingham arts and crafts guild – all the work needed could be designed and made within the local art school. This flavour was continued in the Branch Schools, especially that of Vittoria Street School for Jewellery and Silversmithing opened in 1890 in the middle of Birmingham's 'jewellery quarter'.

Taylor's broad educational ideas can be followed in his two books *Elementary Art Teaching* and *Drawing and Design.* His enthusiasm and astuteness in staff appointments coupled with his belief in the vitality to be gained by working across the traditional boundaries of art, craft and design, maintained Birmingham as one of the most significant art schools of the period. It maintained its high prize winning place in the National Competitions and yet simultaneously practised an extensive hands-on experience in all art, craft and design areas coupled with a greater emphasis on drawing from nature and from memory.

Taylor's reign was the one that succeeded in shifting reliance away from South Kensington's examples of good practice, and in setting an example that was in fact

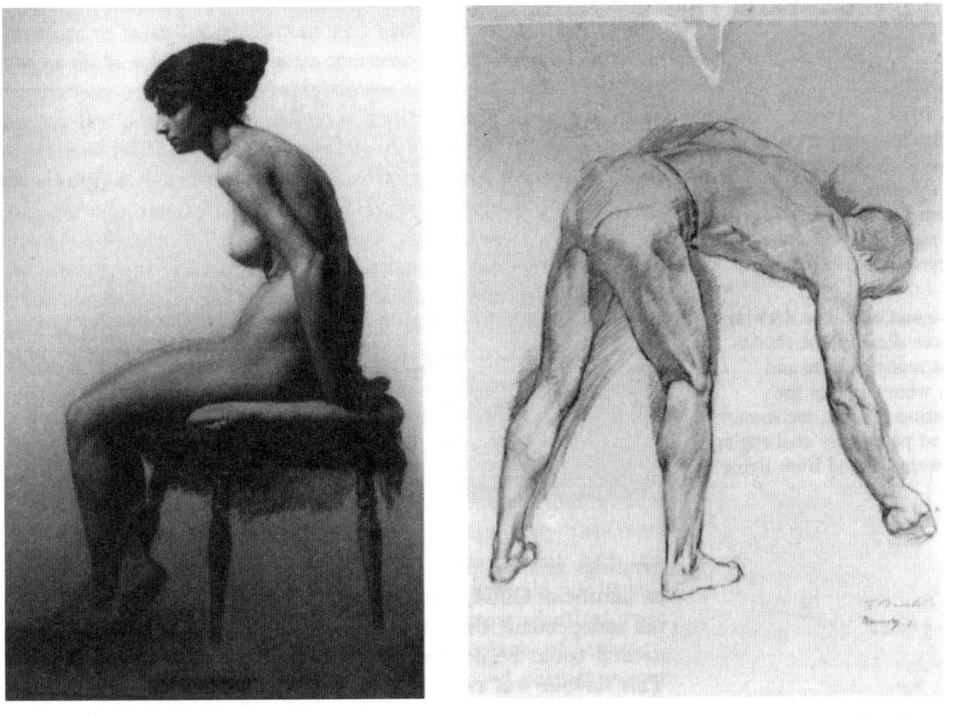

Fig. 2: Left *Shaded drawing from Life 1897 stage 8C2 Florence Camm.* Right *Memory drawing from Life c 1908 Gerald Brockhurst. The main criteria of accuracy, stylistic unity and acknowledged subject- matter were relatively constant; changes in techniques, duration and concepts of finish affected appearance.*

to influence the London schools, especially the new Central School of Arts and Crafts opened in the mid 1890s. Yet, ironically, the reason for the individualism was not the need to be of more use to local manufacturers. There is little evidence that students were eagerly taken from the School. In fact there seems to have been some suspicion of the type of work, the time taken on it, and the philosophy of practice that the students had acquired.[48] The greater independence of the Art School was the result of following the quasi-socialist beliefs of Carlyle and Morris and the artistic and moral credo of Ruskin. The pseudo-medievalism of much of the content of the work produced is ample evidence of the effect of the theoretical and practical progenitors.

The Department of Science and Art had been under increasing pressure to relax its regulations and had done so to some extent, but as far as schools of art were concerned, the National Course of Instruction was still remarkably similar to that of 1853. There had been a few additions and deletions, but the underlying principles, order and criteria were still embedded. Although the students of all schools of art had to be examined within the specified subjects and their criteria, this is not to say that the styles of work remained constant. Despite apparently rigid regulations per stage, the students gained a variety of stylistic approaches to their study from the influence of the teaching staff, the examples circulated by the Department of Science and Art, the growing number of public exhibitions and the increasing circulation of art journals and magazines. Changes can be observed in the approach and manner of students' drawings for each decade from the 1860s to the 1920s, and equally the changing fashions of Arts and Crafts, Art Nouveau and late Victorian mannerism in design are reflected in choice of medium, colours, treatment and selection of subject matter. It is true that constraints existed and that perhaps only the more imaginative were able to manipulate the regulations and still achieve the necessary examination passes, but it would not be true to affirm that such constraints resulted in almost identical work irrespective of location or period. The main criteria of accuracy, stylistic unity within a work, and acknowledged subject-matter were relatively constant, but changes in the acceptability of different media, the amount of time spent on a work and notions of completeness affected outcomes.

Birmingham's stance was to be reinforced when Taylor retired in 1903 to be replaced by the recently appointed headmaster of Vittoria Street School, Robert Catterson-Smith. He had been appointed because of his connections with the Arts and Crafts movement and his success as an educator.[49] He was a natural choice to take over the direction of increasing practical designing and like Taylor before him was also a conscientious organiser. He had already suggested improvements for Vittoria Street School, the most important of which were: that drawing from real objects such as plants, flowers, fish, animals and birds should become the norm rather than the exception and that all these should be live examples; that designing should be done in some particular material and *not* on paper.[50] The prize lists of 1902 show awards for silver-raising, box-making and gold ornaments.[51] Meanwhile Lethaby had extolled the same point in his Examiners' Report of 1900 at the Central School in Margaret Street: 'Ideally, doing "real" things is the best way... the only proper basis for design'.[52] And in 1901 the sub-Committee had suggested that further practical classes were begun in Stained Glass, Bookbinding and Writing

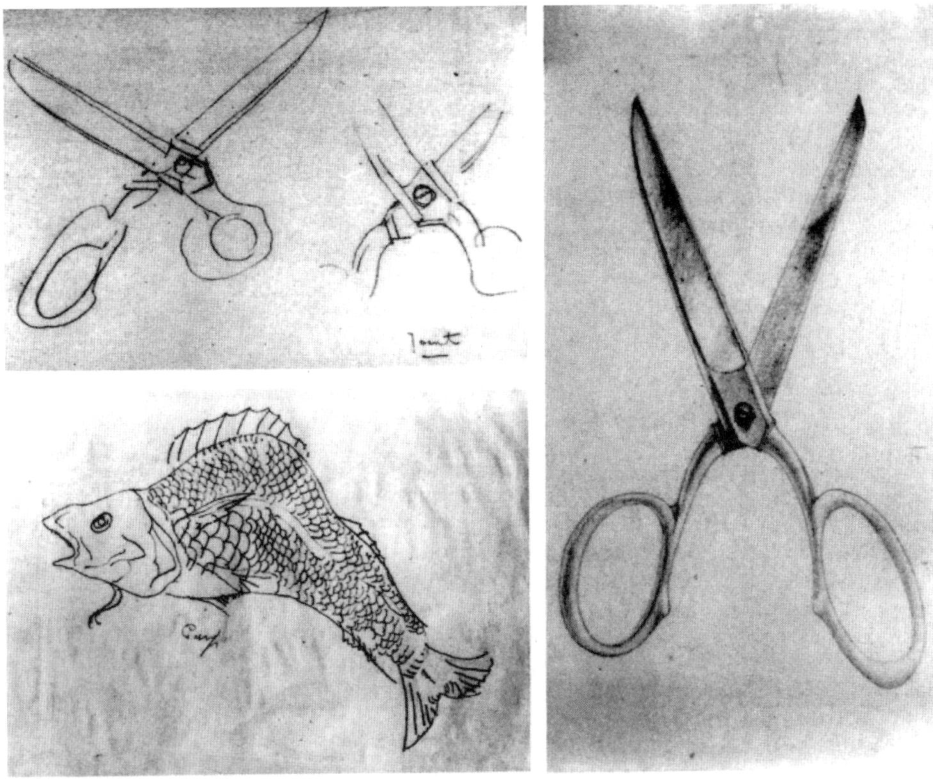

Fig. 3: Top Left *Shut-eye drawing of scissors 1919 L. Morgan.* Right *Open-eye drawing of scissors (same date and student).* Bottom Left *Shut-eye drawing of a carp from life 1921 R.A. Morgan. Shut-eye and open-eye drawings from three dimensional objects. Whereas many sources and subjects were used for the visualisation process, the most lively and potentially challenging results were derived from living objects.*

(Illumination and Calligraphy).[53] Within a few years practical designing had spread to *all* possible areas and was begun early in every student's experience.

The Board of Education's attempt to curtail Birmingham's emphasis on working in materials and drawing from nature was ignored, as the reports of many examiners make evident.[54] Particularly supportive in this role was Henry Wilson, the silversmith. Not only was he an arts and crafts advocate, but he also had radical beliefs in the results of drawing from memory and was an early exponent of child-centred education. The latter are of special interest here, for although Birmingham continued to build on its reputation for practical designing, some other schools of art had rapidly followed suit, e.g., the Central School in London and Leicester School of Art, and by the second decade of the new century, most schools had opened practical workshops for designing. So although Birmingham had helped to realign the direction of design teaching, it was no longer an individual feature of the school. However, the activity of memory drawing shows another departure from centralised control.

Memory drawing had been an aspect of at least three stages of the National Course of Instruction, and Taylor had extended memory exercises for all students at Birmingham. Taylor's policy followed the national example, i.e., it understood memory as a replicating device that could test how much had been learned. Thus Taylor's memory exercises varied from remembering whole objects to remembering the order and the reasons for the order of a sequence of lines in a drawing. Catterson-Smith's early ideas prior to Birmingham and as Headmaster until c.1910, were more or less identical except that he insisted on an even wider and more frequent use, and seemed to have a broader knowledge of earlier memory work.[55] Sometime during late 1909 or early 1910, Catterson-Smith 'discovered' a new method of enabling the student to visualise an object or idea: a method to become known as 'Visualisation' or more commonly 'Shut-Eye Drawing'. Despite the bewildering number of uses to which it was put, the basic activity remained constant.

An 'object' was shown for a couple of minutes, the students being asked to look at it carefully and to try and picture it in their mind's eye. The object was removed and the students asked to draw their internal image with closed eyes on a small piece of paper. The 'shut-eye' drawing was also removed, and the students asked to draw the original 'object' with their eyes open by referring to their mental image and/or making up parts that had 'disappeared'. The 'object' could vary widely: it could be: (a) two dimensional and stable, e.g. a glass slide or picture; (b) three dimensional and stable, e.g. a pair of scissors; (c) two-dimensional and mobile, e.g. a cinema film; or (d) three-dimensional and mobile, e.g. animals, birds, fishes, or humans.[56]

The purpose of these processes was to enable the students to be able to hold, rotate and re-order such images, store them and enhance them in the mind. In so doing Catterson-Smith believed that the images would become 'individualised' through their mingling with other stored memories and that their immediate recall would aid artistic power. A well-stored visual memory would also save the designer time and therefore money. The method created much discussion with polarised positions being taken by those who believed that the proper purpose of memory was precise replication, and those who believed that memory's ability to reconstruct and redefine the original experience was more artistically significant.

The evidence for the efficacy of the method is mixed. There are hundreds of examples in the Birmingham School of Art Archives but they tend towards particular types of design – that of small scale metal work. Their application to larger ideas is not evidenced. Their potential usefulness for the individual is also open to some doubt.[57] The eventual end products are not markedly different from those of other art schools. Rather than the shut-eye drawings leading to individual

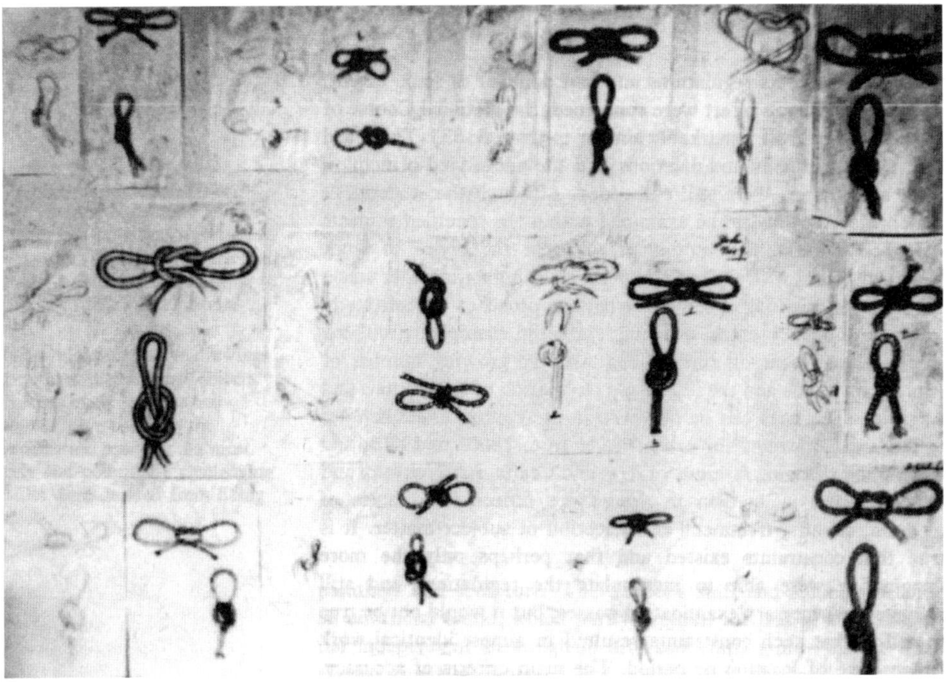

Fig. 4: Shut-eye and open-eye drawings of knotted rope c. *1919. Various students: undated.*

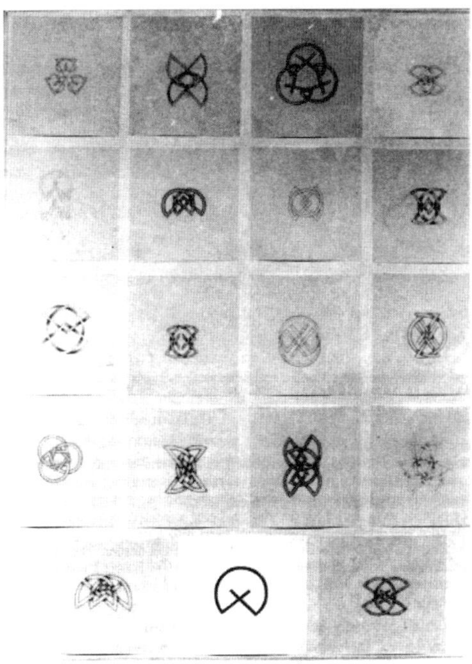

Fig.5: Open-eye drawings for the Combination of Units Exercise c. 1919. Various students aged 15–18, undated. Exercises to improve the visualising capacity involved memorising complicated three dimensional activities, e.g, the tying and untying of specific knots, and the mental rotation of a given shape to form decorative design.

and unique responses as Wilson had argued and Catterson-Smith attempted to realise, the shut-eye works, despite their vividness and spontaneity, tend to be rather similar to each other – there is a strong feeling of family resemblance, and when they are 'converted' to 'open-eye' drawings they differ from their origin and become similar to any other objective study.

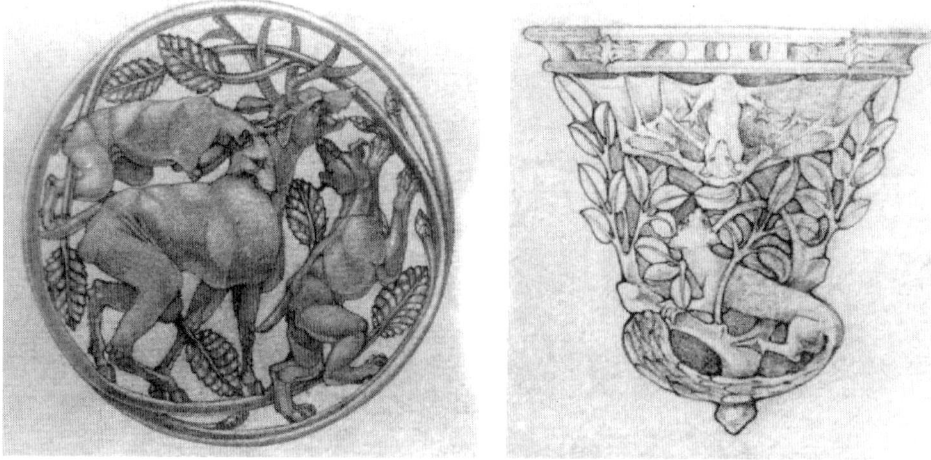

Fig. 6: Space-filling designs preceded by shut-eye drawing. Left *H. W. Watson ND 1916–1924.* Right *Anon c. 1923. Many of the shut-eye drawings of natural forms and animals were used to satisfy two sorts of inter-related exercise – space filling and designs for metal work. Usually scale, overall shape, number and type of ingredients were specified: the student being expected to mentally visualise and organise the constituent parts into a design, make a shut-eye drawing and eventually convert into a finished design. The results rather than revealing individual difference, tend to reflect a family resemblance.*

There are a variety of reasons why the potentially bold experiment failed to justify its expectations (but insufficient space to explore them here).[58] The reason the memory experiments are important, however, is that they are further evidence of the ability of the provincial art school to create a distinctive working method with some shared and some different aims from those of the Department of Science and Art and the Board of Education. The commitment to the Arts and Crafts Movement was still powerful in the Birmingham Art School, but there was an increasing rejection of the over-idealistic purity concerning materials and machinery. The School of Art under Catterson-Smith had increased its liaison with local trades and this by implication suggests that not only tolerance, but also acceptance of mechanical means had taken place.

Discussion

The pattern of increasing autonomy traced from the beginnings of Birmingham art and design education has been identified. The growth was uneven and did not have necessarily common antecedents. From an independent attempt to teach drawing and designing skills in the early 1800s, Birmingham took rapid advantage of the National School of Designs formulation. However, the inherent educational problems within the national system concerning the nature of drawing and designing and the means by which learning should occur, and the organisational difficulties of finance, staffing, student growth and manufacturing dissent, all transferred themselves to the new provincial Schools of Design. During the period of Birmingham's School of Design 1843–1851 little attempt was made to create an individual approach. There was certainly reaction to central imposition, but Birmingham had little to offer in place of what was being suggested other than the obviously sensible request that local industries would respond more favourably to their new School of Design if the teaching staff had actual design experience.

During the second period of 1852–1883, central control of all aspects became more capably planned and administered. As the central body's plans became more concrete, more opportunity arose for alternative suggestions. Certainly during this period there are more frequent requests for local decision-making. Nevertheless, the complex central regulations were sufficient to restrict the hopes of even the most adept. Birmingham's School during this period achieved a little more autonomy in erecting courses independent of examination needs to assist local requirements, but in essence it remained in the situation of making frequent criticism whilst eminently satisfying the National Course's requirements. There is evidence of the groundswell of hostility to the rigidity of the central system, but this is not significantly more or less than that of other schools and was fed by the writings of known critics available to all.

It is really only during the last period under examination here that anything like real independence was achieved. It is not coincidental that the beginning of this period sees the municipalisation of the School of Art, i.e., the ratepayers of Birmingham, via the town council and its committees, become the main financial power. During the years 1885-1920, the Birmingham School pioneered the 'new' method of learning design by using the actual materials; created a whole 'School' of Arts and Crafts practice; and lastly developed new ideas concerning the role and purpose of drawing and its links with memory and imagination.

There are some instructive insights to be gained from this historical examination for present day art and design education. A centrally managed, criterion-referenced, frequently examined, industry-related education system could with ease be mistaken for current plans.

In terms of central management, the example of Birmingham's art school revealed that a substantial degree of independence was gained after achieving some financial autonomy. This is not meant to indicate that 'privatisation' is the answer. Birmingham's autonomy was the result of a powerful, organised, political, cultural, but overall - *local and philanthropic* power-base. Criterion-referencing had an inhibiting effect on all but the most able of students: their work was more noted for its family resemblance than for its personal flavour. However, even within this restrictive, goal-centred activity, eventually different types of influence began to permeate and affect the expectations of the art school teachers and their students.[59]

The nineteenth century system of frequent examination initially led to far too much time being spent on examination-dominated teaching. Gradually schools of art introduced their own separate subject-matter, but it would not be true to suggest that these differed greatly in topic or standard from those they contended with. Slowly, more experimental teaching methods influenced by writers outside the mainstream of education and by the examples to be found at more junior levels of education, began to be implemented. When these were able both to satisfy the school's wishes and at the same time achieve national examination success, both sides were happy.

The original intention of the schools of design was to improve designing capacity amongst the population and by so doing create a healthy balance of payments. Even given that the problem was correctly diagnosed in 1837, why was it repeated for the next 100 years? It *may* have been the case that many artisans and designers pre 1835 were lacking in taste, historically uninformed and mass-market oriented. But how could this remain the case for the next century and a half? By the turn of the new century tens of thousands of students had passed through the widely distributed schools of art, and surely some of them had corrected their supposed deficiencies? I suspect that the diagnosis that design was improvable by increased training had lost its accuracy. This was due to many factors: design training itself; the shift from design to art schools to meet a changing demand; lack of manufacturing confidence in state methods; unimaginative use of designers in industry; too much manufacturing attention to production, marketing and cost to the detriment of function and appearance; the exclusion of the designer from management decisions; and changing concepts of design itself.

This brief history of one provincial art school reveals a lack of cohesion between educational and industrial requirements. It also reveals that the more circumscribed the central policy, the longer it takes to respond to specific and/or local needs. Only the most able students could develop individual flavour and style within a national curriculum, a factor that could well have adversely affected their influence within design trades. Nineteenth century art schools in general, were not noted for their innovative educational ideas. With a few exceptions, the main thrust of educational policies derived from the junior level of education and the emergent psychological and even artistic study of young children's drawings.

Birmingham's art school was untypical in that it called attention to practical designing and new concepts of drawing. It was typical in that it succeeded in challenging centralist control only when it gained financial autonomy via its ratepayers. The success of its challenge was largely due to sympathetic, informed private and public bodies whose artistic tastes and social beliefs coincided with those underlying the new art school ethos, and its developing ability both to offer to industry capable designers and to individual students an art and design education which suited and extended their personal interests and aspirations.

Originally published in the Journal of Art & Design Education, *Volume 7: 1, 1988.*

Notes and References

1. Bell, Q. (1970), *The Schools of Design*, London: Routledge & Kegan Paul; Macdonald, S. (1970), *The History and Philosophy of Art Education*, London: London University Press; Sutton, G. (1967), *Artisan or Artist?,* London: Pergamon; Carline, R. (1968), *Draw They Must*, London: Arnold; Ashwin, C. (1975), *Art Education Documents and Policies 1768-1975*, London: SRHE.
2. Recently a few Schools of Art have celebrated their history through exhibitions and publications. See Clarke, R. (1979, 81), *Cast in the Same Mould: The Origin and History of Coventry School of Art*, Vols. I and II, Coventry Library, Arts and Museums Service; Jeremiah, D. (1980), *A Hundred Years or More*, Manchester Polytechnic; Ashwin, C. *A Century of Art Education 1882-1982*, Middlesex Polytechnic; Kirby, J. (1987), *Useful and Celebrated: the Sheffield School of Art 1843-1940*, Sheffield Polytechnic and Sheffield Arts Department.
3. Birmingham trades included workers in glass, silver, gold, papier mâché, tinware, brass, electro-plating and all types of engineering, with special reference to japanning, enamelling, engraving, die-sinking, medal-making, pattern-making, jewellery, modelling, carving, gunsmithing and 'toy' making.
4. Lines, S. (1862), *A Few Incidents in the Life of Samuel Lines Senior*, Allen, pp. 12–14.
5. Bunce, J. (1877), *Catalogue to an Exhibition of Engravings by Birmingham Men*, Royal Birmingham Society of Artists, pp. 14–16.
6. Lines, S. *op. cit.* pp. 14–16.
7. Langford, J. (1873), *Modern Birmingham and its Institutions*, Vol. I, Osborne, p. 190.
8. The supporters were local hollowware manufacturer A. Kenrick; banker and industrialist S. Galton; and philanthropist Sir R. Lawley.
9. Langford, *op. cit.* p. 196.
10. The Design School was for artisans (handworkers), not professional artists, and as such was deemed a lower establishment on the social scale. Artists had used the same sort of argument in Renaissance Italy to differentiate between the supposedly more mental and spiritual work of the artist and the manual labour of the craftsperson.
11. Muirhead, J. (1911), *Birmingham Institutions*, Cornish, p. 284.
12. This recreated earlier divisions between the practicing artists' section and the remainder of the committee. This resolved itself later the same year by the formation of two separate societies – the Birmingham Society of Arts and School of Design (BSASD) and the Birmingham Society of Artists (BSA).
13. Birmingham Society of Arts: *Minutes* (1843), Vol. 4, pp. 118–20.
14. This was resolved in 1845 when Ambrose Poynter, the new Inspector of Design Schools, advocated that every student should draw the human figure irrespective of involvement in ornamental or industrial work. *Ibid.* p. 119. See also *BSA Minutes* (1845), Vol. 5, p. 133.
15. *BSA Minutes* (1843), Vol. 4, pp. 125–28.
16. In replying to criticism of the Birmingham School, the Committee argued for the 'privilege of judging what is best suited to our circumstances... we ask you to pause before interfering

with the present arrangements'. In conclusion it was hoped for 'a brighter future' if Somerset House would listen to Birmingham's proposals. *BSASD Minutes* (1848), Vol. 6, p. 114.

17. *Ibid.* p. 137.

18. *BSASD Minutes* (1851), Vol. 7, pp. 3–35.

19. He was pressed into being a candidate and advertised himself as being in poor health, only able to work limited hours, needing his own private room and being consulted by and represented on every committee.

20. He demanded cleaner and better-maintained equipment and rooms, more casts and prints, a new prize system for 'general progress, industry and attention', and more individual responsibility for daily decisions. *Ibid.* n. 19, pp. 59–75.

21. It was extensively reviewed in *The Art Journal,* the *Journal of Design* and the *London Illustrated News.* The exhibition was visited by both Cole and Prince Albert and its example must have encouraged plans for the Great Exhibition which closely involved both men.

22. Swift, J. (1983), *The Role of Drawing and Memory Drawing in English Art Education 1800-1980*, Ph.D. Dissertation, Birmingham Polytechnic, pp. 244–5.

23. *Ibid.* pp. 245–8.

24. *BSASD Minutes* (1852), Vol. 7, pp. 94–5.

25. *Ibid.* pp. 217–221. In 1843 the School had enrolled 84 students; by 1846, 355; by 1849, 481; by 1852, 536; and by 1854, 754 (plus another 375 comprising teachers, colleges of education students and school children).

26. In 1858 the Schools' role was analysed in terms of effectiveness for local manufacturers. It listed 4938 students from 1843–1857, 27% of whom belonged to local trades ranging from over 5% for japanning and for engraving, 4% for die-sinking, 3% for jewellery and silver-smithing, about 2% for brass foundry workers, chasers and engineers/machinists and around 1% for modellers and for glass painters. Langford, *op. cit.* p. 230.

27. Untitled volume No. 9: *Minutes* (1859), pp. 3–7.

28. The persons first identified in this crusade were George Dawson, a non-conformist preacher; John Henry Chamberlain, an architect; and William Aitken, an industrial designer. Followers of Ruskin and Pugin, all believed in the role that education could play: in fact Dawson's views of free non-sectarian, public education were more far-reaching than the compromise position eventually reached by the 1870 Education Act. See Timmins, S. (1889), *The History of Warwickshire*, Stock, p. 207.

29. Hartnell, R. (1987), Unpublished research, Birmingham Polytechnic, pp. 3/3–3/5.

30. *The Art Journal* (1867), Virtue.

31. BSA and Government School of Art: *Minutes* (1868), Vol. 11, p. 10.

32. *Ibid.* p. 16.

33. *Ibid.* p. 29.

34. *Ibid.* p. 26.

35. *Ibid:* Insert p. 136. He had appointed two additional pupil-teachers, given more personal attention to students and asked his staff more fully to explain the reasons and principles behind their requests and assessments. Drawing from plants had replaced the customary prints, and a small conservatory had been constructed.

36. *Ibid.* p. 187.

37. *BSAGSA Minutes* (1874), Vol. 9, p. 819.

38. *Ibid.* p. 820.

39. The families involved included Unitarians (Ryland, Nettlefold, Martineau, Kenrick, Beale, Chamberlain); Quakers (Lloyd, Baker, Cadbury, Tangyes); and Anglicans (Bunce).

40. Not all Birmingham industries were sympathetic. Many firms had little contact with the School of Art or the various arts and crafts guilds. However, there was sufficient patronage within these families and firms such as Hope, Lucas and Brampton to support large numbers of arts and crafts people in guilds, as well as the staff of the newly built Municipal Art School.

41. A general Meeting of the Birmingham Society of Arts and the School of Art in February 1883 had minuted '...the success of the competition [design for encaustic and wall tiles] was partly due to the fact that the nature of the design called for no special knowledge of the difficulties of construction... this adds to the weight of proof that the ill success of art students in ordinary designs as applied to manufactures, is due in large measure to their want of technical knowledge.'

42. *BSAGSA Minutes* (1889), Vol. 19, p. 215.

43. *Ibid.* p. 223, *et seq.*

44. *Birmingham School of Art Programme* (1889–90), p. 18.

45. *Ibid.* (1885–86); (1887–88); (1891–92).

46. In 1892 the Margaret Street site was no longer large enough to cope with increasing numbers of students. The growth of day classes for intending art teachers, the control of the drawing classes for all elementary schools in Birmingham and the massive increase of 'leisure' classes, had outnumbered the relatively small groups of artisans who still attended in the evenings.

47. Birmingham Society of Arts and Municipal School of Art (BSAMSA): *Minutes* (1891), Vol. 20, p. 69.

48. The Arts and Crafts philosophy did not always fit happily with the more mechanical means of production to be found in many of Birmingham's manufacturing industries.

49. He had worked as a black and white illustrator for Morris and Burne-Jones at the Kelmscott Press, worked for London County Technical Education Board, had studied metalwork from 1892, taught with Frampton and Lethaby at the Central School of Arts and Crafts, and was a member of the Art Workers' Guild and the Arts and Crafts Exhibition Society. He had testimonials from Burne-Jones, Philip Webb, William de Morgan and Walter Crane, and was a close friend of Henry Wilson and William Lethaby.

50. Vittoria Street School: *Minutes* (1901), Vol. 34, p. 44.

51. *Ibid.* p. 116.

52. *BSAMSA Minutes* (1900), Vol. 22, p. 246.

53. *BSAMSA Minutes* (1901), Vol. 23, p. 9.

54. *BSAMSA Minutes* (1904–06), Vol. 26, Insert p. 117.

55. He was familiar with the technical and educational applications of visual memory in the French mid-nineteenth century work of Lecoq de Boisbaudran, the more psychologically-intended concept of memory drawing that T. R. Ablett had proposed within and without his Royal Drawing Society, and was fascinated by the advanced views of Henry Wilson who linked visual memory and imaginative power, feeling and fantasy – being both unique to individuals and racially determined. Vittoria Street School *Minutes*, Vol. 34, Insert p. 198.

56. There were also other variations which included verbal descriptions with no visual object, and complicated verbal instructions for the internal juxtaposition of mental images.

57. I have interviewed a number of students taught under Catterson Smith's methods and have found a division of opinion. Some found the exercises difficult and avoided them; some found them partially useful; and some claimed the experience lasted throughout their working lives and was still of value.

58. See Swift, J. (1978), *Robert Catterson-Smith's Concept of Memory Drawing 1911-1920*, MA Dissertation, Birmingham Polytechnic.

59. One can demonstrate subtle distinctions between periods and between students, but this is limited by the sparseness of surviving examples. It would be misleading to suggest that all students were able to respond individually. Surviving archives are generally by definition collections of the best works of the past – one is not usually able to study works of students who barely completed courses or failed. I have already suggested that the more elementary levels of art and design training would inhibit individual variation – I would also suggest that 'average' students at any level find difficulty in using their learned skills in a personal manner. It could be argued that nothing would prevent the gifted student from moving beyond imposed orthodoxies.

Chapter 6: Women and Art Education at Birmingham's Art Schools 1880–1920: Social Class, Opportunity and Aspiration

John Swift

Introduction

From 1880 to 1920 was a period of rapid growth in art school education and training, interrupted by the Great War, and increasingly influenced by the demands of trade and industry for art training linked to apprenticeships and allied to mechanisation. The paper uses the archives of Birmingham Municipal School of Art, as one of the largest art schools, to examine its attitude and policy to women as students and staff. It covers the headships of two men, Edward R. Taylor (1877–1903) and Robert Catterson Smith (I903–1920) who both shared an interest and commitment to early years education, drawing, and the Arts and Crafts movement. In common with other large urban art schools, Birmingham had to satisfy many apparently conflicting requirements: local manufacturers' needs for more artistic workpeople and more proficient designers; the teaching of drawing to all local elementary schools; the management and content of branch schools of art (feeders to the central school); the personal fulfilment of middle class students pursuing studies for their intrinsic value; and the initial and further qualification of art teachers. Was Birmingham typical of other art schools and of society in its treatment of women, or did it recognise and use the clear untypicality of middle class women students at the Birmingham Art School?

Birmingham School of Art 1880–1920

Between 1880 and 1920 Birmingham Art School changed its location, size, financial status, theoretical and practical education, and to some extent its purpose. The changes were rapid. One central school, temporarily housed, and six branch schools,[1] developed into a new purpose-built and extended building with fifteen branch schools.[2] From a school typically financed by the Government's Department of Science and Art (DSA), local subscriptions and fees, it became the first municipal art school in 1885. Student numbers grew from c.1,320 in 1880 to 4,268 in 1900, but had dropped to 2,460 by 1917.[3] In 1880 the combined staff of the schools numbered 23, most being part-time, by 1900 there were 87 staff, c.60 being part-time. In 1912–13 of 36 staff, 7 were women (6 being female art-pupil teachers), and using both Central and Branch figures for 1920, of 81 staff 8 per cent were women.[4] The representation of female staff had slightly increased from 4 per cent of 23 to 8 per cent of 81, with between 7 to 9 women teaching the female art-pupil teachers classes.[5] Apart from this class, female teachers were almost exclusively employed to teach needlework and embroidery. In 1880 gender and social class separated classes, after 1900 classes were more mixed, although the social distinctions remained. In 1880 course content, examinations, prizes and teacher training were centrally controlled by the DSA, but financial independence through municipalisation had allowed the pedagogical aspects of the arts and crafts movement to be developed. During the war, the schools' buildings, rooms, and equipment were partly or wholly requisitioned, and staff and students were enlisted. Birmingham dominated the DSA's (and subsequent Board of Education's) annual competitions. Under Taylor, Birmingham had been placed first from 1891 to 1903 inclusive, and under Catterson-Smith this continued until 1906, and in all probability to 1910 and after, until its cessation in 1916.[6] External requests for executed designs made by Birmingham staff and students for national and international arts and crafts exhibitions continued but with a reduction between 1906 and 1912 and after 1916, the latter reflecting a general decline in the popularity of the movement.[7]

Any simple comparison of Taylor's and Catterson-Smith's reigns is made problematic by the inter-related changes within the education system, mechanised industry, trade organisations, and the First World War. Birmingham's economy, built on small industrial trades and the practical application of scientific invention, required a changing art school. Together with pressure from the Board of Education[8] these factors gradually eroded Birmingham Art School's advocacy of the arts and crafts philosophy.

Women's Art Education and the Arts and Crafts Movement 1880–1900

In concentrating now on women's art education, it is important to make a distinction between the social classes and the purpose for which students attended Birmingham art school. For middle class women especially, the art school was one of the few places where advanced study could be undertaken. Before the advent of the arts and crafts movement, the interests of these women tended to fine art with a conventional interest in portrait, flower and landscape study.[9] Those whose finances were more restricted studied to become teachers. Birmingham had introduced branch schools for more working class entry before 1880 to advance the relationship of art to industry. Initially these 'schools' were special classes held in the local schoolrooms with entry at twelve rising to thirteen years. The regulations for free admission favoured boys, resulting in fewer girls competing for places. Female working class students at the Branch Schools were in the minority and this position was continued into the Central School.

Classes were taught according to levels of accomplishment and availability of time. Artisans/designers were taught in the evening after work; Free Admission and Scholarship pupils were initially taught in Elementary classes in both the day and evening, and fee-paying students and teacher-trainees (some 'advanced students') in day classes. Art schools had carefully nurtured their advanced level student numbers, for reasons of esteem and finance.[10] Many of the advanced students at the Central School were women. Most of these were from middle-class backgrounds, fee-paying, and some were the daughters of local 'art industrialists' and other influential people. Across Birmingham's Central and Branch schools the specific mix of students reveals a large number of subsidised or free elementary level pupils (slanted in favour of boys) and evening-only artisans (predominantly male), with a much smaller number of advanced students of which a large section were trainee-teachers, teachers taking further qualifications, and others studying for 'pleasure' (predominantly female) who sometimes attended over many years.[11]

A clear distinction was made between social classes, the ability to pay, and career aspirations. In general, the education offered to all students irrespective of background, was based on the idea of achieving well within their respective social expectations. The position of women as future professional artists was evaded, as it was relatively unusual in that they were expected to marry and raise families as a 'profession'. Thus the education offered was not intended to enable students to challenge their social or gendered background, but to enable them to become capable and skilled within it. Aspirations were linked with and limited by background. Undoubtedly, this dampened ambitions – the clear message was that unless one possessed some unique ability (or wealth), the purpose of art education was to train for a 'suitable' profession – one that fitted within the social norms and expectations of the times and one's social class and sex.

The factor that makes Birmingham particularly interesting in terms of the potential of women's art education is its pedagogic realisation of the Arts and Crafts Movement. The latter's rise and fall, and the role of women in it, is central to this paper.[12] To develop artists as craftspeople and vice versa, a change in art educational methods was effected by Taylor and his supportive Committee. The change was attitudinal and practical – the latter involving executing designs in the materials for which they were intended. The 'hands-on' argument for design was now a widespread movement with powerful and articulate proponents. Whereas students drew, painted, designed for specified materials on paper,[13] and modelled[14] in most large art schools, they did not actually make the designed objects in their intended materials, or have any understanding of design's technical consequences. Birmingham was the innovative art school in introducing executed design in purpose built workshops in an added extension,[15] where appointments for embroidery/needlework, wood-engraving, and enamelling were made and equipment ordered for a wide variety of crafts.[16]

The initial activity had been linked with local metal trades, but many crafts were introduced subsequently as a result of Arts and Crafts enthusiasm and predilection. This diversity of illustrated books, interior decoration and fittings including murals, glass and many other crafts, is testimony to the taste of the new, wealthy middle class patron, especially around the Birmingham area. However, when the same style and work ethic was transposed into small or large commercial workplaces, especially in the metal trades, the result was less enthusiastic.[17]

The increase in executed design work through craft practice, and the stylistic and philosophical influence on students varied. Elementary level students, i.e., apprentices, Free Admission and scholarship pupils at Branch Schools, would have little experience in executing designs at this time, apart from Vittoria Street, which had a more direct relationship with the surrounding metal-trades, and would not necessarily have absorbed an arts and crafts ethos. Advanced classes at the Central School, i.e., those for more advanced artisans and designers, were taught by staff with beliefs in hand-work antithetical to the majority of local metal industries.[18]

What is unexpected is the degree of enthusiasm and success with which the more advanced female students embraced executed design. Working manually, with what could be described as trade materials, would not at first glance seem appropriate. Until the extension opened, many female students won prizes in the traditional areas of drawing, painting and modelling,[19] but after 1894, when new prizes were introduced for paper design work linked to crafts, the percentage for female winners fluctuated between 40 and 60 per cent, with a peak of 74 per cent in 1899–1900, with an average mid 60 percentile.[20] However, it is their success in executed designs from 1890 onwards that is surprising. Ranging from 40 to 100 per cent success, the local prizes won by female students between 1890 and 1900 accounted for 74 per cent of the 157 listed awards, and this success was repeated in external awards.[21] They were out-performing their male contemporaries.

Whilst partly confirming Callen's findings, that generally Arts and Crafts women worked in 'feminine' crafts, the students at Birmingham worked across a wider range, partly countering the socially-determined and conflicting roles of 'woman' and 'artist', and 'lady' and 'work'.[22] The c.307 listings for executed design undertaken by female students reveal that 54 per cent was combined metalwork and enamelling, (40 per cent for a variety of metal crafts and 14 per cent for the three types of enamelling); 28 per cent was needlework and embroidery; 7 per cent was gesso; 5 per cent was book illustration and prints, and the remaining 6 per cent was spread fairly evenly over vase decoration, fan painting, grisaille (glass painting), leatherwork, and carving (usually plaster, but also wood and ivory).[23]

The success of female students disturbed two external examiners. W. J. Wainwright's and W. R. Lethaby's comments from 1897 to 1900 reflect an unease at so many 'amateurs' winning prizes, thus endorsing the popular view that 'amateur' was synonymous with women and 'professional' with men. Wainwright's comments on the preponderance of personal ornament point to the gender of the maker.[24] Lethaby was disturbed by the number of amateurs[25] winning awards planned for artisans.[26] He proposed that every class should be trade linked to local industries. This would have removed almost all female students from executed design classes – as Lethaby put it, keeping the places for 'serious students'.[27] Despite the pointed suggestion, Birmingham did nothing. This was unlikely to be the result of enlightened equity, I suspect it was due to the fear of losing prestige, fees, and the support of the 'art industrialists' whose daughters were part of this group, and remained so, although in diminishing numbers for the next decade.

Birmingham School of Art 1900–1920

By the time Robert Catterson Smith succeeded Taylor in 1903, Birmingham's Arts and Crafts education had become a model for other art schools; initially Leicester, London and Glasgow, and internationally its reputation grew.[28] The School was the midland centre and focus of a strong and virile arts and crafts movement,[29] where a policy of collaborative arts and crafts ventures between staff and students was generated and continued for the first two decades of 1900. But, although the School had fought for and obtained an increasing and untypical independence in its teaching style, content and method, it remained typical in being influenced by the Board of Education's more national perspective, and in its approach to female students and staff.[30] The influence of the Board of Education (which had absorbed DSA) was initially unhelpful. Its early views confused 'hands-on' designing with 'workshop skills',[31] however, it was more helpful in its national outlook,[32] and by 1917 it suggested that art schools' design classes should be directly linked to manufacturing needs.[33]

Catterson-Smith[34] began by re-emphasising some educational factors – more memory drawing at earlier stages of art education and redirecting content to natural things, and planning for change by extending the arts and crafts classes,[35] with additional ones where a representative trade association would in consultation devise and implement courses, and sponsor students. He had also been innovative in planning new local teaching qualifications, reorganising the scholarship scheme, and trying to increase entry from the poor and from girls.[36] Due to falling rolls after 1906 and increasing pressure to satisfy trade related industries, he retained the arts and crafts practices but partly reorganised them as trade-linked classes where technical instructors were inevitably, and increasingly skilled artisans from the local trades.[37]

Increasingly, during the latter part of his headship, several areas seemed to have two aspects – one traditional arts and crafts, the other more trade related, for example, embroidery as distinct from needlework, murals and other applied arts as distinct from interior decoration, and wood carving as distinct from furniture design. Many arts and crafts courses continued from 1903 to 1920 seemingly unaffected by changes, for example, advanced surface design, advanced figure design, bookbinding, writing/illumination and heraldic drawing, embroidery, metalwork and enamelling, modelling and casting, and book illustration. Some were interrupted for the war period when apprentices were not forthcoming, for example, woodcarving (furniture trade) closed 1915, brasswork and stained glass 1916, and house painting and decorating 1917. Wood engraving closed as a separate class in 1906, although it probably continued within book illustration.

The effect of this on female middle class students is partly obscured by the reduction of interest in the Arts and Crafts style and the counter attraction of the University of Birmingham from c.1900. The female art pupil teachers' classes had thrived throughout the first decade, and the onset of war had not affected female enrolment as much as male, so that student numbers had become a little more equally balanced within a decreasing total. There is little evidence that such matters were in the minds of the staff or Committee – faced with falling rolls, and the appropriation of parts or the whole of the Central school and branch schools for war use, they had pressing needs to increase the student population and this was via trade classes. This had the effect of devaluing the role of the middle class women students, but would in a few trades, e.g., leather, actually increase the number of working class women.

Following the pattern of organisation at Vittoria Street, joint consultative sub-committees comprising of members of the Birmingham School of Art Committee, and the respective trade organisation, were developed for each trade-related course. The School's relationship with trade associations was mixed. Despite having begun discussions with several trade associations, the Board of Education requested a progress report in 1912.[38] The rate (and quality) of implementation did not satisfy them as they questioned the 'so-called trade classes' in 1913.[39] Numbers in some trade classes had diminished due to a lack of new apprentices, and the outbreak of war closed several classes, however not all trades were equally affected.[40] Reading between the lines, one senses a reluctance to be hurried by either circumstances or by the Board of Education.[41] In the late 1918 spirit of 'rebuilding', the School's Sub-Committee discussed the re-opening and re-starting of classes in architecture, house-painting and decorating, brassworking, enamelling, and furniture design.[42] Many trade-related classes re-opened as day classes on a full-time basis of one year's release. In 1919 day classes for printers, house painters, and a newly constituted school of architecture started in the Central School, and day classes for silver and jewellery at Vittoria Street.[43] In 1920 the Central School re-opened its art laboratories for enamelling, metalwork, modelling and casting after their wartime requisition.[44]

Catterson-Smith's changing position on the relationship between art and industry (specifically local manufacturing trades), from a defence of the arts and crafts tradition, slowly moved, or was forced, towards an acceptance of linking design classes with relevant trades, and the consequent necessity of introducing machinery into the art and design education procedure. Catterson-Smith's central function was the problematic balancing of an innovative system of 'hands-on' designing within an Arts and Crafts philosophy to which many of his teaching staff subscribed, with a need to give students a relevant education for the changed, mechanised world of industry in which most of his technical instructors worked. His assessment of the value of female students as the School's most valuable arts and crafts practitioners is ambivalent, as is his view of the balance between the educational and industrial needs of art or design.[45]

Conclusion

What affected the role of women in Birmingham Art School and how aware were they of the context? It would be too simplistic to blame any one factor, e.g., the rise of trade-related classes, (although the number of middle class women attending arts and crafts based classes dwindled as the number of trade classes increased). There is little to suggest that the women had been empowered and were therefore dissatisfied with a male-dominated situation, (although the proportion of female staff and students had not grown significantly since 1900). Few women were enabled by their art education to change their original ambitions or expectations – the majority of middle class women appear to have trained as teachers, and only a small minority had the conviction, ability and money to set up as independent artist/designers. There is no evidence of the working class woman or artisan improving her prospects outside the horizons that she had been set and unwittingly accepted. There is evidence of increasing opportunity to attend and study, although women students in advanced classes were proportionately far more successful in gaining scholarships than working class girls were in gaining Elementary Free Admissions.

It would be foolish to expect one provincial art school to stand in the face of the general mores of society. Despite the current belief that art schools have been hotbeds of radical thinking, in reality, and especially in the period under discussion, they were rather reactionary. Nowhere is this more evident than in the marginalisation of women's ambitions, a situation which has been slow to change. The reasons for the decrease of middle class women students whose success in arts and crafts gained fame for Birmingham, were in part due to changing tastes in art, the post-war emphasis on machined design and trade-related courses, the closure of the art laboratories during the war, and alternative opportunities offered by the recently opened Birmingham University. The Birmingham Art School either failed to recognise the significance of the female middle class students or simply did not care.[46] The evidence suggests that Birmingham Art School from 1880 to 1920 failed to take advantage of its most able female students as potential teachers, observed the gradual erosion in numbers due to altering taste and alternative cultural milieus, and rather than challenging the social expectations of the student body, effectively prolonged them by matching aspiration with social conditioning to effectively maintain the status quo of the female student.

Originally published in the Journal of Art & Design Education, *Volume 18: 3, 1999*

Notes and References

1. The branch (elementary) schools fed the central (advanced) school. In 1880 all branch schools were housed in rented rooms in Birmingham's School Board elementary schools.
2. Two were untypical – one was jointly run by trade and another purpose built. Vittoria Street School for Jewellers and Silversmiths opened in 1890, and Moseley Road Branch School opened in 1899.
3. Some of the 1,300 were elementary students admitted by competitive scholarships offered by the School and various legacies. Over 1,300 attended the Central School in 1900. Student numbers in total increased and then decreased, rising to 4,477 during 1905–6, and dropping to 3,205 in 1909–10, to 2,279 in 1914–15, and rising slightly to 2,460 in 1916–17. Figures taken from Birmingham Municipal School of Art Management Committee; [BMSAMC] Minute books, Volumes 25 to 29.
4. BMSAMC Sub Committee Volume 27A, 1909–1916, pp. 285–6: BMSAMSC Volume 29, Appended 148–53: and Appended 419.
5. Birmingham Society of Arts and School of Art Minutes [BSASA] Volume 14, 1881–1884, p. 9; BMSAMSC Volume 21, 1893–1897, Appended 131, p. 6; BMSAMSC Volume 22,1897–1900, Appended 273–4 & 94, pp. 7–8.
6. There is no comparative data for 1906–10, 1911 and 1912, and results for 1913–15 have lower totals, but are probably sufficient to retain Birmingham's position. National Competitions ended in 1916.
7. Requests from Dublin; St. Louis, USA; Boston, USA and Arts and Crafts Exhibition Society, London; Milan and New Zealand were received in 1903, 1904, 1905, and 1906. BMSAMSC Volume 25, 1903–04, pp. 183–4; BMSAMSC Volume 26, 1904–06, pp. 30–1, 208, 224–5, 282; BMSAMSC Volume 27, 1906–08. pp, 28–9. Requests received from 1nternational Art Congress 1912, British Arts and Crafts Exhibition in Paris 1914, and Arts and Crafts Exhibition Society, London in 1916. BMSAMSC Volume 27A, 1909–16. pp. 152, 437 and 703.
8. BMSAMSC Volume 26, 1904–06, Appended 117–8. Board of Education Report on Birmingham's art education system. Individual attempts to reform drawing in general schooling were overtaken when the Education Act of 1902 gave the Board of Education control over the content of school syllabuses, but allowed the old County Boroughs (renamed Local Education Authorities) freedom in implementation. Whilst this affected the teaching of drawing at a junior level (up to the school leaving age of normally thirteen or fourteen), it had no effect in the art schools' more advanced classes. By 1905 *Suggestions for the Consideration* of *Teachers and Others Concerned in the work of Public Elementary Schools* placed its educational emphasis on the child's needs, rather than technical or vocational requirements. Within the new liberalism, drawing (and memory drawing) was used to encourage more personal observation, although initial evidence is rather contradictory. The tension between the personal needs of the learner, and technical and vocational needs, was felt at the art school level – it engaged Catterson-Smith's attention throughout his headship.
9. The art schools replaced the drawing masters of the eighteenth and early nineteenth century, who after some preparatory skill-based teaching, usually turned to portrait heads, landscape and flower studies – these being seen as more seemly subjects for women and other amateur artists.
10. Some art schools in the mid nineteenth century were bankrupted; the lesson had been learned.
11. One such long-attendee was Florence Camm who with her brothers and sisters were students at the art school. A daughter of the local stained glass firm of T. W. Camm & Co, Florence undertook an enormous variety of art and craft activities, eventually specialising in painted/stained glass. She was registered as a student from 1892 almost continually until 1912, during and after which she was regularly commissioned to supply stained glass windows for churches and secular buildings.

12. Swift, J. 'Birmingham and its Art School: Changing Views 1800–1921' *Journal of Art & Design Education*, 7: 1, p. 14. (See Chapter 5 of this book). See Swift, J. 'The Arts and Crafts Movement and Birmingham Art School 1880–1900', in Thistlewood, D. (Ed.) (1992), *Histories of Art and Design Education: Cole to Coldstream*, Longman & NSEAD, for a more detailed explanation of why and how the Arts and Crafts Movement appealed to Birmingham. There is a multitude of literature on the Arts and Crafts Movement, its philosophy, practices and practitioners. For a simplified introduction see Crawford, A. (Ed.) (1984), *By Hammer and Hand: The Arts and Crafts Movement in Birmingham*, Birmingham Museum and Art Gallery

13. The 'designs for specified materials' included 'certificates, wallpaper, fans, and stained glass, to jewellery, silverware', utensils, and rooms containing the above. Such prizes for 'designs for' continue throughout the 40 years under scrutiny and form an increasingly specific and numerous feature of Birmingham's prize lists.

14. 'Modelling' involved the manipulation of clay and other materials in figurative or ornamental work. The students handled the materials, but did not understand anything of firing, casting or mould-making. The model was sent to specialists and returned completed. The modelled designs could be intended for a wide variety of different materials with specific characteristics, but nothing apart from lectures on technical matters informed students' awareness of these implications.

15. The plan to extend the new building of 1885 was agreed to satisfy increasing student numbers, (from five branch schools in 1884, the number had risen to eleven by 1891; the consequent pressure for places at the Central School); to realise the implications of Walter Crane's Examiners Report, BMSAMSC Volume 19, 1888–1890, Appended 215, p. 28 & Volume 20, *op. cit.,* Appended 111, p. 7: and to implement the Technical Instruction Act of 1889 making modelling obligatory, BMSAMSC Volume 19, *Ibid.,* Appended 223, pp. 4–5. Technical instruction was designed not to interfere with trade skills but 'shall mean instruction in the use of tools, processes of agriculture, and modelling in clay, wood and other materials'. This would build on the practical tuition of silver and jewellery students. *Ibid.* pp. 237–240, and BMSAMSC Volume 20, *op. cit.* pp. 7–12. BMSAMSC Volume 20, Appended 15, pp. 5 & 8–9. The Report describes increases in numbers, Board School drawing supervision and teaching, the proposed opening of Vittoria Street School for Jewellers and Silversmiths, and an increase in free admissions and types of students attending as reasons for the new extension; and to extend the success of executed design work in outside competitions. BMSAMSC Volume 20, *op. cit.* p. 6. In the Armourers and Braziers Exhibition of May, 1890, Birmingham students won eight prizes for executed design, three by female students, in repoussé, engraved, etched, chased, and embossed metalwork and brasswork. In March 1891, Taylor made radical proposals for facilities to carry out designs in a wide range of materials. *Ibid.* Appended 69. 'proper facilities... to carry out... designs in, (a) repoussé and kindred subjects. e.g., niello, chasing, etching and engraving on metal, damascening and filigree. (b) Enamelling: *Cloisonné*, *Champlevé* and Limoges, and (c) Wood-carving, wood-engraving, needlework, terracotta, encaustic painting, the making of decorative cartoons, and working in fresco, tempera and sgraffito, etc.'; and allotted space for two Art Laboratories [workshops] in the basement linked with the modelling and casting rooms, and a cartoon and fresco room on the first floor. *Ibid.* Appended 70, 3 sheets.

16. The new extension was added in 1892 and opened in 1893. It contained the Art Laboratories. Mary Newill, Bernard Sleigh and Louis Joseph had been appointed to teach embroidery, wood engraving and enamelling respectively. New equipment had been ordered for enamelling, annealing, etching. lithography, wrought and beaten ironwork, terracotta, glazing and stained glass work, and carpentry BMSAMSC Volume 21, 1893–1897, pp. 208, 233 & 267, also appended 255–6.

17. From a few existing records and on stylistic grounds only four or five local metal manufacturers actively welcomed Birmingham School's approach to commercial needs, and this is hardly surprising if the students adopted the typical arts and crafts aversion to machine manufacture. See Crawford. A. (Ed.) (1984), *op. cit.* pp. 33–4 & 110–8.

18. It is difficult to be precise – records are rare, and so is evidence of any short or long-term effect.

19. Until 1884 a maximum of 2 per cent of female students had won design prizes, although their success in pictorial art had grown from 16 per cent to 32 per cent in four years. Whilst their success overall grew from c.30 to over 40 per cent by 1893–1894, their design prize percentage increased to 27 per cent.

20. Birmingham awards for women from the DSA, although not completely documented, show a parallel growth, from 18 to 35 to 44 per cent in 1880, 1883, and 1893 respectively. The female prizewinners in design rose from zero for the first two years to 64 per cent in 1893.

21. This trend is repeated in external awards, e.g., the Armourers and Braziers Awards from 1890 to 1893 showed female students winning 47 per cent of the executed design prizes; in the Arts and Crafts Exhibition of 1893, 58 per cent of all executed designs; and at the Paris Exhibition of 1901, 77 per cent of all executed designs. BMSAMSC Volumes 14, 18,19, 20, 21 and 22 – figures extracted from details of Prize Lists, Awards and other documents.

22. Callen, A. (1979), *Angel in the Studio*, Astragal, pp. 218–21.

23. Some areas although practised, were rarely undertaken by Birmingham students during this period, e.g., mosaic, terracotta, ceramic murals, stained glass, poster designs, bookbinding, and metal casting. Some were mainly practised at an elementary level, e.g., chipped metal and die-sinking, leaving a few areas where perhaps male-dominated trades inhibited female entry, e.g., cabinet and furniture making, iron foundry work, stone-carving, and house painting [male only class].

24. BMSAMSC Volume 21, 1893–1897, Appended 140, pp. 6–8.

25. *Ibid.* p, 7.

26. *Ibid.* p. 6.

27. *Ibid.* p. 12.

28. *Ibid.* Appended 84, pp. 14–24. Local executed design categories were ironwork, engraving on metal, repoussé, wood-carving, woodcuts, stencilling, needlework, leatherwork, gesso and enamelling; 70 per cent of which were won by female students. The DSA awards totalled 76, of which 30 were for design, 14 being won by female students. Crawford, A. (Ed.) (1984), *op. cit.* pp. 157–160, states that by 1895 illustrated works had been published by Birmingham artists, one book being directed by A. J. Gaskin and comprising of fellow staff and student work. Quite apart from the Kelmscott links, by 1900 over 70 books had been illustrated by Birmingham's arts and crafts workers, most of whom were staff or students at the art school. BMSAMSC Volume 22, *op. cit.* pp. 255 & 289–291. Executed design work was requested for the 1901 Paris International Exhibition – thirteen works were selected of which ten were by women, in crafts as diverse as wood-carving, chased copper, *champlevé* enamel, gesso, silver repoussé, steelwork, lace, needlework, and embroidery. Glasgow requested works accompanied by preparatory studies and designs, 'and any other such work... (which will)... illustrate the course or courses of study pursued'.

29. See Crawford, A. (Ed.), *op. cit.* For example pp. 27–30, 37–9. 43, 62–5 *et seq.* 85–6, 90–3, 103 *et seq.* & 120–8.

30. The majority of its students were elementary level, and consisted of mostly male school-aged children, apprentices, trade-released designers, and teachers; classed as 'artisans' by the School. The advanced sector and its middle-class element was a largely female minority. The School was happy to maintain the latter's number, but their untypicality was increasingly clashing with a growing pressure to satisfy other requirements. BMSAMSC Volume 20, *op. cit.* Appended 15, pp. 5 & 8–9. 'All the students at the Branch Schools are artisans, and the great majority of them directly apply to their trade the knowledge which they acquire in the classes. Most of the students of the Central School also are artisans (including)... architects, builders, designers for all local manufactures, artists in stained glass, brass-workers, die sinkers, modellers, lithographers, draughtsmen, machinists, persons in training to become art teachers, etc.... at Ellen Street... a special class... [of 155 students]..., for the Jewellers and Silversmiths Association... (and)... over 300 female Pupil and Candidate Pupil Teachers at Bristol Street Board School.'

31. BMSAMSC Volume 26, 1904–06, Appended 117–8. Board of Education Report on Birmingham's art education system.

32. The Board of Education promoted a more balanced curriculum for Branch Schools of Art in 1913, (BMSAMSC Volume 27A, 1909–16, pp. 271–2 and 331–4) the grouping of courses of study in age bands, and art educational institutions in three progressively advanced stages in 1917. BMSAMSC Volume 29, 1916–21, Appended 34. Circulars 897 and 972.

33. *Ibid.* Form 491T.

34. Catterson-Smith's previous success as head of Vittoria Street School, as an educator in drawing, and his extensive experience in the Arts and Crafts Movement, made him well qualified as the next Head in 1903 on Taylor's retirement. This specialist Branch School linked with the jewellery and silver trades had led to the purchase of a suitable building, and a School that had joint responsibilities – to the Municipal Art School Sub-Committee, and to the Birmingham Jewellers and Silversmiths Association.

35. The majority of his testimonials were from eminent Arts and Crafts practitioners – see Swift, J. (1988), *op. cit.* p. 29.

36. Catterson-Smith attempted some innovations of his own, e.g., a Diploma of Art Instruction in1904, and a combined University and Art School pedagogic syllabus for art teachers in 1913 and 1917. BMSAMSC Volume 25, 1903–04, pp. 252.*ff.* He had reorganised the scholarship and free admission system to encourage more entries from poor backgrounds in 1910/11, and from girls in 1914 and 1919. BMSAMSC Volume 27A, 1909–16, pp. 392–6; Volume 29, 1916–21, Appended 78, respectively. This may have been connected with falling student numbers beginning c.1906, and increasing from 1914 onwards. (See reference 3 above).

37. This paper cannot cover Catterson-Smith's particular treatment of memory drawing and visualisation except to comment that he saw it as a valuable tool in storing images and speeding up future designers', craftworkers' and artists' abilities to design. It was a particular and educationally interesting approach that has a bearing on his ideas about art education as a whole especially in the visualisation and realisation of ideas. Catterson-Smith, R. (1921). *Drawing from Memory and Mind-Picturing*, Pitman, is his own explanation of the idea and methods, and for a later interpretation see Swift, J. 'Robert Catterson-Smith's Concept of Memory Drawing 1911–1920', unpublished MA dissertation. University of Central England; Swift, J. (1990), 'Memory Drawing and Visualisation in the Teaching of Robert Catterson-Smith and Marion Richardson' in Soucy, D. & Stankiewicz, M. A. (Eds.), *Framing, the Past: Essays on Art Education*, National Art Education Association; and Swift, J. (1992), 'Robert Catterson-Smith's Theory and Practice of Memory Drawing 1900–1920' in Amburgy, P. *et al.* (Eds.), *The History of Art Education*, National Art Education Association, USA.

38. The National Amalgamated Furnishing Trade Association (NAFTA) complained about the quality of teaching and unfair competition from staff. The complaint over staff taking outside contracts in competition with trade workers, struck at the heart of Birmingham's arts and crafts philosophy of a guild-like co-operation between staff and students on professional jobs. The School refused to alter its practice. BMSAMSC Volume 24, 1901–03, *op. cit.* pp. 258–9; Volume 26, 1904–06, *op. cit.* pp. 6; Volume 27, 1906–08, *op. cit.* pp. 65–6 and 98. Specialist instruction in lace-making, metalwork, house-painting and decorating, brasswork and interior decoration was introduced between 1903 and 1909. BMSAMSC Volume 25, *op. cit.* pp. 32 and 134, lace-making; Volume 26, *op. cit.* pp. 79 and 91, ironwork p. 170, and Volume 27, *op. cit.* p. 21 carving, chasing, chipping and damascening; *Ibid.* p. 98 house-painting and decorating: *Ibid,* pp. 101–2, 114–5, 146, 165 and 209 brasswork; *Ibid.* pp. 210 and 216 interior decoration. The Birmingham Master House Painters Association and Birmingham Brass Makers Association began discussions in 1906, a joint-committee between the Birmingham Technical Education Committee and the Art School was proposed in 1909*, op. cit.* Volume 27A, p. 30, and NAFTA and the Cabinet Makers Trade Association began discussions in 1911. *Ibid.* pp. 107–8.

39. *Ibid.* p. 201 and BMSAMSC Minutes Volume 26, 1904–06, pp. 236–7.

40. Classes in woodcarving and architecture closed in 1915, brasswork and stained glass in 1916, and house-painting and decorating in 1917. Other trades were not adversely affected, for example, discussions with the Birmingham Master Printers Association and Birmingham Typographical Society resulted in new classes for printing in 1914, and in 1916 discussions were started with the Birmingham and Walsall Leather Trade Association. *Ibid.* pp. 420–2 and 522–4.

41. A staff and committee meeting in 1917 concluded that the full-time trade classes were meeting the needs of the City's industries appropriately, but the part-time classes were problematic. BMAMSCM 1904–06 *Ibid.* Volume 26, Volume 29, p. 19. The Board of Education's Form 491T had already made suggestions concerning future training, but Birmingham was reluctant to be hurried or controlled, and sent a deputation to the Board arguing that the best way of retaining the confidence of employers was not by following their proposals blindly, but through consultation and compromise. *Ibid.* pp. 75–7.

42. *Ibid.* p. 284.

43. *Ibid.* Appended 322, and pp. 333–4 and 372–3.

44. *Ibid.* p. 447.

45. By 1915 he was criticising 'pass-time' students as making the School less efficient. *Ibid.* 1909–16, Volume 27A, Appended 592. In *Birmingham Institutions* he argued that whilst the School should try to meet trade requirements, 'it must not allow itself to make mere commercial tools of the students' and implied that the pursuit of art 'in the highest sense' would somehow

percolate through to industrial art. Catterson-Smith. (1911), 'Birmingham Municipal School of Art' *Birmingham Institutions* edited by Muirhead, J. H. Cornish Brothers UK, pp. 304–5.

46. The latter might explain the lack of opportunity offered to outstanding women ex-students as members of staff. Birmingham's attitude was typical in so far as I have been able to ascertain, only Glasgow School of Art had the foresight to employ some of its most talented female students, and this only for a brief period around1900 to1910.

Chapter 7: The Early History of the NSEAD: the Society of Art Masters (1888–1909) and the National Society of Art Masters (1909–1944)

David Thistlewood

On 25 July 1888 some 60 prominent members of the art teaching profession met at the South Kensington Museum to inaugurate the *Society of Art Masters,* the NSEAD's direct forebear. It was formed to represent the interests of qualified Art Masters throughout Great Britain, and to be their medium of communication with the Department of Science and Art in London. The initiator was Edward R. Taylor, Head Master of the Municipal School of Art, Birmingham, reflecting provincial frustration at the lack of any direct means of influencing the Department on matters deriving from practical teaching experience except through School Committees and their Honorary Secretaries – 'a cumbersome, inefficient and sometimes impracticable process'.[1] Taylor was elected founding Chairman (the Chair was to become the Presidency in 1909), and in his *Introductory Address*[2] he set forth the objectives of the SAM as being 'to preserve the interests of Art Education, of Schools of Art and of Art Masters', regarding the former as a subject of the highest national importance.

There had been earlier attempts to organise the profession, and these had been largely ineffective because of the rigid hierarchy legated by the National Course of Instruction then in force. This was so finely gradated in its recognition of competence (there were 23 stages comprising over 50 separate parts) that it had resulted in an academic caste system of almost infinite complexity, and a great deal of confusion about professional co-equality. In 1887, however, a Committee of 'Masters in Training' at the National Art Training School, South Kensington, had circulated all 122 Head Masters of Schools of Art, seeking support for their efforts to gain graduate status on successful completion of their studies.[3] All but eleven expressed favour for an Art Degree; and it was this unprecedented (virtual) unanimity which provided the necessary cohesion for the founding of the SAM, giving expression as it did to a great desire for more tangible academic recognition for Art on the part of the subject's most distinguished holders of diplomas and advanced certificates. The Head Masters themselves then took advantage of the common interest that had been highlighted by their humbler colleagues and formed the SAM; though ironically it was decided at inauguration that it would be unseemly to be cohering merely for the purpose of self-decoration. The issue of graduate status was set-aside until six years later when the Annual Meeting carried a motion requiring the Society to pursue all possible means towards this end. The first tangible progress in this direction came in 1896, when the Society was instrumental in the National Art Training School's transformation into Royal College of Art, and in the acceptance of its Associateship as being degree-equivalent.

This was not the only pressing issue of the time, and others featured prominently in Edward Taylor's *Introductory Address.* There was grudging acceptance that Art no longer had a government department to itself but now shared with Science, but there was anger that Science was the more favoured of the two, consuming greater resources in spite of Art's substantially superior contributions to the national economy. It was argued that Art could provide, at less cost and with reduced risk of failure, the kind of skilful technical education for which hopes were being pinned on Science. There was a suspicion, too, that Science examinations were tactically easier to pass, resulting in larger emoluments for its teachers in a time of 'payment by results'; and there was frustration at the fact that a promised and almost – won national museum of Art Education had been lost – again to the benefit of Science. The first step towards correcting such imbalance was to be the petitioning for access to the corridors and smoke-filled rooms of power.

This the SAM did remarkably successfully. By the end of its first decade it was an accepted part of the educational establishment, few prominent members of the profession having chosen to disregard it. From the outset there were shrewd appointments to honorary membership – the Lord President of the Council, the

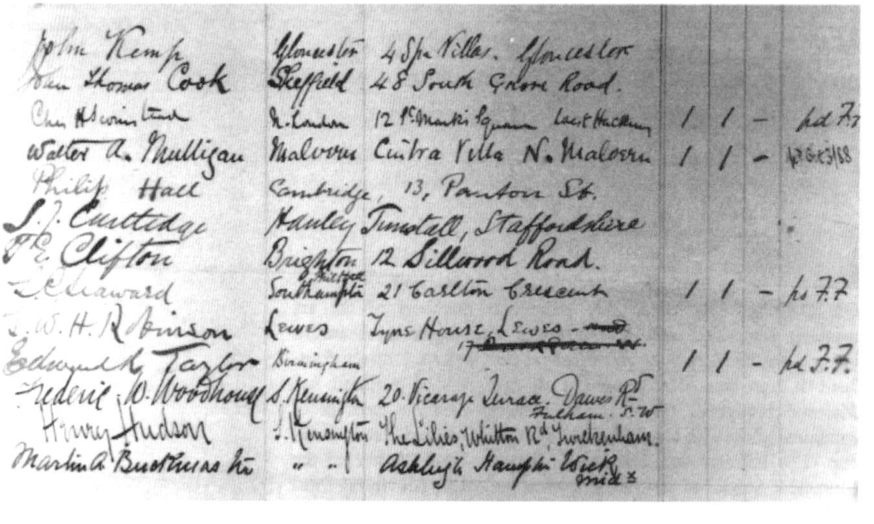

Fig. 1: A leaf from the SAM's first subscription files, recording that Edward Taylor, the first Chairman, and others had paid their one-guinea dues (NSEAD/A/7).

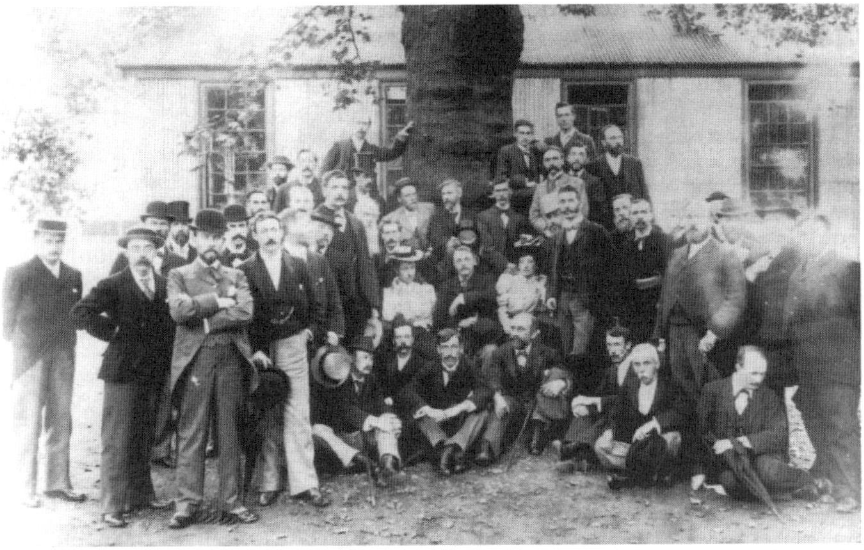

Fig. 2: The SAM membership photographed at the 8th Annual Meeting at South Kensington in 1895 (NSEAD/A/19).

Vice President of the Committee of Council on Education, the Principal (John Sparkes) and the Visitor (Edward Poynter) of the National Art Training School, the Director of the South Kensington Museum, and the Secretary of the Science and Art Department together with his Director and Assistant Director for Art. It was considered proper to control the quality of the general membership by strict exclusion of all except 'gentlemen' (two women, the first of a growing number, were in fact admitted in the Society's first year) who were Head Masters of Schools of Art, holders of the Art Masters' Certificate (Group One), or (as they began to graduate) Associates of the Royal College of Art. And, in return for enshrining the Art Masters' Certificate in its principles of membership, the Department of Science and Art promptly recognised the Society's representative significance with an assurance that:

> *The Lords of the Committee of Council on Education will always be glad to give the fullest consideration to any communication from your Society, as representing the views of so large a body of gentlemen deeply interested in the progress of Art instruction, and well qualified by their position and experience to form most valuable opinions on various matters connected therewith.*[4]

The first occasion on which this assurance was tested was in January 1893 when the Society made its first considered approach to officialdom. A deputation of the SAM, consisting of the current Chairman Michael Sullivan and almost all of the officers, was received by its honorary member the Rt. Hon A. H. Dyke Acland MP, Vice President of the Committee of Council on Education, in the presence of other honorary members, Major-General Donnelly C. B., Secretary of the Department of

Science and Art, and Mr Armstrong, the Director for Art. On the Society's agenda was the complaint that scientific aspects of Geometry had infiltrated courses leading to Art Teaching qualifications, emphasising theory and downgrading draughtsmanship, and at the same time debarring teachers without Science qualifications from offering certain courses in Geometry in return for payment (though permitting tuition unpaid). There was also confusion over whether the remuneration of teachers of Modelling would receive payment on results in examination or on attendance totals. There was annoyance at the recent poor manufacture of cast reproductions used in Drawing from the Antique (a cost-paring measure on the part of the Department), which had inevitably led to inferior copying, a lowering of Drawing standards (and of paid rewards). There was a tentative suggestion that more spontaneous draughtsmanship might be credited in Drawing from Nature. And among several administrative issues was the publication of examination marks obtained in the Department's annual National Competition (much desired by the SAM as even teachers were denied this information) and the provision of Department circulars for dissemination to the membership (many School Secretaries being negligent in this regard).

What of course was being criticised, without such words being used, was the monolithic clumsiness of the prevailing centralised system of controlling curriculum, examination and remuneration. Acland's response, recorded in a SAM printed memorandum, had obviously been prepared in advance and was clearly unexpected. He said:

> *My hope is that we are moving towards the time when secondary education in the broader sense, including both scientific and art instruction, is going to be, at any rate in part, put more effectively upon what I may call a municipal footing... I think that it is impossible not to feel that however admirable was the original conception of our work here, we could never in future adequately carry on the whole work needed in Science and Art by a central grant, central inspection, central examination, and so on. We must look to our work becoming modified in various reasonable directions in accordance with the movement of public opinion... On the other hand you are well aware that it is not easy for us to interfere with the local authorities... Certainly some three-quarters of a million a year is a sum we must look to with a great deal of interest... Your body represents a very important part of our work in connection with industry. I am always hoping, as I think that you must always hope, that we shall do more and more in the way of bringing our designing work into closer contact with the work of the country.*[5]

He also urged the SAM to discourage the kind of art education which aimed to teach students how to paint pictures which would 'fetch five pounds', but this admonishment was submerged in his enormous hints at an imminent dismantling of bureaucracy. The SAM deputation withdrew speechless but no doubt happy at having had Acland's ambitions revealed to them. These were remarkably prophetic, anticipating as they did a proposal of the Bryce Commission (the creation of Local Education Authorities), which was not, formally recommended until the *Report* of 1895[6] and not finally implemented until the *Education Act* of 1902 (the Balfour-Morant Act) came into force.

Elation at the Society's access to the centre of power in 1893 was dampened later the same year by a temporary loss of financial equilibrium, with the collapse of the London and General Bank in which all its capital assets had been invested. Twelve shillings in the pound – a restoration of 60 per cent – was recovered in 1894. Nevertheless over £50 was lost, and the potential calamity of this may be judged against current income and expenditure. Annual subscriptions amounted to only a little over twice this amount; the Secretary, Francis Ford, was paid £6 per month; postage for the year cost £7. 15s. 0d. and stationery £1. 10s. 4d.; parliamentary papers were purchased for the library for 3s. 0d.; and a river excursion to Hampton Court showed a deficit of £3. 19s. 0d. Potential disaster was avoided only because the Society's servant and chief creditor, Francis Ford, was content to receive nominal payments while the crisis lasted.

Its financial stability restored, the Society resumed activities 'in the interests of Art Education, of Art Schools and of Art Masters'. *Annual Reports* reveal a host of minor representations to the Department of Science and Art, often resulting in changes to curricula and examinations. The proposed devolution of powers to municipal authorities was welcomed, especially because it meant that Schools of Art might respond positively to the needs of local industries; but from its very first intimation of the government's thoughts in this direction – and until it grew exasperated at the centre's poverty of ideas – the Society used all its influence to advocate retention of national examinations, run by the Department of Science and Art (later the Board of Education), in order to ensure comparability of standards throughout the country. That such an arrangement was in fact put into effect for Art was both a tribute to the SAM's persuasive arguments and the reason why one of its main ambitions – to establish Art degrees – was incapable of early realisation.

The paradoxes of esteem were regularly noted. There was obvious pride at the fact that Art examinations were administered by government, for this pointed-up the subject's strategic importance. There was often anger, however, at the principles of administration. The 1897 Chairman, Samuel Cartlidge, referred in his *Address* to an issue which had festered at several Annual Meetings, namely the refusal by the Department of Science and Art to consider appointing Art specialists to Inspectorships, while relying on men of Science to oversee the national provisions for Art. The Meeting duly deplored this fact, as it had done before, Cartlidge asserting the unlikelihood of ever effecting changes to the system.[7] The Annual

Meeting of the year following, however, celebrated Cartlidge's own elevation to the Inspectorate, and his passing from Ordinary to Honorary Membership.

The Society's greatest honorific act, in the sense of reflecting more on the bestowing than the bestowed upon, took place on 18 May 1899 when Edward Prince of Wales was pleased:

> *To accede to the prayer of (a tendered) petition and accept the post of Honorary President of the Society of Art Masters.*[8]

This seemed to herald a return to conditions which, 50 years earlier, had given rise to the revival of Art led by the Prince's father Albert; and possibly because of this the Society was emboldened to state publicly the principles it would hold forth in connection with the Education Bill still making its protracted journey towards enactment. These included well-established policies – the creation of more Art Inspectorships, separate and distinct status for Schools of Art within the national provisions for technical education, and the retention of centralised control over examinations. But this last requirement was complemented by a curious piece of kite-flying on the part of Walter Scott, the Chairman in 1899, who quoted an official memorandum stating that the certificates awarded by the Department of Science and Art were comparable to university degrees, took note also of rumours to the effect that London University was to be re-sited around South Kensington, and speculated:

> *it is possible that ere long London may be the educational centre of the empire, and the Department at South Kensington affiliated thereto. Then degrees for attainments in art would be given, and Art Masters would at last take their fair and just position.*[9]

It may have been rash to envisage such an eminence for the capital, but furthering the cause of Art Degrees demanded drastic measures. Walter Scott was diffident about accepting his right to an Associateship of the Royal College of Art because this privilege was denied others who, while not having trained at South Kensington, were his equal in respect of ability and service. Many members regularly expressed their views in favour of the Society's instituting its own academic qualifications, and, while there was a certain distaste for a proposed course of action which was apparently tainted by self-indulgence, its ramifications were thoroughly explored.

Francis Black, a Member of Council, seems to have been the prime initiator here. During the Annual Meeting of 1905, addressing what had become a routine topic of discussion, he moved:

> *That the Council be instructed to take the necessary steps to incorporate the Society under the Companies Acts, and to obtain thereby full powers to issue diplomas.*[10]

This was subsequently withdrawn, but the side issue was pursued in a successful motion (proposed by Alfred Shuttleworth and seconded by Charles Ripper) requiring Council to enquire as to the advantages and cost of incorporation and to take any desirable action. This was done, and at a Meeting of Council on 21 October 1905 it was moved unanimously that:

This Council, having made full enquiry, are of opinion that incorporation under the Companies Acts would be of no value whatever in so far as the granting of diplomas or certificates of membership is concerned, and defers the further consideration of the possible value of incorporation in other respects.[11]

Not discouraged by this, Francis Black wrote to the current Chairman, Frederick Marriot, on 23 November, linking his objective to another of the Society's preoccupations, an intention to petition for the prefix 'Royal' to be added to the Society's title. On King Edward VII's accession in 1901 he had ceased to be Honorary President and had become Patron (in which capacity the Throne was to be linked to the Society until after the death of King George V). But sections of the SAM deeply desired the royal appellation, and this had been sought fruitlessly from Queen Victoria and was now about to be petitioned to her son.[12] Black wrote:

I have spoken to a very high personage who is in communication with our Sovereign the King; and he declares that the first consideration that will weigh with His Majesty will be the stability of the Society.

When he heard how we are constituted, he replied that Incorporation would remove the chief stumbling block.

In answer to my enquiry whether an intimation to His Majesty that the Society contemplated taking steps to Incorporate and become an Examining Body issuing Diplomas would suffice; he declared no! It might prevent a direct negative; but the actual stability of the Society is a matter of the first magnitude when approaching the Sovereign for such a purpose.

In view of the above, I must ask you to at once request the Council to rescind their decision of last Saturday; and to take immediate steps to Incorporate the Society under the Companies Act, keeping back the petition for the present.[13]

This worried Members of Council sufficiently to require Black to reveal his informant, but this he resolutely refused, saying:

I have no authority to divulge the name; but, I may say, if it will be of assistance to the Council that the personage in question is sufficiently high to be the direct means of conferring Royal Patronage on Educational Institutions; and this, without the slightest difficulty.[14]

Maintaining the initiative, he wrote once more to Marriot, who reported to Council on 13 January 1906 that Black had been to Somerset House and met a 'high official' who had affirmed an ability to empower the Society to grant diplomas. Marriot then communicated directly with the Controller of the Companies Registration Office at Somerset House, and was informed that there would be no objection to the inclusion, in a *Memorandum of Articles of Association,* of a provision to award diplomas, but if the Society did not already possess such powers incorporation, in itself, would not confer them.[15] By a circuitous chain of events, then, the Council came to adopt the view that it must first formulate a scheme for recognising academic and professional excellence, and then pursue the formalities of incorporation, before seeking its ultimate objective of the royal appellation.

This was put to the Annual Meeting in August 1906 and it was agreed to institute Associateships and Fellowships, although Council's proposals that these should be awarded automatically – the ASAM after two years of membership, and the FSAM either after ten years or (in the case of Head Masters) after two years – met with general disapproval. The meeting expressed an overwhelming desire to attach distinction to these awards by limiting them to successful examinees, the relevant examinations being set at substantially higher levels than the Art Masters' Certificate (Group One), so that they might become proper badges of merit. Council was therefore empowered to establish Associateships and Fellowships on the understanding that it would take cognisance of the feelings of the meeting. This it did, tendering compromise proposals that were accepted the following year. Accordingly Associateships became available after two years of membership without examination, and Fellowships were awardable after seven years (Head Masters two years) and successful examination by submission of works of art or a written thesis on Art Teaching. The membership list of 1908 reveals a full complement of 295, of which 45 individuals had passed the tests of Fellowship and 29 had availed themselves of their automatic rights to Associateships.

Thus the academic ambitions of the SAM were eventually realized, but by this act it effectively ruined, for the time being, its chances of gaining incorporation. After the Society's solicitor presented a *Draft Memorandum and Articles of Association* to the Board of Education in 1907, he was obliged to report this body's substantial objection to a scheme of examination which seemed to rival its own. The main problem was the Society's name – the *Society of Art Masters* - which had always intentionally reflected as a condition of membership the possession of an Art Masters' Certificate (Group One) or its recognised equivalent. To the Board of Education the Society seemed to be creating its own equivalents, or at least the possibility for an unqualified member (in the Board's eyes) to gain through

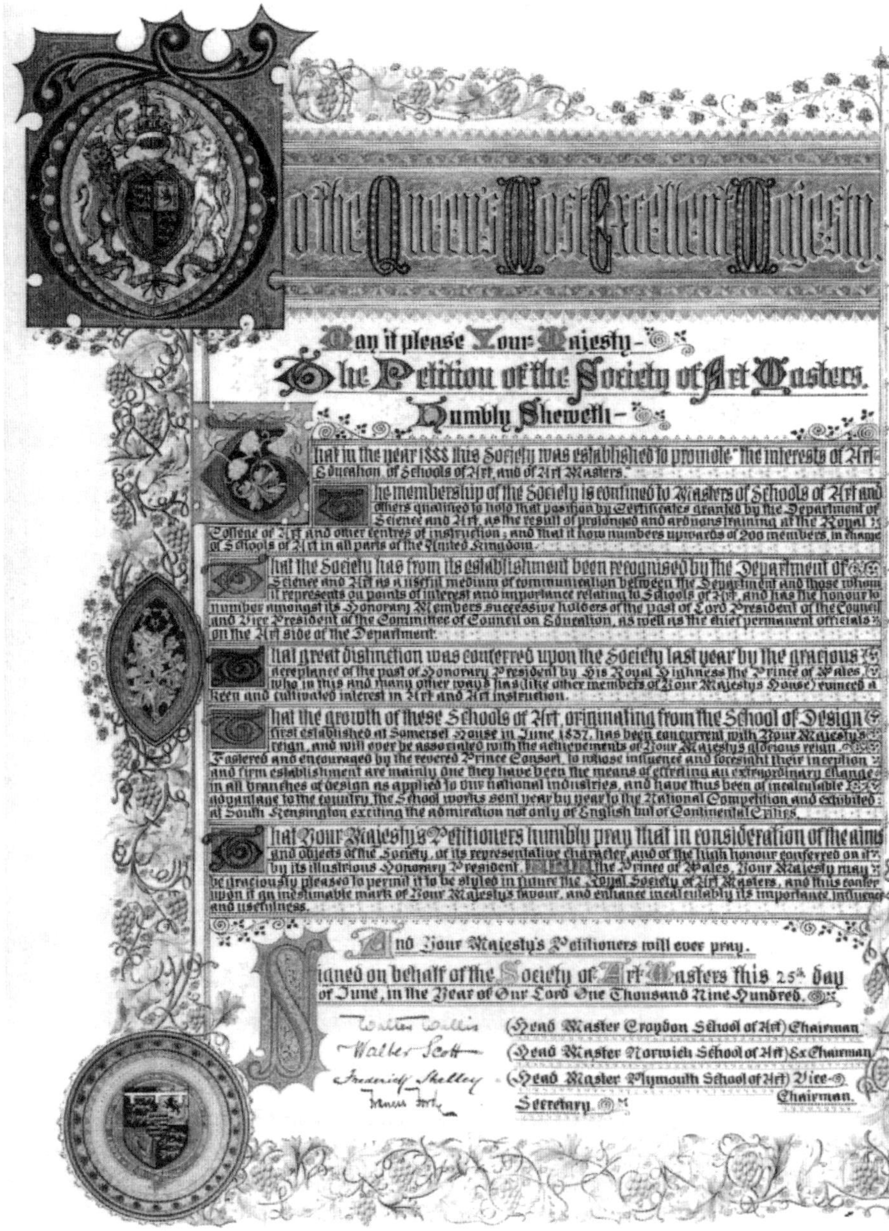

To the Queen's Most Excellent Majesty.

May it please Your Majesty—

The Petition of the Society of Art Masters.

Humbly Sheweth—

That in the year 1888 this Society was established to promote "the interests of Art Education, of Schools of Art, and of Art Masters."

The membership of the Society is confined to Masters of Schools of Art and others qualified to hold that position by Certificates granted by the Department of Science and Art, as the result of prolonged and arduous training at the Royal College of Art and other centres of instruction; and that it now numbers upwards of 200 members, in charge of Schools of Art in all parts of the United Kingdom.

That the Society has from its establishment been recognised by the Department of Science and Art as a useful medium of communication between the Department and those whom it represents on points of interest and importance relating to Schools of Art, and has the honour to number amongst its Honorary Members successive holders of the post of Lord President of the Council and Vice President of the Committee of Council on Education, as well as the chief permanent officials on the Art side of the Department.

That great distinction was conferred upon the Society last year by the gracious acceptance of the post of Honorary President by His Royal Highness the Prince of Wales, who in this and many other ways has (like other members of Your Majesty's House) evinced a keen and cultivated interest in Art and Art instruction.

That the growth of these Schools of Art, originating from the School of Design first established at Somerset House in June 1837, has been concurrent with Your Majesty's reign, and will ever be associated with the achievements of Your Majesty's glorious reign. Fostered and encouraged by the revered Prince Consort, to whose influence and foresight their inception and firm establishment are mainly due they have been the means of effecting an extraordinary change in all branches of design as applied to our national industries, and have thus been of incalculable advantage to the country, the School works sent year by year to the National Competition and exhibited at South Kensington exciting the admiration not only of English but of Continental Critics.

That Your Majesty's Petitioners humbly pray that in consideration of the aims and objects of the Society, of its representative character, and of the high honour conferred on it by its illustrious Honorary President, [illegible] the Prince of Wales, Your Majesty may be graciously pleased to permit it to be styled in future the Royal Society of Art Masters, and thus confer upon it an inestimable mark of Your Majesty's favour, and enhance incalculably its importance, influence and usefulness.

And Your Majesty's Petitioners will ever pray.

Signed on behalf of the Society of Art Masters this 25th day of June, in the Year of Our Lord One Thousand Nine Hundred.

Walter Wallis (Head Master Croydon School of Art) Chairman

Walter Scott (Head Master Norwich School of Art) Ex Chairman

Frederick Shelley (Head Master Plymouth School of Art) Vice-Chairman.

Francis Ford Secretary.

Fig. 3: The SAM illuminated petition to Queen Victoria dated 25 June 1900, signed by Walter Wallis (Chairman), Walter Scott (Ex-Chairman), Frederick Shelley (Vice-Chairman) and Francis Ford (Secretary), requesting permission to adopt the style Royal Society of Art Masters.

Fellowship a mark of distinction that was deemed to be superior to Group One. As a condition of supporting the SAM for incorporation the Board required its Certificates of Associateship and Fellowship to disclaim the existence of authorised statutes or charters, thus rendering the awards useless for academic purposes. As an alternative it suggested a change of name – to the *Society of Teachers of Art* - but this was immediately rejected, not because it would open doors to the great majority of teachers who were unqualified (the Society was keen to recruit such individuals to less than full membership), but because it would seem to advertise a lowering of standards.[16]

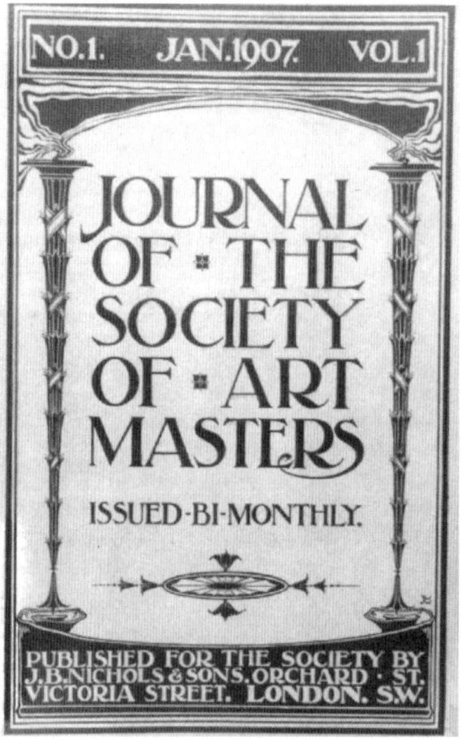

Fig. 4: Title page of the Society's first Journal.

It was therefore announced to the Annual General Meeting of 1908 that the issue of incorporation had been put into abeyance principally because the Board of Education had been obstructive. In many ways this cleared the air for a dispassionate consideration of the Society's future supported neither by corporate status nor, realistically, royal appellation. It seemed to dawn on the membership for the first time that its relatively close association with the Department of Science and Art had been superseded by a more distant and probably more antagonistic relationship with its successor, and by the necessity now to make representation to the host of Local Education Authorities, the unknown quantities of recent creation. In the course of a single Annual Meeting, the twentieth, then, the Society underwent fundamental changes, revoking procedures which had been designed chiefly for lobbying Whitehall and South Kensington, and adopting machinery for acting in the interests of Art Education wherever needs might arise. This transformation was symbolically encapsulated in a change of name – to the *National Society of Art Masters* – adopted on 1 August 1908;[17] and it was put into practical effect by the creation of a system of regional organisation devised by Frederick Burridge, Vice-Chairman elect and Head Master of the Liverpool School of Art.

This had been on agendas – official and unofficial – for several years; and when Burridge bemoaned that 'the Society had no local branches which might deal with the local authorities, and it had no system for gaining local information'[18], he was merely expressing issues which others had attempted to force by extraordinary action as early as 1899. Then Charles Swinstead and Francis Black had proposed a scheme for reorganisation, described by the Chairman of the day, Walter Scott, as dangerous and revolutionary, which had included the creation of a regional system of electing officers, and the formation of a General Purposes Committee resident in London and having advisory responsibilities towards Council and the Chair. These ideas had been canvassed in secret. Thirty signatories had called for a Special General Meeting, and, though Council had initially refused this, it was persuaded by a threatened legal injunction (at the delicate moment of the Prince of Wales' becoming Honorary President). The meeting took place on 20 May at the Midland Hotel, Birmingham, surviving a point of order intended to establish its illegality, as well as hostile opening remarks from the Chair.

Swinstead's case was this:

> *The leading idea all through with everybody concerned has been the strong desire to strengthen the Society by helping in all ways that we can to bind together the members in conscious unity. The bulk of us are so many detached atoms whose connection is of the frailest description, a connection which with half of the members has been limited to the payment of a guinea per annum and the receipt in exchange of the official notices. We seek therefore to give to every member an available vote which shall be effective, entirely irrespective of distance, and which cannot be lost except by inaction on the part of the member himself. By dividing the country into constituencies we hope to make a local connection as well as a corporate union effective, and we also think this will be a means of getting rid of any suspicion that any part of the country shall be over represented.*[19]

His constituencies were to have been a Northern Division containing Scotland and counties south to Nottinghamshire, a Western Division embracing all parts of the country south of a line from Cheshire to Hampshire, and an Eastern Division including London and everywhere else. These would have generated business in local meetings for submission to Council, in whose assistance a General Purposes Committee would have been established to speed things up and cope with the inevitably increased demands. These proposals came to nothing, being referred by resolution to the attention of Council (whose feathers had been ruffled by the scheme's conspiratorial origins and its implied accusations of Council's tardiness).

The issue of regionalisation had next arisen in response to the fact that immediately after the 1902 Act scores of local specialist teacher-associations had formed to cope with the autonomy of the LEAs. Many members of the SAM had also joined their local societies and were making strong representations that the Society should organise a scheme of affiliation, accepting the principle of less than full attachment for unqualified persons. The Annual Meeting of 1905 had therefore adopted strategic regulations to provide for this eventuality,[20] and these had been put into effect for the first time on 8 January 1906 when the *West Riding Society of Teachers of Art and Art Technology* applied successfully for affiliation.[21]

At the time of Frederick Burridge's proposals for a regional organisation in 1908 the *West Riding* was still the only affiliate but he had prepared his own *North Western Association of Head Masters of Schools of Art* for a positive approach, and the *Staffordshire Society of Art Teachers* had expressed approval for his outline scheme. Representatives of the *London Association* and the *Midland Association of Head Masters of Schools of Art* were also present at the Annual Meeting. The time seemed therefore ripe to institute District Branches, which would at once regionalise the Society and provide receptacles for these and other local associations. There would be a financial burden of course, but the *North Western Association* had conducted its entire business for £3. 15s. 0d. in 1907. It was not a question of the Society sponsoring the ambitions of less qualified people out of its by-now respectable reserves. The point was that the Society needed to organise functioning divisions of itself in every part of the country to exert its influence wherever and whenever required, linking these divisions to its centre by means of formal representation on Council, and reciprocally providing a mechanism for senior officers to intervene directly in local matters as and when necessary.[22] All of this was accepted in principle and Council was empowered to draft the details.

The chief problem was the Board of Education's recurring objection to the NSAM's consorting with inappropriately qualified persons, and a neat solution was found for presentation to the Annual Meeting of 1909 when Council reported back. It was a fact that there were numerous individuals teaching Art and allied subjects at all levels of education by virtue of qualifications other than the Art Masters' Certificate (Group One) or the ARCA, and it was agreed that all these teachers ought to be adopted as integral to the Society's future plans. However, so long as the Society was an organisation of members having passed exclusive examinations, those so distinguished had to maintain a position in it beyond and above that of others. Therefore Burridge's committee proposed the creation of a class of 'junior' membership of the NSAM, permitting potential colleagues of different backgrounds to become attached to thirteen electoral divisions of the parent Society distributed throughout the country. These individuals were to be christened 'District Members of the NSAM', and permitted to hold any of its offices except where they bore upon the affairs of full members. This would be seen as preparing judiciously for the future, for as Burridge predicted:

> *Art instruction and its administration, the schools, the National Competition, their diplomas – all, all would change, and the Society must be elastic and ready for change also.*[23]

Burridge's scheme, as refined by Council, was given approval at the Annual Meeting of 1909 and was put into effect soon afterwards, the success of its reception indicated by an increase in the Society's ranks from 312 members in 1909 to 340 Full and 160 District members in the following year, raising subscription income from £327. 12s. 0d. to £390. 0s. 0d. The Society regionalised itself and opened its doors to wider membership not a moment too soon, for within four years Burridge's fears had been realised, the Art Masters' Certificates being abolished by the Board of Education, and the Royal College of Art losing its absolute pre-eminence because of a reluctance, for the moment, to embrace industrial design.

Having been largely responsible for turning an inward-looking SAM, preoccupied with its own inner circle and its special relationship with the centre of administration, into an NSAM of expansive outlook, Burridge became the first President in 1909, revealing in his *Presidential Address* that the changes he had desired for the Society had been but an aspect of his ambitions for Art Education as a whole. Chief among these was the desire to nurture a healthy relationship between Art, industrial design and the creative crafts, and this he now introduced into the Society's mainstream policies, remarking:

> *Never has there been so critical a period for Art Education; apparently the whole scheme is in the melting pot, may it emerge remoulded in accordance with the requirements of modern conditions and, while preserving the highest Art ideal, be of direct value to industrial and commercial work.*

This concern immediately became the crux of the NSAM's advice to the Board of Education's Committee of Inquiry into the functions and constitution of the Royal College of Art and its relation to Schools of Art throughout the country. Arguing first for the abolition of unequal competition between Art Schools in small communities and in the more densely populated areas, the Society suggested a network of provision that echoed its own revised constitution. It put forward the idea that numerous Art Schools in small communities should belong to co-operative geographic groupings, focusing upon major schools, or 'Provincial Centres', which, having large hinterlands to draw upon and the very best equipment of the day, would be able to develop scholarly and practical aspects of creative work as never before. These larger provincial Schools would in turn act as feeders to the Royal College of Art, but this would necessitate changes to this institution because the excellence coming forward in this way would include expertise in a whole range of necessary design and craft skills rather than the exclusive expertise in Drawing ability the RCA had traditionally respected. 'The point I wish to make and insist upon', Burridge said:

is that as the Provincial Centres have realised the necessity for provision of Art trade instruction, the Royal College of Art must be prepared to afford to the trade students who go there equal facilities for the continuance of their education, which cannot at that stage become only theoretical but has an even greater need for the testing of increased Art knowledge by practical experiment.

Existing examinations for students outside the RCA, of course, geared as they were towards outmoded Art Teaching ideals irrelevant to the design industries, would need to be replaced by a series of specialist subject diplomas, and ideally these would be recognised for entry purposes by the RCA. These lower or ordinary diplomas would require central moderation and, the Art Inspectorate being insufficiently wide-ranging in its expertise, this task would be best shouldered by the most fitting body available, the NSAM. And as to instituting *relevant* qualifications in Art Teaching, the most appropriate way to provide for these would be for suitable students to progress from the RCA to London University to take Bachelors' or Masters' degrees.[24]

There are no records of the Board of Education's reaction to the NSAM's offer of diploma moderation, nor to its suggestion about higher teaching qualifications. It is perhaps significant, however, that on the one hand the Society developed its own direct involvement in teacher-education (receiving in 1912 over twelve hundred papers in its examination *Drawing for use in Secondary and Other Schools*), and that on the other hand the Board abolished the Art Masters' Certificate in 1913, replacing it with a comprehensive system of (a) Intermediate Drawing Examinations in such categories as Life, Antique, Architecture and Anatomy, (b) Advanced Examinations in Painting, Pictorial Design, Modelling or Industrial Design; and (c) courses leading to a qualification entitled the 'Teaching Certificate for Teachers in Schools of Art'. Intermediate courses were then provided in the majority of Art Schools, Advanced courses in what came to be known as Regional Art Schools, and courses in *Principles of Teaching and School Management,* leading to the Teaching Certificate, in newly-approved centres attached to most of the upper tier of Art Schools. These latter institutions only admitted students who had matriculated and already possessed Intermediate and Advanced Art School Certificates, and this meant they automatically ruled out the artisan classes, who could not afford full-time study beyond the school leaving age of thirteen.

Because the NSAM Council had tacitly supported this principle without reference to the general membership it had given rise to great controversy at the Annual Meeting of 1912,[25] which was only resolved by a great deal of subcommittee work over the next twelve months. However Hubert Schröder, who succeeded Burridge as President, was able to announce at the 1913 Annual Meeting plans substantially to increase the Society's own involvement in examinations, providing appropriate subjects for artisans in place of normal scholastic Intermediate courses, and offering alternative teacher-education courses for candidates excluded from conventional training through financial hardship.[26] The Society's syllabuses for these were in place by 1914.[27] In the same year the Oxford Local Examinations Board recognised the NSAM's Certificate for Secondary Teachers as a prime qualification within its jurisdiction.[28] And as its importance as an examining body grew the Society also came to demand responsibility for monitoring the standards of Art Schools as institutions, requiring the Board of Education to 'group and grade' them only in response to initiatives taken by NSAM District Committees.[29]

Now the most significant aspect of all this activity, seen in the context of what is known of the major developments of Art and Design Education in the early twentieth century, is the NSAM's insistence on elevating craftwork, and design for industrial applications, to levels of acceptance afforded to those subjects featuring in the Board of Education's Intermediate examinations – Drawing from Life and the Antique, and Anatomical and Architectural Drawing. This insistence was the natural expression of a Society whose chief officers had invariably been Heads of provincial Art Schools in contact with trades and industries [see Appendix]. The ways in which their schools had served these industries, promoting fine craftsmanship, high quality execution, and appropriate though often restrained decoration, had created a kind of educational subculture, overlooked by the Establishment because of the consistent excellence of responses to 'official' academic programmes as revealed by the annual National Competition.

The true value of practical alternatives, however, had been perceived by other governments: Germany, in particular, had positively emulated them. And when Hermann Muthesius had made his celebrated survey of the work of Art Schools in Britain, on behalf of the Prussian Board of Trade, reporting in 1907, it had mainly been the schools of members of the SAM he had visited and their provisions for crafts and industries he had seized upon.[30] His report had initiated the creation of the *Deutscher Werkbund*, an organisation of teachers, writers, designers and industrialists, dedicated to raising the quality of German design and production in order to compete more effectively with Britain in world markets. This in turn had given rise to the complete revision of German design education, and the formation of regional schools, usually serving the needs of local industries, the most famous of which now is the Weimar Bauhaus. Five years before the Bauhaus became an actuality though, many of the principles now associated with its work (and accepted as having been revolutionary) were evident, unsung, in the NSAM's craftwork examination syllabuses.

For example, artisan students of Plasterwork, Cabinet Making, Pottery, Silversmithing, Metalworking, Textile Design and Lithography were required to *make* (not *draw*) simple geometric constructions, concentrating on accuracy and soundness of manufacture, as their introductions to their respective trades.

Decorators were required to explore geometric construction applied to pattern making and the setting-out of spaces, and to do exercises in lining, matching and colour harmony. Typographers were examined in 'rough sketches of arrangement of lines and masses'; Woodcarvers explored the relationships of tool-cuts, timbers and resulting patterns; and throughout all craftwork courses the emphasis was on practical realisation of finished artefacts rather than conventional drawn representations.

While it may come as a surprise, then, that an *Exhibition of German and Austrian Industrial Art* was held at Goldsmiths' Hall, London, in 1915, at the height of First World War hostilities, it is not surprising to find this event being reported as a matter of special importance to the Society. Members were reminded that German design had formerly been 'undesirable', that Muthesius had not missed anything of possible advantage in English working methods, and that the German ideal of *Qualität* was thus directly descended from Arts and Crafts principles as practised in English Art Schools.[31] Echoing this sentiment, and also referring to the German exhibition, the President for 1914–15 William Dalton (who had established Camberwell School of Arts and Crafts as a centre of excellence in the craft of Pottery), said that whereas British art education had endeavoured towards the ideal of the decorative masterpiece, efforts in Germany had been geared to influencing everyday things of life and improving commerce in as wide a way as possible. This would be the arena of competition after the War: it was therefore urgent for the Society now to institute appropriate policies, noting with regret that the government had negligently sought to reduce its investment in Art Schools, using the War as an expediency. The policies Dalton urged the NSAM to adopt were astonishingly far ahead of their time. He said:

> *Our schools in relation to industrial life must perform fuller functions; they must, of course, be centres of education, but they must also be laboratories for the cultivation of ideas, where ideas could be worked out and treated not for markets, but as suggestions for manufacture... School workshops should be replete not only with the best... historical examples, but with examples that are not considered the best, and of course modern work should find its way to these thought centres as regularly as it makes its appearance in the markets... [For example] analyses should be made of all the forms now in use, or that have been used in the past, of jugs, coffee pots, cups, and so on, to see from a re-examination whether shapes could not be devised more complete in their beauty of form, and in their utility, to our everyday requirements... It is obvious... that the pottery chemist could play an important collaborative part, and that the schools of ceramic chemistry should be in constant correspondence with the schools of art... and these remarks could be applied, with proper modification, to each individual industry – like typography, metalwork, cabinet-making, and other subjects in industrial art...*[32]

The German exhibition travelled the country, causing outrage at the national enemy's apparently superior use of the weapon of design.[33] Local Schools of Art invariably bore the brunt of press criticism, and this focused minds on Dalton's ideas in many District meetings of the NSAM. The Head Master of Leeds School of Art, Haywood Rider, took a populist stand against 'the pernicious effect of cubism, futurism, etc.', to prove he was right-minded, but he was nevertheless respectful of German industrial and commercial design.[34] Such a balancing act was typical of the Society as a whole, and when the debate gradually filtered back from the regions to the Annual Meeting there was general support for a London District plan for the complete reconstruction of British industrial education, aimed at meeting post-war German competition on equal terms rather than heaping it with moral criticism.[35] The London plan was refined by the Society and submitted to the President of the Board of Education in April 1917. Impatient at the slowness of his response, however, the Society made direct representation to the Prime Minister's Reconstruction Committee in September, tendering the most far-reaching, comprehensive proposals for coordinating Art and Design provisions in Primary, Secondary, Technical and Continuing Education since Henry Cole's *National Course of Instruction* of the 1850s. As evidence of its own willingness seriously to enter the field of continuing education the NSAM became affiliated to the *Workers' Education Association* in 1917.

Among the numerous innovations suggested by the NSAM were the following. Art Education should cultivate aesthetic appreciation and knowledge of 'the achievements of Art', besides developing aesthetic practice, as a first step in the training of public taste. It should be obligatory at all levels, requiring vast numbers of specially-trained teachers and the creation of LEA Advisers to identify and promote good practice. The school leaving age should be raised to fourteen, and pre-apprenticeship courses in Art subjects be provided for all pupils of artistic aptitude. All young workers entering manufacturing trades and industries should be required to attend day classes in Art Schools for between ten and twenty hours per week, 40 weeks per year, until the age of eighteen. Scholarships would provide access from Secondary Schools to Schools of Art, Schools of Art to Provincial Colleges, and Provincial Colleges to a central national institution (the Imperial College of Art) in London. All young persons working in trades or industries would similarly be enabled to re-enter full-time training in Art, Crafts, Trades or Teacher Education at age eighteen. The National Competition (suspended as a wartime economy in 1915) would be reinstated to act as a recruitment forum for British industry. In order to attract men and women of ability and ambition, teaching was to be regarded as a strategic profession and its paid rewards revised accordingly.[36]

This campaign of the Society's suddenly ceased to be a pressing issue at District and Annual Meetings, suggesting its sympathetic reception. In fact it received no further mention in the Society's proceedings until February 1919 when Henry

Cadness, Principal of Manchester School of Art, rose at the Annual Meeting to congratulate the government on the passing of the 1918 Education Act (the Fisher Act) embodying virtually everything the NSAM had wished for.[37] National scales of remuneration had been agreed for the first time, and superannuation provisions had come into force. There was a general sense of pride in the Society having influenced the most far-sighted and socially just educational reforms ever conceived. After the years of war, during which the Society lost about twelve per cent of its membership (falling into financial deficit from which it had to be rescued by voluntary subscription) it seemed that a time of unprecedented prominence for Art Education was about to begin.

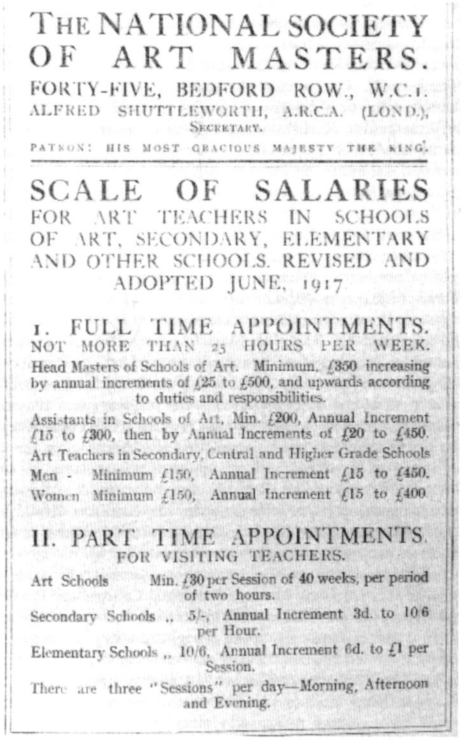
THE NATIONAL SOCIETY OF ART MASTERS.

FORTY-FIVE, BEDFORD ROW., W.C.1.

ALFRED SHUTTLEWORTH, A.R.C.A. (LOND.), SECRETARY.

PATRON: HIS MOST GRACIOUS MAJESTY THE KING.

SCALE OF SALARIES

FOR ART TEACHERS IN SCHOOLS OF ART, SECONDARY, ELEMENTARY AND OTHER SCHOOLS. REVISED AND ADOPTED JUNE, 1917

I. FULL TIME APPOINTMENTS.

NOT MORE THAN 25 HOURS PER WEEK.

Head Masters of Schools of Art. Minimum, £350 increasing by annual increments of £25 to £500, and upwards according to duties and responsibilities.

Assistants in Schools of Art, Min. £200, Annual Increment £15 to £300, then by Annual Increments of £20 to £450.

Art Teachers in Secondary, Central and Higher Grade Schools

Men - Minimum £150, Annual Increment £15 to £450.

Women Minimum £150, Annual Increment £15 to £400

II. PART TIME APPOINTMENTS.

FOR VISITING TEACHERS.

Art Schools Min. £30 per Session of 40 weeks, per period of two hours.

Secondary Schools ,, 5/-, Annual Increment 3d. to 10/6 per Hour.

Elementary Schools ,, 10/6, Annual Increment 6d. to £1 per Session.

There are three "Sessions" per day—Morning, Afternoon and Evening.

Fig. 5: The Scale of Salaries for Art Teachers which became effective in 1917, but which because of abatements and erosion remained little more than a distant objective for more than a decade.

What the records describe, however, is a period in which an incoming government clawed back many of the celebrated gains. The required army of new teachers and the very necessary buildings failed in large measure to materialise. The legislation covering continuing education for design trades workers was relaxed and unofficially withdrawn in many LEAs. A 'voluntary' five per cent abatement of salaries was requested in 1923 and made mandatory two years later. It may not be surprising then that the NSAM's fourth decade (which spanned the Great Depression and the General Strike) was graced by few great strategic issues, but rather a sequence of tactical encounters with authorities seemingly committed to the contraction of Art Education and the demeanment of its teachers. For example, relations between the NSAM and the newly established Burnham Technical Committee (on which it had four representatives) were often awkward. The 1918 Act had provided for enhanced emoluments for graduate teachers: this necessitated a great many individual applications for degree equivalence in respect of Art Education's vast array of qualifications (as a first step towards rationalising its own certificates the Society suspended the Associateship in 1921). A Council Minute of 1923 records rare success and illustrates what was required to establish honours degree equivalence. A particular candidate possessed an Art Master's Certificate (less one examination); was a Travelling Scholar; had been awarded one Gold and 'fifteen to eighteen' Silver and Bronze Medals in the National Competition; was a full member of the *Royal Watercolour Society;* 'had decorated a large Hall'; was a special teacher of painting and figure painting; and was recognised for posts of Special Responsibility (with three Assistants).[38] All this was traded for honours graduate standing.

In keeping with the self-defensive tenor of the times, the Society involved itself with an eclectic mix of other organisations. With the *Federation of British Industry* it established an Art Students' Employment Bureau. It accepted representation on the *Royal Institute of British Architects'* Education and Examination Boards in 1925.[39] Co-ordinated action was taken with the *Art Teachers' Guild* to press the claims of Art as a matriculation subject for University entrance, the ATG resolving in 1925 to consider how the two societies might move towards amalgamation.[40] A Standing Joint Committee was also formed with the *Association of Teachers in Technical Institutions* and the *Association of Principals in Technical Institutions* to establish common policies on matters of mutual interest – the so-called 'Joint Three Committee' becoming the most influential pressure group for pay and conditions of service. There was regular collaboration with the *Design and Industries Association* and with the WEA, and through the latter the Society was drawn towards the fringes of the *Labour Movement.*[41] As it may be imagined, this reciprocation caused a vast increase in the Society's use of the mails, and to economise on time and postage the President 'authorised the Secretary to have the telephone instrument installed' in 1924.[42]

In the mid-I920s the Society produced another broad scheme for the revision of what was still called 'Technical Education', but even this was essentially defensive in tone. It originated when the Society's attention was drawn to the fact that the Teaching Pedagogy course offered by the Royal College of Art was ill constructed and undemanding, comparing quite unfavourably with Teaching Certificate courses operating under the Board of Education. The NSAM took an intense interest in what might otherwise have been seen as the RCA's domestic problem, chiefly because teaching qualifications had always been regarded as the pinnacle of Art Education, marking the standard of comparability to university degrees. The Society's first reaction was to suggest to William Rothenstein, Principal of the RCA, that his students ought to take externally moderated courses like their counterparts elsewhere. Rothenstein was not unsympathetic, but in effect he widened the Society's involvement in the issue by enlisting support for his own argument that RCA Diplomas gained in its Schools of Architecture, Painting, Sculpture and Design should themselves attract graduate status, while an improved Pedagogy course for intending teachers would be regarded as a postgraduate supplement. The NSAM and the RCA then formulated joint proposals which were put before the Board of Education in June 1925.

These were as follows. The Royal College of Art should forthwith become a central 'University of Art'. The larger Provincial Schools of Art should be designated 'Colleges of Art', their recognition and validation entrusted to the Governing Body of the 'University'. This would assume responsibility for all examinations in Art previously conducted by the Board of Education. The Diplomas it would then award in Painting, Modelling, Pictorial Design and Industrial Design would enjoy degree equivalence. The Board of Education's jurisdiction would be confined to teacher education, but would cover all such professional courses, even those provided by the 'University'.[43] This scheme, substantially worked out by the NSAM, would have established the principle of graduate studies in Art and, particularly, the Design trades, conducted throughout the country and validated by a central regulatory body. It is an organisational model familiar today, but in the 1920s it was too far-reaching and it came to nothing. However, it remained a long-term policy of the Society occasionally reviewed and revised. So for example when, in 1930, the RCA's standards were once more 'Perceived to be diminishing (or rather changing at the expense of Design and in favour of Fine Art), the Society felt entitled to call for a revision of its policies, and to demand advisory powers in respect of the RCA's governance.[44]

In October 1940 the Society's rented office at 29 Gordon Square, London WC1, which had been occupied since 1922, was destroyed in an air raid, and most of its records for the preceding decade were lost. The Council and Examination Board Minute Books and the Membership Records survived because the Secretary had had the foresight to take them home to Berkhamstead, but these are factual and unelaborated, and they mean little without such corresponding documents as Journals, Presidential Addresses and Reports of Annual Meetings, which are normally relied upon to bring the strictly factual records to life. One or two line references are therefore the only allusions to events which clearly would have generated intense discussion, as for example when the President was commended for his response to the Government's intention to impose salary reductions,[45] or when it was noted, as a matter-of-fact, that King Edward VIII had decided to discontinue the Royal Patronage in 1936.[46] In this way too the foundation of the *New Society of Art Teachers* was recorded. This was later to combine with the *Art Teachers' Guild* to form the *Society for Education through Art* (the SEA of course was to amalgamate within the NSEAD in 1984); but in 1938 the NSAM decided to have nothing to do with the NSAT because it was suspected of being principally a commercial organisation for hiring out pictures to schools.[47] There is thus a substantial gap in the Society's history, bridged only by the Minute Books; and what emerges on the other side of this divide is not only a rather curious picture of the NSAM living in an outhouse in the Secretary's back garden, but an image of a Society having radically revised its outlook.

In its modest new quarters the Society experienced one of its most productive periods, taking full part in the heady debates preceding and shaping the 1944 *Education Act.* A series of booklets was published outlining an ideal future - *Art Education After the War; Art in General Education After the War;* and *The Curriculum and External Relations of the Art Schools.* These took as their initial text the passage from a Board of Education *Memorandum* which defined its objective as:

> *establishing a state of society where the advantages and privileges, which have been enjoyed only by the few, shall be more widely shared by the men and youth of the nation as a whole.*[48]

To the Society this meant enlarging the availability of creative education in general, but more particularly for the 11–16 age group. This would be achievable in two ways: by substantially increasing the provision of Junior Art Schools as one means of maintaining a link between Elementary and Technical education, or by defining and giving massive support to an art and design education tailored specifically for the Secondary sector. In either case it was felt necessary to stress the importance of 'education', in and through art, as opposed to artistic 'exhibitionism' (the former enhancing pupils' receptivity to the wider curriculum, the latter merely serving the interests of 'showy accomplishment' so beloved by Governors, Headmasters and Headmistresses) even if in practice this required some compromise between teaching 'expressional exercises' and 'representational technique'.[49] It will be seen that this constituted a sea change for a Society previously committed to the highest standards of technical accomplishment in art and in design. The new emphasis was to be upon a kind of education in which *appreciation* - 'a sense of form, rhythm and colour, structure, grace and growth, of harmony and fitness' – would be the equal of production. As it was noted:

> *Not many years ago the teaching in secondary schools of what we now call art, was nothing more than a very elementary course in the technique of drawing. The teaching of drawing in this manner maintained a prolonged defence on the plea that drawing, being a language, its teaching in schools was necessary, as an alternative means of communication either of facts or ideas. On the intellectual side, it was claimed as a unique vehicle for the training of observation...*
>
> *It is generally not in doubt that some measure of technique should enter into art education even in general education. As we might expect there are art teachers who do not accept such a claim. The view sometimes reaches the extreme of regarding any semblance of technique as a disquieting symptom... The two extreme attitudes might be described approximately as (a) where the pupil is allowed to express himself in line, form and colour, unfettered in any way, unrestrained and even unguided, relying only upon the pupil's emotions and native imagination and his intuition for*

graphic representation; (b) where the pupil is led through a course of drawing and painting, craftwork and such-like, progressing through stages of graded technicalities with the objective of his acquiring executive competence.

As with most extremes of theorising the practicable course lies somewhere between the two extremes.[50]

This would consist in including within the general curriculum 'a greater measure of cultural content' defined as 'the appreciation of historical and contemporary art in its many manifestations'. That the accent was to be placed upon the latter is revealed in a statement which demonstrates how completely the NSAM had changed its outlook.

The public conception of the full and proper function of art and the art schools is still too Victorian in character. Art must take its place in this age of machines and mass production as it has in all the ages that are past. Neither art nor the art schools can be vital in the present age if they are circumscribed by the tenets of a dissimilar age of a century ago. Art in the mass for the masses means mass production and mass production signifies machines. Machines and industrial methods are constituents of equipment and curriculum essential to the schools.[51]

Council had debated intensively in 1942 its pronouncements on art in general education and in the art schools, and in the course of this the conclusion had been reached that the Society ought to sectionalise its interests. This idea was also partly a reaction against a District proposal in 1941 that the Society should spawn a separate *Association of Principals of Schools of Art.* Accordingly the 1943 Annual Meeting was asked to consider a resolution organising the NSAM's membership into two broad panels: (1) of Principals and Assistants in Schools of Art, and (2) of Art Teachers in Schools of General Education. The Secretary, Marlborough Whitehead, put this to the meeting, as he was obliged to do, but he added his own advice that the recommendation would be divisive. It may be thought ironic considering the eventual outcome, but his stated desire was to establish an *Institute of Art Education,* dedicated to 'educational' development, and coexistent within the NSAM which would otherwise confine itself to 'professional' matters. The *Institute's* two chief functions would have been to foster intensive research and to facilitate its dissemination through publications and national exhibitions; and its work as an *integral* part of the NSAM's functioning would have enabled the Society's complementary mechanisms to concentrate upon 'trades union' interests.[52]

Framed as an amendment to the Council's resolution, this scheme was carried unanimously; but in the course of being polished for implementation it became subtly, though fundamentally, changed. It emerged as the *Association of Art*

Institutions, initially financed and administered by the NSAM, with Whitehead as its Secretary and having its provisional officers elected by the Society's own Council. Its constitution, however, bore no reference to integral status, and so from its foundation it was an independent national body of Principals of Schools of Art and representatives of the LEAs.[53] Ostensibly it had a research foundation, and it seems clearly to have been Whitehead's intention to separate this out from what he saw as the NSAM's main involvement in trades unionism. In this latter respect it was still thought necessary for the Society to sectionalise; and therefore in 1944 two separate Councils were created (one of fourteen representatives of Principals and Teachers in Art Schools; the other of seven representatives of Teachers in General Education) within a Society now bearing a new name, the *National Society for Art Education.* This marked a new beginning for the 56 year-old organisation in ways that are so numerous as to require a separate history. One of these, however, must be mentioned as a postscript to the NSAM in case it is thought this was somehow diminished in the transformation. Though originally intended (perhaps only by Whitehead) to be exclusively a professional cohort the NSAE was thankfully caught up in the general euphoria at war's end and the sense of reconstruction, and in fact never relinquished its responsibilities to scholarship. As we know, it continued its dual involvement in the worlds of learning and legislation, and it is this remarkable feat of balancing, as well as its centenary, that was celebrated in 1988.

Originally published in the Journal of Art & Design Education, *Volume 7: 1, 1988*

Notes and References

1. Society of Art Masters: *Foundation and Objects*, pamphlet 12 pp. (London, 1907) p. 2. [NSEAD/D/32].
2. Edward R. Taylor: *Introductory Address,* 1888, pamphlet 8 pp. (London, 1889) [NSEAD/D/l].
3. A. Fisher's annotated letter from the Committee of Masters in Training, with subsequent analysis of responses. [NSEAD/A/1].
4. *Ibid.* n. 1.
5. Marked 'Private – for members only': Society of Art Masters; *Interview with the Rt. Hon. A. H. D. Acland, MP, Vice-President of the Committee on Council for Education. Saturday 14 January 1893,* pamphlet 24 pp. (London, Women's Printing Society Ltd., 1893) pp. 21–2. [NSEAD/D/6].
6. *Report of the Commission on Secondary Education* (the Bryce Commission), 1895.
7. *Proceedings at the Ninth Annual Meeting of the Society of Art Masters*, 1897 (London, Women's Printing Society Ltd., 1897) pp. 27–8. [NSEAD/D/15].
8. Holographed letter 2 pp. to Walter Scott from Dighton Macnaghton Probyn, Comptroller and Treasurer to the Prince of Wales, dated 19 May1899. [NSEAD/A/97].
9. *Proceedings at the Eleventh Annual Meeting of the Society of Art Masters,* 1899 (London, Women's Printing Society Ltd., 1899) p. 8. [NSEAD/D/I8].
10. *Proceedings at the Seventeenth Annual Meeting of the Society of Art Masters, 1905* (London, J. B. Nichols & Sons, 1905) p. 14. [NSEAD/D/28].
11. Holographed notes 7 pp. entitled *Incorporation of the Society;* p. 1. [NSEAD/ A/34}.
12. See the various petitions in draft, copy and final forms and their responses [NSEAD/A/98–115] (18 items).

13. Carbon copy of a letter 1 p. from Francis Black to Frederick Marriot dated 23 November 1905. My italics. [NSEAD/A/17].

14. Carbon copy of a letter 1 p. from Francis Black to Frederick Marriot dated 27 November 1905. [Attached to NSEAD/A/17].

15. *Ibid.* n. 11, p. 2.

16. *Ibid.* n. 11, pp. 4–7.

17. *Proceedings at the Twentieth Annual Meeting of the Society of Art Masters, 1908* (London, J. B. Nichols & Sons, 1908) pp. 26–7. [NSEAD/D/33].

18. *Ibid.* n. 17, p. 18.

19. *Proceedings at a Special General Meeting of the Society of Art Masters at the Midland Hotel, Birmingham,* 20 May 1899 (London, J. B. Nichols & Sons, 1899) p. 9.

20. *Ibid.* n. 10, pp. 44–53.

21. Stamped application signed on behalf of the *West Riding Society of Teachers of Art and Art Technology* by its officers John Swire (Chairman) and J. H. Farran (Secretary), dated 8 January 1906. Appended Regulations of the SAM as approved 4 August 1905. [NSEAD/A/33].

22. *Ibid.* n. 17, pp. 17–46.

23. *Proceedings at the Twenty-First Annual Meeting of the National Society of Art Masters, 1909* (London, J. B. Nichols & Sons, 1909) pp. 37–59. [NSEAD/D/35].

24. *Proceedings at the Twenty-Second Annual Meeting of the National Society of Art Masters, 1910* (London, J. B. Nichols & Sons, 1910) pp. 4–8, 24–5. [NSEAD/D/38]. These passages summarise the NSAM advice to the BoE Inquiry: the Society's official report on the subject, however, has been lost.

25. *Proceedings at the Twenty-Fourth Annual Meeting of the National Society of Art Masters,* 1912 (London, J. B. Nichols & Sons, 1912) pp. 11–24. (NSEAD/D/42].

26. *Journal of the National Society of Art Masters* 1, 1 Oct 1913, pp. 39–51. [NSEAD/D/60].

27. As listed in the *Journal of the Society of Art Masters* 1, 2 Feb 1914, pp. 89–96. [NSEAD/D/62]. See also *ibid.* 1, 3, May 1914, pp. 115–18.

28. *Journal of the National Society of Art Masters* 1, 4, Oct 1914, p. 127. [NSEAD/D/64].

29. *Ibid.* n. 28, pp. 175–6.

30. The chief exception being the Central School of Arts and Crafts, London, which was not headed by an NSAM member until Frederick Burridge of Liverpool succeeded William Lethaby in 1911.

31. B. J. Fletcher (1915), 'Art and Trade' *Journal of the National Society of Art Masters*, 1:6, pp. 244–6. [NSEAD/D/69].

32. *An Address by W. B. Dalton Esq., ARCA, President of the National Society of Art Masters,* pamphlet 7 (London, NSAM, 1915) pp. 5–7. [NSEAD/D/66].

33. For a selection of letters to newspapers see *Journal of the National Society of Art Masters* 2, 2, 1916, pp. 67–72. [NSEAD/D/72].

34. *Journal of the National Society of Art Masters* 2,1, 1915, p. 50. [NSEAD/D/71].

35. *Journal of the National Society of Art Masters* 3, 1, 1917, pp. 33–49. [NSEAD/D/74].

36. *Journal of the National Society of Art Masters* 3, 3, 1917, pp. 108–17. [NSEAD/D/76].

37. *Journal of the National Society of Art Masters* 4,1, 1919, pp. 67–70. [NSEAD/D/80].

38. Council Minute 238, 27–28 April 1923. [NSEAD/C/l].

39. Council Minute 490, 4–5 December 1925. [NSEAD/C/I].

40. Council Minute 421, 20 March 1925. [NSEAD/C/l).

41. Council Minute 178, 3 January 1923. [NSEAD/C/l].

42. Council Minute 337, 8–9 February 1924. [NSEAD/C/l].

43. Council Minutes 438 (5–6 June 1925), 458 (2–3 October 1925). [NSEAD/C/1].

44. Council Minute 855, 27–28 June 1930. [NSEAD/C/3].

45. Council Minute 864, 26–27 June 1931. [NSEAD/C/3].

46. Council Minute 1122, 19–20 June 1936. [NSEAD/C/3].

47. Council Minute 1265, 24 June 1938. [NSEAD/C/3].

48. NSAM: *Art Education after the War;* pamphlet 16 pp., nd (1942); p. 3. [NSEAD/D/156].

49. NSAM: *Art in General Education after the War,* pamphlet 14 pp., nd (1942); pp. 4–5. [NSEAD/D/155].

50. *Ibid.* pp. 10–12.

51. NSAM: *The Curriculum and External Relations of the Art Schools;* pamphlet 20 pp., nd (1942); p. 19. [NSEAD/D/157].

52. *National Society of Art Masters Conference Journal* XIV, 3 June 1943, pp. 72–80. [NSEAD/D/151].

53. *Ibid.* pp. 98–100.

Appendix

Chairmen of the Society of Art Masters

1888–90 Edward R. Taylor	Birmingham School of Art
1890–91 J. Nichol Smith	Bristol School of Art
1891–93 Michael Sullivan	Hastings School of Art
1893–95 William H. East	Dover School of Art
1895–97 Samuel J. Cartlidge	Hanley School of Art
1897–99 Walter Scott	Norwich School of Art
1899–00 Walter Wallis	Croydon School of Art
1900–02 Frederick Shelley	Plymouth School of Art
1902–04 Charles Stephenson	Bradford School of Art
1904–05 John T. Cook	Sheffield School of Art
1905–06 Frederick Marriot	Goldsmiths' College
1906–08 Joseph A. Pearce	West Bromwich School of Art
1908–09 John Fisher	Kensington School of Art, Clifton, Bristol

Presidents of the National Society of Art Masters

1909–10 Frederick V. Burridge	Liverpool School of Art (1911 Central School of Arts and Crafts)
1910–11 Richard G. Hatton	Armstrong College, University of Durham
1911–12 H. Barret Carpenter	Rochdale School of Art
1912–13 Alfred Shuttleworth	Handsworth School of Art
1913–14 Hubert Schroder	Acton and Chiswick Polytechnic
1914–15 William B. Dalton	Camberwell School of Arts and Crafts
1915–16 W. H. Milnes	Coventry School of Art

1916–17 Charles Ripper	Lancaster School of Art
1917–18 Joseph Harrison	Nottingham School of Art
1918–19 R. T. Mumford	Willesden Polytechnic
1919–20 G. P. Gaskell	Regent Street Polytechnic
1920–21 George Rushton	Ipswich School of Art
1921–22 R. A. Dawson	Belfast School of Art
1922–23 W. H. Milnes	Coventry School of Art
1923–25 William H. Evans	Brighton School of Art
1925–27 Robert R. Carter	Walsall Schoo lof Art
1927–28 W. H. Meggs	Bradford School of Art
1928–29 Osmond E. Gollins	Birmingham Central School of Arts and Crafts
1929–30 Walter M. Barnes	School of Art, West Ham Technical Institute
1930–32 John C. Moody	
1932–34 Douglas S. Andrews	Derby School of Art
1934–36 W. Marlborough Whitehead	Burnley School of An
1936–38 W.T. Blackband	
1938–41 H. P. Huggill	
1941–43 A. Seaton White	Cheltenham School of Arts and Crafts
1943–44 Charles W. Hobbis	Norwich School of Arts and Crafts
1944 A. Sallis Benney	Brighton School of Arts and Crafts

Secretaries of the SAM and the NSAM

1888–1907 Francis Ford

1907–1914 Francis Charles Ford

1914–1931 Alfred Shuttleworth

1931 R. T. Mumford (Acting Secretary)

1932–1939 Robert Radcliffe Carter

1939–1958 W. Marlborough Whitehead

Chapter 8: InSEA: Past, Present and Future

John Steers

The Past

'The past', wrote the novelist L. P. Hartley, 'is a foreign country: they do things differently there.'[1]

In this brief history [2] I wish to consider just how different the world was over 50 years ago – what inspired art educators in 1951 when the idea of International Society for Education through Art (InSEA) was formulated? But first a caveat: 'History isn't what happened. History is just what historians tell us.[3] The verbal histories of the events of over half a century ago are becoming lost. It is becoming more urgent to order some insights into the past as a way of providing both a key to understanding the present and as a source for constructive speculation about the future.

InSEA, like its parent organisation the United Nations Educational, Scientific and Cultural Organisation (UNESCO), was founded in the aftermath of the 1939–1945 world war. Richard Hoggart explains how UNESCO was conceived in a spirit of hope, in a heady confidence that a new style of international relations could be developed:

> *The world had just come through a terrible and protracted war, one initiated by false philosophies working on ignorance through massive control of free speech. The impulse, in 1945, to try to ensure that it did not happen again, and that people should* understand *each other better through education and all forms of cultural and scientific exchanges, the passionate emphasis on truth, justice, peace and the importance of the individual – these impulses were irresistible.*[4]

At UNESCO's first and second general conferences, held in 1946 and 1947, resolutions were adopted to inquire into art education. In 1948, Dr Herbert Read from the United Kingdom was appointed as chairman of a 'Committee of Experts' to look into this matter. This small group comprised Thomas Munro from the USA; the Hungarian composer Zoltan Kodaly; two government education inspectors, Georges Favre from France and Edward O' R. Dickey from the United Kingdom; a professor of philosophy from the Sorbonne, M. Bayer; two aestheticians, Professors Souriau and Lalo; and Mme. Langevin, an art teacher from France.

From these beginnings followed the UNESCO seminar on 'The Visual Arts in General Education', held from 7–27 July 1951 at the University of Bristol, England, at which some twenty countries were represented. The delegates included a significant number of people who continued to take leadership roles in InSEA as the organisation developed. For example Dr Edwin Ziegfeld from the USA, who was a 'Specialist-Consultant' at the seminar became the first president of the Society (as well as being coincidentally the first president of the National Art Education Association in the USA). Charles Dudley Gaitskell from Canada directed the seminar (he subsequently became the first president of the Canadian Society for Education through Art). The programme included general sessions, guest speakers and visits to schools and schools of art. One such visit was to the newly founded Bath Academy of Art at Corsham Court:

> *Through the kindness of Mr Clifford Ellis (Director of the Bath Academy) and Lord Methuen, the participants were able to make a thorough exploration of the academy proper, as well as of the experimental school for children. The programme of the school was admitted to be the most advanced and informative. Design in both art and crafts was highly original and ingenious, and the craftsmanship of the highest order. In the experimental school for children, the use of visual material, and the spirit of enquiry and intellectual adventure evident in the children's work, drew forth much praise.*[5]

There is no doubt that the seminar was seen as a significant event at that time. Ziegfeld wrote, 'The effects of this seminar will leave an indelible mark on our future'.[6] Whether he was right in this assertion is one of the questions I wish to consider.

It seems evident from all accounts of the 1951 seminar that Sir Herbert Read (1893–1968) was central to proceedings as a leading figure in the avant-garde of art, literature and aesthetics.[7] Read had been a soldier in the 1914–1918 world war and was decorated with the Military Cross and the Distinguished Service Order, but he later became a pacifist and a self-proclaimed anarchist. He regarded himself primarily as a poet, but literary and art criticism became his predominant activities.

Read spoke of the human need to strive toward self-realisation, of the importance of developing full human potential, the need of individuals to be active and productive, true to themselves, and to relate to others in a spirit of mutuality. Read set out his view of the aims of aesthetic education:

- To preserve the natural intensity of all modes of perception and sensation.
- To co-ordinate the various modes of perception and sensation with one another and in relation to the environment.
- To express feeling in communicable form.
- To teach children how to express thought in required form.

The UNESCO report of the seminar summarises Read's conclusions:

...Dr Read said that in order to communicate human reaction as completely as possible, it is necessary to employ not only 'the infinite subtleties of verbal expression, but also various forms of symbolic expression'. Our educational systems have tended to ignore the various types of symbolic communication. However, we are beginning to question the adequacy of our verbal modes. The movement which has led to the liberation is beginning to recognise the fact that human beings are dependent upon symbolic as well as conceptual means of thought. Since the purpose of education is to liberate the force of spontaneous growth, and since growth is only made apparent in expression, then education is a matter of teaching children and adults how to express themselves in sounds, images, tools and utensils. In other words, 'the aim of education is, therefore, the creation of artists – of people efficient in the various modes of expression and communication'.[8]

In 1968, shortly after Read's death, Ziegfeld wrote fondly about his impressions of Read and the Bristol seminar:

To all his utterances he brought clarity of thinking and brilliance of insight. Added to this was the impact of his delivery. The clear, thin, and only slightly modulated voice seemed at first a model of understatement. But as one listened one was aware of an almost incandescent intensity which burned behind it, and hearing Sir Herbert Read became both an intellectual and aesthetic experience.

The highlight [of the 1951 seminar] however, which gave the whole show its impetus and meaning, was the address delivered by Herbert Read. We all remember the occasion vividly. We still see him, slight, unobtrusive, modest, his manners friendly and courteous, his humour quiet, introverted, his speech quietly voiced, but flowing, in words and phrases that brought out all the beauties of the English tongue. His delivering [sic] in itself was a work of art.[9]

The idea of an international organisation for art education was not exactly new. An international congress was held in Paris in 1900 and the 'International Federation for the Teaching of Drawing and of the Arts Applied to Industry', which had aims that were not so disparate from InSEA, was founded in 1904. A further seven congresses followed between 1904 and 1937 when its activities were suspended until 1955. The organisation adopted the shorter name '*Fédération Internationale pour l'Éducation Artistique*' (FIEA) in 1957. After a good deal of wrangling the FIEA merged with InSEA in 1963 at the Montreal World Congress. (It is the existence of the FIEA, overlapping as it does with InSEA, which partly explains the curious numbering of InSEA tri-annual world congresses – for example the Brisbane event in 1999 was designated as the 30th World Congress. The congresses are numbered from 1900, not the 1950s, but there is also some dispute about which events can properly be designated 'World Congresses').

Read's seminal text 'Education through Art' was published in 1943. The British Society for Education *in* Art (SEA) was founded in 1946, springing from what had been seen as a temporary merger of existing organisations during the 1939–45 war: Read was its chairman and president for 28 years. The title of the British organisation, the Society for Education *through* Art, was only adopted in 1953 after a protracted debate – at much the same time that InSEA was coming into existence. While it is evident that Read influenced the name of the international organisation, it is not clear how much this was a matter of debate in the international forum. The idea of 'Education *through* Art' is now often taken for granted but Read saw it as revolutionary. He wrote in the SEA context:

> *We declare that our foremost aim is 'the establishment of an education in art which will develop the imaginative and creative powers of children', and that, to the outside world, must seem as harmless as any cause that ever brought two or three people together. But those who have followed through the implications of this aim know that it is packed with enough dynamite to shatter the existing educational system, and to bring about a revolution in the whole structure of our Society.*[10]

InSEA formally came into being with the adoption of its constitution at the First General Assembly held in Paris in July 1954. Read opened the meeting with an address entitled 'The Future of Art Education' – certainly not the last time such a title has been used at InSEA congresses. The preamble to the Constitution (which in the intervening years has only been subject to minor amendments) reveals the idealism of the founding members of InSEA and their belief that:

> *Education through art is a natural means of learning at all periods of the development of the individual, fostering values and disciplines essential for full intellectual, emotional and social development of human beings in a community;*
>
> *Association on a worldwide basis of those concerned with education through art is necessary in order that they may share experiences, improve practices and strengthen the position of art in relation to all education;*
>
> *Co-operation with those concerned in other disciplines of study outside the teaching profession and domains of education would be of mutual advantage in securing closer co-ordination of activities directed to solving problems in common;*
>
> *International co-operation and the better understanding between peoples would be furthered by a more completely integrated design and permanent structure for the diffusion of beliefs and practices concerning education through art, so that the right of man [sic] 'freely to participate in the cultural life of the community, to enjoy the arts' and to create beauty for himself in reciprocal relationship with his environment, would become a living reality.*[11]

In a spate of initial enthusiasm InSEA embarked on an ambitious programme that included preparing recommendations on the teaching of art in primary and secondary schools addressed to the ministries of education of all UNESCO members. A large international touring exhibition of children's art was assembled for UNESCO and sets of colour transparencies of children's work were distributed internationally. An international list of resource material was compiled and later extended and InSEA published regular newsletters. A key ambition was to encourage the establishment of National Committees of InSEA with a view to the Society becoming a federation of such organisations. Plans were laid for the Second General Assembly that took place in The Hague in August 1957. Not for the last time the difficulties of organising and financing a World Congress became apparent. Nevertheless, a pattern of world and regional congresses has developed over the years:

The importance of its international congresses to the life of InSEA can hardly be over-estimated. Congresses have been its lifeblood, the more or less regular focus of activity that has held the organisation and an international community of art educators together for 50 years. They are an embodiment of InSEA's aim to promote worldwide co-operation in the exchange of ideas in visual arts education and the published proceedings of these events form a valuable resource. The organisers of the 1999 World Congress expressed their purpose succinctly:

> *[to] ...provide a forum in which teachers, academics, artists, specialists and others concerned with the promotion and advancement of creative education, may meet and exchange information. ...an opportunity for educators, academics, artists and representatives to evaluate current ideas and experiences, debate relevant and topical issues, and establish working relationships with colleagues in associated fields.*

In later years regional congresses were held in the intervening years between world congresses and these more 'local' events facilitated wider participation.

Every successive president has brought a particular emphasis and focus to the work of the Society and to some extent has placed their particular stamp on the Society for the period of their presidency. However one fact is inescapable: the domination of InSEA by the Western world and by the English language – a majority of InSEA's presidents have spoken English as their native tongue. This is a precedent that is overdue for change.

Jane Rhoades Hudak, InSEA's archivist, has provided a thumbnail sketch of the achievements of each presidency. Throughout the early period from 1951–1960 Edwin Ziegfeld served as president and by the end of his presidency the Society had some one thousand members. He established a sound organisational structure and achieved the majority of the goals established at the early General

Table 1: FEA and InSEA World Congresses 1957-2002

Fédération Internationale pour l'Éducation Artistique	
1900	Paris, France
1904	Berne, Switzerland
1908	London, United Kingdom
1912	Dresden, Germany
1925	Paris, France
1928	Prague, Czechoslovakia
1935	Brussels, Belgium
1937	Paris, France
1955	Lund, Sweden
1958	Basle, Switzerland
1962	Berlin, Germany
International Society for Education through Art	
1957	The Hague, The Netherlands
1960	Manila, The Philippines
1963	Montreal, Canada
1966	Prague, Czechoslovakia
1969	New York, USA
1970	Coventry, United Kingdom
1972	Zagreb, Yugoslavia
1975	Sevres, France
1978	Adelaide, Australia
1981	Rotterdam, The Netherlands
1984	Rio de Janeiro, Brazil
1987	Hamburg, German Federal Republic
1990	Manila, The Philippines – Cancelled for political reasons
1993	Montreal, Canada
1996	Lille, France – Cancelled for financial reasons
1999	Brisbane, Australia
2002	New York, USA

Table 2: InSEA Regional Congresses 1980-2000

1971	Otaniemi, Finland
1980	Baden, Austria
1982	Nicosia, Cyprus
1983	Sofia, Bulgaria
1985	Bath, United Kingdom
1986	Vancouver, Canada
1988	Lagos, Nigeria
1988	Stockholm, Sweden
1989	Cairo, Egypt
1992	Helsinki, Finland
1994	Lisbon, Portugal
1995	Taichung, Republic of China
1995	Manila, The Philippines
1997	Glasgow, Scotland
1998	Tokyo, Japan
2000	Poznan, Poland
2001	Sun Moon Lake, Taiwan ROC
2003	'InSEA on Sea', Stockholm, Helsinki & Tallinn
2004	Istanbul & Cappadocia, Turkey
2004	Beijing, People's Republic of China

Assemblies. Indeed, the basic structure of the organisation today would easily be recognised by Ziegfeld as it has essentially changed very little in the intervening years.

The records for the presidencies of Gaitskell, Soika and Kurata have not survived. However a key achievement of Gaitskell's term was the merger of the FEA and InSEA. Soika presided over an exceptionally successful conference in Prague, attended by over 2000 people. Kurata's presidency was marred by financial irregularities of which, I should emphasise, he was unaware and uninvolved. He presided over the first New York World Congress and was characterised by Jane Rhoades Hudak who met him late in his life as '...one of the most extraordinarily intuitive, gentle and sensitive people I have ever had the chance to meet'.[12]

Subsequently Eleanor Hipwell was faced with re-establishing the Society. Jane Rhoades Hudak concluded that she: ...'saved' InSEA. The organisational structure and processes were broken down. She put the organisation back into the black financially and reorganised the Society.[13] The 1970s marked a period of consolidation with much of the focus of activity on organising a sequence of

Table 3: Presidents of InSEA

1951–1960	Edwin Ziegfeld	*USA*
1960–1963	Charles D. Gaitskell	*Canada*
1963–1966	J. A. Soika	*Federal Republic of Germany*
1966–1969	Sabura Kurata	*Japan*
1969–1973	Eleanor Hipwell	*United Kingdom*
1973–1976	Aimée Humbert	*France*
1976–1979	Al Hurwitz	*USA*
1979–1982	Jack Condous	*Australia*
1982–1985	Brian Allison	*United Kingdom*
1985–1988	Marie-Françoise Chavanne	*France*
1988–1991	Elliot Eisner	*USA*
1991–1993	Ana Mae Barbosa	*Brazil*
1993–1996	John Steers	*United Kingdom*
1996–1999	Kit Grauer	*Canada*
2000–2002	Diederik Schönau	*The Netherlands*
2003–2005	Doug Boughton	*Australia*

significant world congresses. The detailed records of the Humbert and Hurwitz era are lost but from Condous's time on there is a detailed and continuous record. Allison was a particularly energetic and ambitious president. He established the InSEA regions and set up a structure of Recognised National Organisation and Affiliates, very much in the spirit of the founders' intentions. The constitution and rules were revised and guidelines for various activities, such as organising congresses, were drawn up. Boards of Council were established to deal with research, affiliations and publications and, for a time, a relationship flourished with the Bulgarian international 'Banner of Peace' movement.

In 1982 Allison brought me into the InSEA Executive Committee as secretary and I served as a member of the committee continuously in one capacity or another until 1999. I have had the privilege of working with eight world presidents between 1982 and now, as well as serving myself for a term as president. I can testify to the commitment and dedication to the Society of all these individuals and from personal experience I learned how demanding it is to try to lead an international organisation with far-ranging ideals and ambitions but with very limited financial resources. Chavanne strengthened links again with UNESCO, Eisner secured funding for an initiative that lead to publication of one of the most substantive published documents in InSEA history: 'Evaluating and Assessing the Visual Arts in Education: International Perspectives'.[14] Barbosa very significantly raised the profile of the organisation in Latin America and Grauer's lasting achievement may well prove to be the establishment of InSEA on the Internet. Schönau consolidated this work, strengthened the Society's finances and worked to re-vitalise relationships with UNESCO. The current president, Doug Boughton has a long association with InSEA: his fine work as co-editor of the assessment publication was followed by two further titles for InSEA where Boughton was instrumental in seeing these works through to publication.[15] The key initiative at the present time is the imminent publication early in 2005 of the 'International Journal for Education through Art'.

The Present

Everywhere our world at the beginning of the twenty-first century is very different to that of 1951 in countless and often unimaginable ways. An obvious change is our growing awareness of the threats and immense opportunities that are presented by increasing globalisation. The word lacks precise definition, but clearly globalisation has something to do with the notion that we all now live in one world with increasingly shared experiences, economies and cultures. We are aware of processes that tend to centralise economic power. Some people believe that the era of the nation state is over and that politicians have lost their capacity to influence major international events. World trade drives globalisation and its scale is such that just for once the term 'awesome' is justified. Anthony Giddens has pointed out a fact that '...more than a trillion dollars is now turned over each day on global currency markets'.[16]

At the core of this transformation is the development of digital communication that has significance in many ways beyond global economics. I recently read an account and saw a photograph of members of a remote tribe living near the head waters of the Amazon settling down in their otherwise unchanged stone age surroundings to view a DVD of the destruction of the World Trade Center. It is hard to comprehend what they could have made of these events having never seen skyscrapers or aircraft before. As Giddens reminds us:

> *Instantaneous electronic communication isn't just a way in which news or information is conveyed more quickly. Its existence alters the very texture of our lives, rich and poor alike. When the image of Nelson Mandela may be more familiar to us than the face of our next door neighbour, something has changed in the nature of our everyday experience.*[17]

Globalisation may be one root cause for demands for increasing political devolution and the revival of local cultural and ethnic identities in many parts of the world. In the arts, there is ample evidence of transcultural practice in the international art market. A 'school' of artists no longer needs to congregate in a particular geographical location: a print-maker in Tokyo may have close contacts with artists working in a similar idiom in Rio de Janeiro or London and might sell her work in

Paris or Chicago. Transculturalism seems dependent on the opportunity to recognise 'self-similarity' between groups and individuals and the new technologies allow a meeting of minds, a meeting of worlds, uninhibited by distance, cost and increasingly, language.

But globalisation is not necessarily benign in all its consequences:

> *To many living outside Europe and North America, it looks uncomfortably like Westernisation – or, perhaps, Americanisation, since the US is now the sole superpower, with a dominant economic, cultural and military position in the global order. Many of the most visible cultural expressions of globalisation are American – Coca-Cola, McDonalds.*[18]

Perhaps we need to be alert to the dangers of the potential development of an insidious international pedagogy and recognise that alternative approaches to curriculum and assessment are increasingly being erased by the dominant ideologies of some governments and influential, wealthy organisations. For example, there are some extraordinary similarities of approach to curriculum design among the majority of the Organisation for Economic Co-operation and Development (OECD) countries. Governmental thinking, understandably, is dominated by concerns about how to sustain economic growth and national competitiveness, and how to maintain social stability, cohesion and harmony. As Skilbeck has remarked, this is often manifested by:

> *The remarkably rapid accession of 'knowledge', 'skill', 'competence', to the prime place on the totem pole of national survival/development, combined with economic anxiety and with the susceptibility of public schooling to political/administrative control, combine to provide impetus to the current reform movements. A fear – often exaggerated – of falling standards fuels these concerns and helps explain the pervasive emphasis on quality.*[19]

In the sphere of state-maintained education and training, central or provincial governments tend to exercise curriculum control through legislation. However, they may just as effectively choose to work through the influence or control they exercise over intermediary bodies such as curriculum councils and development agencies, syllabus committees, examination boards, awarding bodies and so on. Linked to this are inevitable demands for greater accountability from the teaching profession leading inexorably to ever-tighter control of the curriculum and its assessment and, through these mechanisms, to control of teachers in the vain search for a 'teacher proof' education system. This can be very destructive for creative and cultural education: we need to resist the search for some kind of a universal panacea, and to learn to tolerate a rich variety of curricula appropriate to the needs of diverse people and cultures.

Through InSEA, a relatively small organisation, there exists an international and supportive professional community of art educators that has had a disproportionately significant role in disseminating ideas and research internationally – not least through the success of its congresses and published proceedings. But, crucially, our aim must be to encourage, appreciate and tolerate diversity, and to resist any moves towards a stultifying international uniformity devoid of all real individuality, originality and creativity.

The Future

How well founded was the founders' idealism and has InSEA lived up to expectations? Or has it become what economists call a 'shell institution', that is an organisation that has become inadequate for the tasks it is called upon to perform? Sometimes it is necessary to reconstruct the institutions we have or, maybe, create new ones, in a form that is both appropriate and capable of taking advantage of the opportunities presented by the global age.

I am not suggesting that InSEA has had its day, but I do believe we can re-visit some of the original intentions, review the achievements, recognise weaknesses and look for new opportunities. For example, membership numbers are still similar to the early years. A well-organised and well-attended congress boosts membership for a year or two in that region. How can we account for this? Perhaps InSEA does not have enough to offer the classroom teacher? But is that beginning to change with the launch of the InSEA web site? Does InSEA have at last a relatively cheap and immediate means of communicating effectively with members and prospective members? Another intractable problem that concerned InSEA from the outset was membership subscriptions. How to set a fair rate when faced with the inequalities of teachers' salaries in different parts of the world and currency restrictions that often prevented payment in 'hard' western currencies? Electronic transfer of money is helping to solve the problem although, depressingly, the gap between the richest and poorest countries shows no sign of closing.

The original intention of InSEA's founders was to create an International Federation for Art Education and an 'International Institute for Information and Research in Art Education' both of which were expected to have the '...full co-operation and financial help of UNESCO'.[20] A few years ago, Bill Barrett, the New Zealand representative and last survivor of the 1951 seminar, reminded me:

> *Another focus not yet realised. The idea that InSEA needed a permanent base as a research centre, a clearing house and a place for art educators. 'A hub of the wheel', as it were... Maybe this should be revisited?* [21]

In recent years the Society has had semi-permanent homes with the National Society for Education in Art and Design (NSEAD) in the United Kingdom and with the Dutch Institute for Educational Measurement (CITO) in Arnhem. But these are dependent on individuals and the goodwill of the host institutions. I agree that a new initiative should be launched and although a physical base is needed for the secretariat, the research centre, clearing-house for information and 'a place for art educators' might best be located in cyber space at www.insea.org.

At the outset it was fully expected that UNESCO would fund the organisation on a permanent basis, or at least until such time as its future was secure. The founders' shopping list include the launch of an international journal, although as an interim measure they expected UNESCO to sponsor '...a popular inexpensive illustrated bulletin devoted to the furtherance of art education' while supporting a range of other publications and the necessary translation facilities. It seems that 'the interim' was destined to last for half a century, but now at last the Society is about to launch a peer-reviewed academic journal.[22] Although UNESCO has supported some InSEA activities from time to time – the occasional publication grant and more recently some support for the new web site – the reality is that UNESCO backing has never been consistent.

Some of the initial aims have been realised; for example, the exchange of exhibits, often in association with congresses, and the international interchange of teachers and students. Although the latter exchanges are extensive, they develop as a consequence of informal links between those members that have an opportunity to meet, often on a surprisingly regular basis, at InSEA and other international events. InSEA has sometimes been accused of being an international travel organisation for rich art educators – although that excludes most InSEA members I know! Time as well as money was a factor – when Bill Barrett attended that 1951 seminar in Bristol he relates how at that time it took six weeks to travel from New Zealand by sea, or, for the privileged, nearly two weeks by flying boat. Today travel problems are lessening in an era of increasingly mass travel and tourism. Even so, the accusation of exclusivity contains more than a grain of truth seen from the perspective of classroom teachers from many parts of the developing world.

Up to now InSEA has succeeded in establishing a relatively small but often influential community of art educators. But we may be on the brink of establishing – in fact it is already happening – a virtual network of transcultural art educators. For example, we can have on-line seminars, virtual galleries of children's art, on-line research databases and Internet portals to a vast range of teaching and learning resources. These include access to the majority of the great and less well known museums and galleries world-wide or to a host of curriculum materials such as those available for example from www.nsead.org or the Getty Center for the Arts. One of the Society's future roles should be to try to bring some order, or at least to map a way to navigate the plethora of art and art education sites that are springing up on the World Wide Web. A very modest start has been made but InSEA must not be caught unawares. For good or ill growth in use of the web will continue to expand exponentially. Giddens points out that it took 40 years for radio to gain an audience of 50 million in the USA. By contrast, only four years after it was made available 50 million Americans were using the Internet.[23]

Ziegfeld held the view that Herbert Read's ideas on education would become more relevant as time passes rather than less so. He believed Read saw in clearer and more humanistic terms than most, the nature of what they both perceived as a profound cultural crisis. Ideas for the resolution of this crisis are at the core of *Education through Art*, a book that Ziegfeld believed:

> *is a distinctly prophetic work dealing as it does with what the nature of education should be. Furthermore, Read, during the last several decades, has been almost the sole world figure who has spoken out on the place of the arts in all of education. Indeed, Sir Herbert's ideas on education may well be his most important legacy, not only for Americans but for all art teachers. The fact that they are not yet clearly understood is a testament of their ultimate validity and proof of the fact that they require basic changes in the outlook and the values of modern man [sic]. The fact that the world organisation of art teachers has incorporated into its name the basic idea of Read's educational views is proof that they have a universal, rather than a national or regional validity.*[24]

I believe that InSEA is needed now more than ever provided it is capable of adapting to the challenges of ever-changing global circumstances. We have to realise, 'Globalisation is not incidental to our lives today. It is a shift in our very life circumstances. It is the way we live now'.[25] My experience of InSEA has confirmed my belief that we should strive for truly idealistic and humanistic forms of art education that at their core value diversity. What emerges from interaction with art educators from other countries is not just the realisation that we share many concerns, but appreciation of the rich multiplicity of ideas and solutions worthy of consideration. One of the key qualities of creative individuals (but one seldom shared by organisations) is the ability to tolerate ambiguity and to forestall closure – to keep a range of possibilities in play. If art education is to avoid atrophy we need to cherish multiple visions of teaching and learning *about, for* and *through* art. In his book 'Celebrating Pluralism: Art, Education and Cultural Diversity', InSEA colleague Graeme Chalmers, draws attention to the need to accept and respect the '...co-equality of fundamentally different frames of thought and action characteristic of diverse cultures'.[26] This, I suggest, should be a fundamental tenet of all InSEA's actions.

Notes and References

1. Hartley, L. P. (1953), 'The Go Between', London: Hamish Hamilton.
2. For this account I am indebted to my late friend and colleague Professor David Thistlewood for his work on the archives of the Society for Education through Art. I am also very grateful to the

InSEA archivist, Dr Jane Rhoades Hudak (Georgia Southern University), and Professor Irena Wojnar (University of Warsaw) both of whom commented on drafts of this paper. I have also drawn on records held at the National Arts Education Archive: Bretton Hall for which I thank the Director Professor Ron George and Sonja Kielty. My records from serving on the executive committee in one capacity or another from 1983–1999 have also proved useful.

3. Barnes, J. (1989), 'The History of the World in 10 Chapters', London : Jonathan Cape.

4. Hoggart, R. (1978), in Rhoades, J. (1987), 'A History of InSEA' unpublished Ph.D. dissertation, Columbus, Ohio: The Ohio State University.

5. UNESCO (1952), 'The Visual Arts in general Education: Report on the Bristol Seminar, United Kingdom, 1951', UNESCO/CUA/36 Paris, 12 May 1952, p. 12.

6. Ziegfeld, E. (1951), 'A report to American art education: The UNESCO seminar in art education, Bristol, England, 7–29 July 1951' *Art Education*, The Journal of the National Art Education Association, 4: 4, 1951.

7. Thistlewood, D. (1984), 'Herbert Read: Formlessness and Form', London: Routledge & Kegan Paul.

8. *ibid*. n. 5. p. 22.

9. Zeigfeld, E. (1968/9), 'Symposium' *Athene* (Special issue dedicated to Sir Herbert Read 1893–1968) London, Society for Education through Art, 14: 1, Winter, 1968–9, p. 24.

10. Read, H. (1965), 'Education through Art: A Revolutionary Policy', A lecture given by Sir Herbert Read at an Open Meeting at University, College London, 3 January 1965 (Pamphlet published by SEA – no other details available).

11. Preamble to the Constitution of the International Society for Education through Art ratified at the First General Assembly, held at UNESCO, Paris in July 1954.

12. Rhoades, J. (1987), 'A History of InSEA' unpublished Ph.D. dissertation, Columbus, Ohio: The Ohio State University.

13. *ibid*. n. 12.

14. Boughton, D., Eisner, E., Ligtvoet, J. (Eds.) (1996), 'Evaluating and Assessing the Visual Arts in Education: International Perspectives', NY: Teachers College Press.

15. See: Boughton, D. & Mason, R. (Eds.) (In Press), 'Beyond Multicultural Art Education:

International Perspectives' in the Series European Studies in Education (Christoph Wulf, Series Editor). Munster, NY: Waxman; and Congdon, K. & Boughton, D. (Eds.) (1998), 'Evaluating Art Education Programs in Community Centers: International Perspectives of Conception and Practice', Vol. 4 in Series Advances in Program Evaluation (Robert E. Stake, Series Editor), Connecticut, USA: JAI Press.

16. Giddens, A. (1999), 'Runaway World', BBC 1999 Reith Lectures on Globalisation broadcast on 11 April 1999.

17. *ibid*. n. 16.

18. *ibid*. n. 16.

19. Skilbeck, M. (1992), 'National Curricula: Within the OECD' *Unicorn*, 18: 3, September 1992, pp. 9–13.

20. *ibid*. n. 5.

21. Barrett, W. (1999), unpublished letter to the author dated 28 June.

22. The first issue of InSEA's new *International Journal of Education through Art* is due to be published by Intellect Books in the spring of 2005. See http://www.intellectbooks.com/journals/eta.htm for more information.

23. *ibid*. n. 16.

24. *ibid*. n. 9.

25. *ibid*. n. 16.

26. Chalmers, G. (1996), 'Celebrating Pluralism: Art, Education and Cultural Diversity', The Getty Education Institute for the Arts, Los Angeles CA, p. 45.

27. Earlier versions of this revised and updated paper were published in: *Journal of Research in Art & Education*, Volume 1, 2000, pp. 1–19 (Korean Society for Education through Art. ISSN 1229–747X); *Congress proceedings of 30th* World Congress of InSEA, Brisbane, Australia, AIAE, Elsternwick, Victoria. ISBN 0-646-39274-3; and in Samoraj, M. (Ed.) *Education through Art: Time Passing and Time Enduring*, Warsaw University, 2002, pp. 18–29. Another version with the title 'InSEA: a brief history and a vision of its future role' was published in the *International Journal of Art & Design Education*, 20: 2, 2001, pp. 215–229.

Chapter 9: Looking, Drawing and Learning with John Ruskin at the Working Men's College

Ray Haslam

In early November 1854 the writer and critic John Ruskin (1819–1900), then aged 35, began work on Thursday evenings 7 p.m. until 9 p.m. as teacher of elementary and landscape drawing at the newly established Working Men's College in London. By this time in his career he had completed the first two volumes of *Modern Painters* (1843, 1846); *The Seven Lamps of Architecture* (1849); *The Stones of Venice* (1851, 1853); and numerous other articles and lectures on scientific, religious and artistic matters.[1] He was held in high regard 'by the general cultured public and its representative critics' and this new activity involving practical art teaching with working men was, perhaps, rather unexpected for a man of Ruskin's stature.[2] However, with the benefit of hindsight, Ruskin's participation can be seen as an inevitable part of his driving need to teach and learn in many different contexts, combined with a public expression of his growing social concerns. His teaching at the college is also interesting in that it aimed, in part, to provide a practical criticism of certain aspects of art teaching, especially the *National Course of Instruction,* introduced in 1852, by the Department of Science and Art for children in schools, adults and teachers in training. What Ruskin particularly objected to was that it was a mechanistic approach, which emphasised the acquisition of 'hand power' in a purely utilitarian manner. This involved copying from flat diagrams in hard outline, the use of ornamental casts (rather than natural forms) and the representation of simple geometrical solids in outline alone. All such work was expected to be 'strictly imitative'; the result being that of the 23 Stages of Instruction; 'Only a minority of the students ever reached Stage 10 (and) sometimes about half the students were only at Stage 2'.[3] Nevertheless, the 'South Kensington System' as it became known, was to continue, with minor changes, until the beginning of the twentieth century.

Ruskin's contribution to the development of art education in Britain, especially to practical studies, has tended to become obscured. This is largely due to his undoubted failure to gain much influence on the practice and thinking behind the huge confederation of Government Schools of Art, led by Cole and Redgrave from South Kensington[4] and secondly because of the subsequent advancement of a more expressive approach based on the nature of the child, pioneered by Cooke and Ablett towards the latter part of the nineteenth century. This paper considers Ruskin's practical teaching within the framework of the aims of the Working Men's

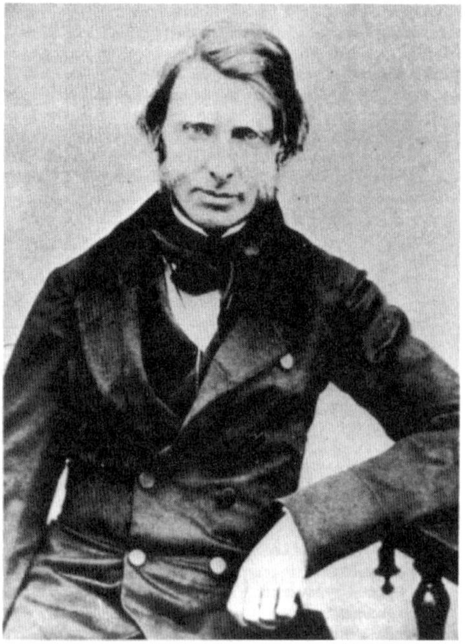

Fig. 1: John Ruskin photographed c. *1856 by Mr Jefferys, Working Men's College; reproduced by kind permission of 'The National Trust' (Wallington).*

College, as evidenced in the recollections of his pupils and his own statements in letters, books and lectures during the period of his active involvement. What emerges is a highly original approach for the period, which, in many ways, can be seen to be pertinent to issues in art education today.

Part One

The Working Men's College opened on the 31 October 1854 in an old house at number 31 Red Lion Square, London. It grew out of the Working Men's Associations of the time and was established by F. D. Maurice, F. J. Furnivall, T. Hughes, C. Kingsley, R. B. Litchfield, C. Lowes Dickinson and others. Central to the college's foundation was the aim of providing a serious liberal education for working men; a form of education previously only available to the wealthy. In this sense, its conception was very different from that of the Mechanics' Institutes which had largely concentrated on utilitarian, informational and commercial aspects. Frederick Harrison, (1902) a biographer of Ruskin and teacher at the college, makes it clear that the aims were also much broader than the provision of the best academic training possible, within the limitations of evening classes. The central spirit of the college was based on co-operation, Christian fellowship and a joining of social classes; 'Carlyles' *Sartor,* Kingsleys' *Alton Locke,* Hughes' *Tom Brown,* and Maurices' Broad Church *Sermons* were the literary forms of the new idea – a cultured, orderly, respectable type of Social Democracy'.[5] The founders held Christian Socialist beliefs, were opposed to the effects of the current political economy on the lives of working people and conceived of education as a life enhancing activity, rather than simply a means to a livelihood. They were determined to place educational opportunities within the grasp of the less fortunate.

Ruskin's introduction to the Working Men's College was made through his friend, F. J. Furnivall, who surmised that he would have considerable sympathy for their plan to aid the educationally underprivileged. A note and a prospectus was sent in the hope of gaining a subscription and with a specific request for permission to reprint Ruskin's central chapter on 'The Nature of Gothic' from *The Stones of*

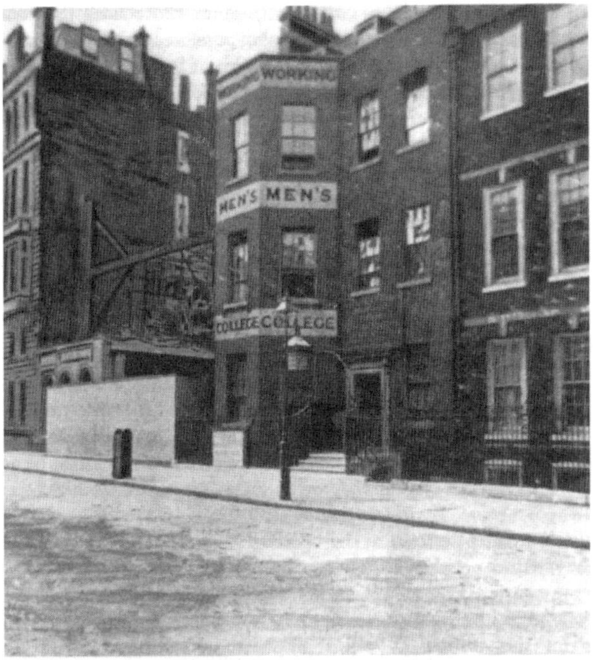

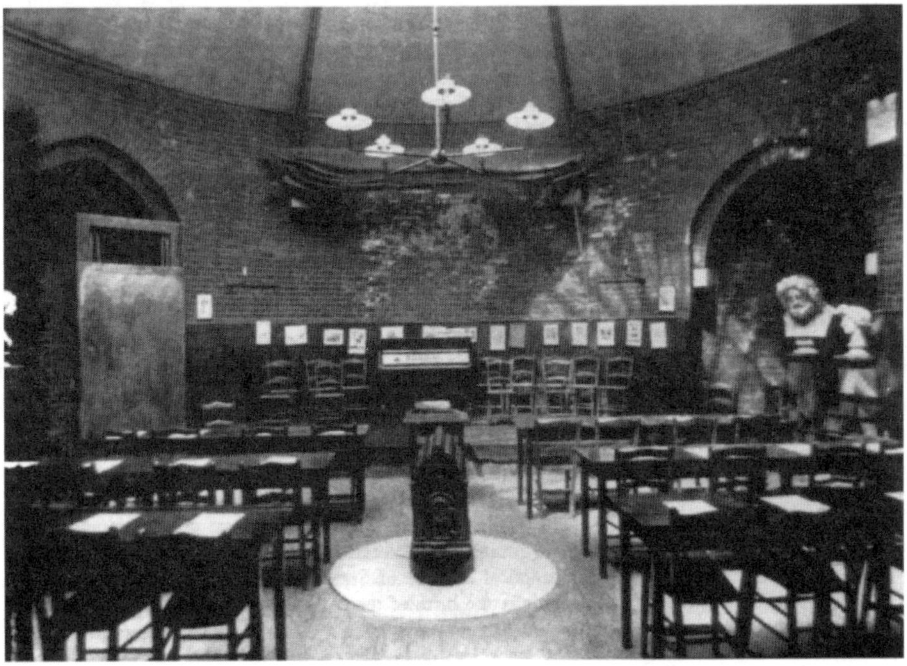

Fig. 2: Exterior view of the Working Men's College, Great Ormond Street, London (its second address) reproduced by kind permission of Macmillan & Co. Ltd (Original photograph property of The Working Men's College, Crowndale Road, St Pancras, London). Interior view: the Oval Room of Working Men's College, Great Ormond Street; reproduced by kind permission of Routledge & Kegan Paul Ltd (Original photograph property of The Working Men's College, Crowndale Road, St Pancras, London).

Venice to serve as a kind of manifesto to be distributed to the men at the opening meeting. It is possible that the chapter, with its praise of the crucial value of creative workmanship was seen as being an ideal expression of some of their aims, whilst being essentially non-political. Ruskin replied 'Print the chapter as you think best' and with characteristic generosity promised Furnivall 'If you lose by it, I will stand the loss; if you make anything, give it to college funds' (36.178).[6] He also offered to take an evening class himself each week in elementary drawing.

It is clear that Ruskin's particular views on both religion and politics were unlikely to be completely in tune with the founders of the college, but it is also evident that his name was a valuable publicity asset which 'helped the enterprise as a whole by letting the world know that one of the greatest Englishmen of the time was in active sympathy with it.'[7] F. D. Maurice, the college Principal, had already disagreed with some of Ruskin's theological views outlined in his *Notes on the Construction of Sheepfolds* (1851) although the two must have felt able to work together. Ruskin's central drive and interest was, however, to be entirely directed towards his art teaching and not the wider aspects of policy and administration. He explained to Furnivall, in May 1855, that he was not prepared to worry himself about the constant pressures to revise plans for the college, stating that Maurice should 'manage the college' whilst he would teach there minding his own business (36.212).

The Working Men's College may appear a rather strange venue for the future Slade Professor at Oxford to begin his teaching and his practical critique of State directed practice in art education. Essentially the birth of the college came at an appropriate time in the development of Ruskin's thought when he needed an additional focus and direction. As early as 1844, he had told Osborn Gordon, his Oxford tutor, that in his writing he was trying 'to spread the love and knowledge of art among all classes' (3.665) and this was to be a major aim throughout his career. He had recently been abroad, in part, to escape the publicity surrounding his divorce, and on the return journey his thoughts were clearly directed towards a more active involvement with education. Writing from Paris, on 24 September, he told Pauline Trevelyan that he wanted to 'give short lectures to about 200 at once in turn, of sign painters and shop decorators – and writing masters and upholsterers and masons – and bricklayers and glassblowers and pottery people'.[8] He asked Rossetti, least he misunderstand his motives, not to see his work at the college as being 'in any wise an endeavour to *regain* position in public opinion' and that the work was concerned with doing what he had always set out to do (5.xliv). Rossetti, for his part was somewhat amused by the idea of Ruskin teaching workmen and informed William Allingham: 'Ruskin is back again. He has written saying he wants to consult with me about plans for "teaching masons"; so you may soon expect to find every man shoulder his hod with upturned fervid face and hair put back'.[9] Ruskin was clearly looking forward to the venture and explained to Sarah Acland on the 19 October that he was 'going to begin a steady course of drawing teaching to workmen on 2

November' and to amuse her suggested he was considering whether to make 'Peruginos – or Turners – or Tintorets or Albert Durers of them'.[10]

Rossetti was soon swept along with Ruskin's enthusiasm and joined the teaching staff along with Lowes Dickinson. Perhaps in order to set his mind at ease Ruskin told him 'all the men want is to *see* a few touches done and to be told where and why they are wrong in their work, in the simplest possible way' (5.xxxviii). At first they worked together with a steady attendance of 40 to 50 men.[11] In the Easter term of 1855 the class divided, Rossetti taking the figure drawing on another night. By 1856, there was a further sub-division, Lowes Dickinson moving to Tuesday evening while Ruskin continued on Thursdays with the assistance of a former pupil William Ward. He taught on a regular basis until May 1858 and from then on more intermittently, teaching for a term in 1860 and continuing his association through lectures (three in 1865) and informal addresses, as time and other commitments would allow.

In 1854 therefore, the Working Men's College offered the ideal opportunity for Ruskin to explore a new, more direct means of communication through practical work, demonstrations and informal lectures. It offered, more crucially, a different audience from the one which normally came into contact with his ideas through his publications. He saw the college drawing classes as an opportunity to put some of his developing ideas about art and education to the test.

Part Two

There is no doubt about the energy and seriousness with which Ruskin carried out his teaching at the college. He soon made arrangements for the third floor studio, consisting of two small rooms knocked into one, to be left open during the day, in order for any who had the time to continue with their studies. He provided specially made, best quality drawing paper and easels, at his own expense and brought in a wealth of stimulating material from which the men could observe and make drawings. His intention, in keeping with general college policy, to provide a form of liberal education in art is emphasised in a manuscript outline (undated) setting out his aims for men who wished to join the class:

> *The teacher of landscape drawing wishes it to be generally understood by all his pupils that the instruction given in his class is not intended either to fit them for becoming artists, or in any direct manner, to advance their skills in the occupations they at present follow. They are taught drawing, primarily in order to direct their attention accurately to the beauty of God's work in the material universe; and secondarily, that they be enabled to record with some degree of truth, the forms and colours of objects, when such a record is likely to be useful. (16.471)*

The content and teaching strategies employed by Ruskin appear quite remarkable when due account is taken of the fact that these lessons took place almost 150 years ago. His teaching certainly had a profound effect upon the lives of many men who attended the classes several of whom described the lessons and methods Ruskin employed. A number of common memories emerge and what is clear is that he went to enormous lengths to make the work interesting, challenging and individualistic in nature.

The actual objects for Ruskin's programme of study were organised with some attention to both level of difficulty and the degree to which individual students might give a positive response. In the Preface to *The Elements of Drawing,* (1857) he pointed out that at the Working Men's College, pupils were 'set at *once* to draw from a solid object' (15.14). This was normally what may appear at first to be a rather daunting exercise; the drawing of a white leather ball. William Ward was set the problem on his first visit to the class and recorded his reactions:

> *I was first set to copy a white leather ball suspended by string and told to draw exactly what I saw – making no line but merely shading the paper where I saw shade. The result was a rather feeble affair; but I remember Mr Ruskin was much taken with my attempt... After the ball came plaster casts of leaves, fruit and various natural objects (36.lviii–lix).*

The exercise was probably used as a diagnostic tool for both visual and executive skill. Certainly, Ruskin was unconcerned at this stage about the accuracy of the sphere itself and wished to demonstrate the transforming effect of tone on a flat surface. He explained:

> *This he learns most satisfactorily from a sphere; because any solid form, terminated by straight lines or flat surfaces, owes some of its appearance of projection to its perspective; but in the sphere, what without shade was a flat circle, becomes merely by added shade, the image of a solid ball; and this fact is just as striking to the learner, whether his circular outlines be true or false. (15.14)*

Ruskin constantly took in all manner of interesting things from his various collections and also 'anything associated with any work of his in progress, if he thought it would interest the men', as George Allen recorded (5.xxxix). Much of this material was available for examination, discussion and drawing. The range is both imaginative and challenging and re-creates in some way his own interests and artistic development. His aim was, essentially, to lift the perception of his students by focusing their attention in different and at times, original ways. Thomas Sulman recalls:

> *For one pupil he would put a cairngorm pebble or fluor-spar into a tumbler of water, and set him to trace their tangled veins of crimson and amethyst. For another he would bring lichen and fungi from Anerley Woods. Once, to fill us with despair of*

colour, he brought a case of West Indian birds unstuffed, as the collector had stored them, all rubies and emeralds. (5.x1)

Here we see the method of stimulating vision through the placing of objects in an unfamiliar context which in turn helps to focus the viewer's attention. Colour is also enhanced. Another method utilized by Ruskin in order to isolate colour or tone for the purposes of careful analysis was the (now) familiar viewfinder, cut from a piece of card. Large scale drawing was also undertaken, again in order to provide a method of sharpening perception and to give a different range of visual and graphic problems. Ruskin describes one such project, with some amusement in the fifth volume of *Modern Painters* (1860):

I set one of my pupils at the Working Men's College (a joiner by trade) to draw, last spring, a lilac branch of its real size, as it grew, before it budded. It was about six feet long and before he could get it quite right, the buds came out and interrupted him. (7.92)

On another occasion when, for a change of subject he wanted the men to draw cordage, he sent George Allen to a shipbreakers' yard at Rotherhithe in order to collect some old ships' hempen cable; whilst William Ward recalls that Ruskin had 'A tree cut down... from Denmark Hill and fixed in a corner of the classroom, for light and shade studies.' (36.1ix). The degree to which Ruskin encouraged a broad interpretation of these exercises is still open to some speculation. His pupil J. P. Emslie considered him to be 'patient and indefatigable, and greatly interested... in the development of whatever gift each particular pupil might possess'.[12] In the *Elements of Drawing* Ruskin is strongly opposed to the use of recipes in art and argues that 'there is no general way of doing anything' (15.97). He dissuades his 'reader' from an over-concern with making a drawing look 'nice', the essential thing being 'to make it look right and to learn as much in doing it as possible' (15.107). William Ward believed that Ruskin made 'everything living and full of interest and disliked servile copying and niggling' (36.1ix).[13]

Throughout the evening Ruskin would talk 'discursively but radiantly' (5.xl) with an easy manner which filled the two hour sessions with compelling interest. Tim Hilton (1985) suggests that his teaching style was '...improvised and freely expository; his thoughts were paradoxical and returned upon themselves in apparent contradiction; he employed anecdote, aphorism, and dramatic questions; the tone was both rhetorical and intimate'.[14] There is no doubt that Ruskin was an excellent teacher, Rossetti informed William Allingham that the 'class has progressed astonishingly and I must try to keep pace with him'.[15] Even Ford Madox Brown, who was no friend of Ruskin's described him in 1857 as being 'eloquent as ever', and 'wildly popular with the men.'[16]

His lifelong interest, observation and study of the forms of nature manifested itself in his teaching of drawing. He had 'a gift for perceiving a feature not immediately apparent in an object (which) gave charm or character to the whole' wrote J. P. Emslie (38.187). Such observations might be expressed in a commentary while making a small analytical study on the edge of the paper, which quickly extracted and explained the essential character. This aspect is stressed in *The Elements of Drawing*:

> *Try always, whenever you look at a form, to see the lines in it which have had power over its past fate and will have power over its futurity. Those are its* awful *lines; see that you seize on those whatever else you miss. (15.91)*

The method stressed a perceptual-cognitive approach which moved the learner beyond the more obvious visual qualities to the nature and causation underlying appearance and hence towards greater understanding and perhaps expressive power. The genesis of the approach may in part, have stemmed from his old drawing teacher Charles Runciman (1798–1864) who had taught him as a child '...the habit of looking for essential points in the things drawn so as to abstract them decisively' (36.77). His own searching drawings done during the course of the evening were seen by J. P. Emslie as being 'masterly, giving the prominent features of an object in exceedingly few, slight, but most expressive touches' (38.187).

Not all of the work was confined to the small room at Red Lion Square, nor later at the art room in Great Ormond Street, when the college moved in 1857. Ruskin would invite members of the class to see the Turners at his home at Denmark Hill[17] and in addition he organised sketching expeditions for members of the class into the countryside around London. Colleagues were sometimes invited to join them and see the work in progress. The group would take 'Cabs at Camberwell Green, at half past three, Tea at the Greyhound Inn Dulwich at seven' (5.xxxviii). Furnivall considered it 'a treat to hear and see him with his men'.[18]

The concern for both practical and critical studies as a means of developing a more refined perception and appreciation of art is always in evidence (as it was to be later in his drawing school at Oxford). Working methods of artists would be demonstrated, for example 'one evening (he) took for his subject a cap, and with pen and ink showed us how Rembrandt would have etched and Albert Durer engraved it' (36.lix). The men might then be set to copy a few square inches of a wood-cut by Durer or to examine a Gothic missal. Turner watercolours would appear and he would 'point out the subtleties and felicities in their compositions, analysing on a blackboard their lines and schemes' (5.xl). In addition, examples from Turner's *Liber Studiorum* were made available for study in order for the men to make copies of small sections. Sometimes a '*Liber*' subject might be taken for a specific demonstration and 'with a large sheet of paper and some charcoal' Ruskin would 'gradually block in the subject explaining at the same time the value and effect of the lines and masses'.[19] Paintings were commissioned by William Hunt of the Old Water Colour Society to show the class how a professional artist tackled and made something of simple subject matter, such as the objects they were working from.

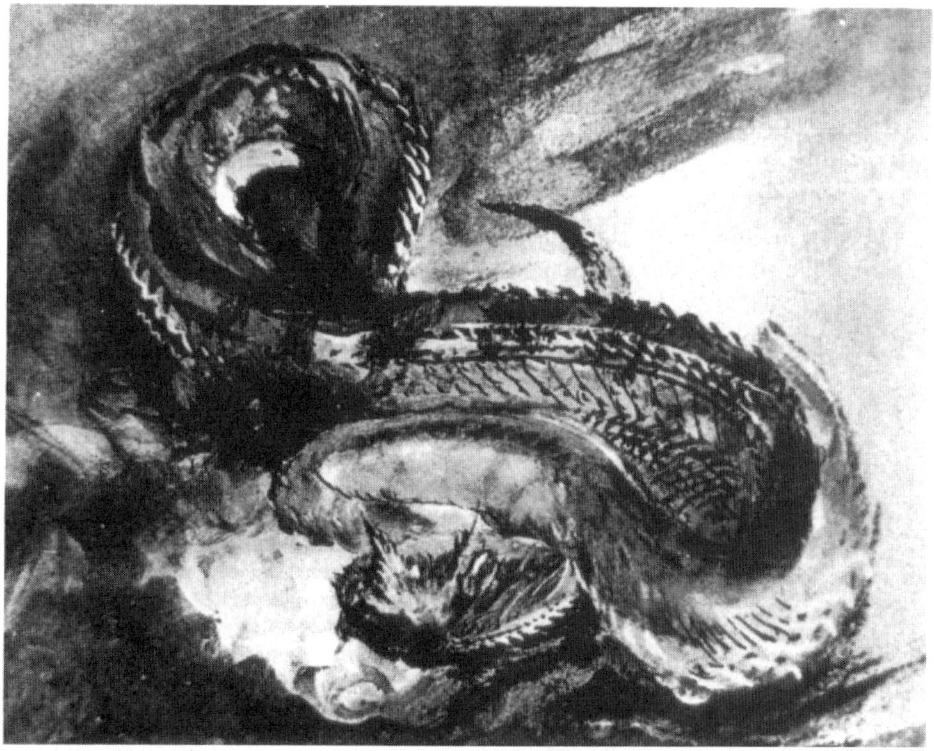

Fig. 3: Study of Cerastes Cornutus *by John Ruskin; reproduced from Deucalion; Vol II, by kind permission of George Allen & Unwin Ltd and the Ashmolean Museum, Oxford.*

Ruskin taught each member of the class on an individual basis considering their problems and encouraging each in turn. This was not without its difficulties as the room was small and the class generally large. Thomas Sulman described it as being 'so closely packed as to deny elbow room'. Ruskin told Lady Waterford, 'I can't see as much of the men as I should like. Their weekly lesson is broken into five minutes to each'.[20] He was very conscious that the time most of the men could afford to devote to drawing was extremely limited and he agonised about the problem, not wishing to direct them too far from their means of earning a livelihood. His lectures at the college were delivered to large audiences with 'continual bursts of applause which greeted his simply chosen but frequently eloquent remarks'.[21] He was held in high regard by both staff and students and Lowes Dickinson considered that 'to teach under the great master was to learn and I hope never to forget my indebtedness for all I learned from him' (36.178).

Part Three

Ruskin's approach at the Working Men's College was shaped by the educational objectives of the institution; by his own training and practice in art, and conditioned by his intense interest and capacity for sight. His training in the practice of art was conducted by his father, and by a number of professional artists and drawing masters who taught him a wide range of technical skills in pencil and watercolour. Most of his teachers were from a new generation who had gained much from the example of J. M. W. Turner and were aiming to rid themselves of the former picturesque tradition.[22] By the time of his commencement at the Working Men's College, he was a highly accomplished draughtsman and had come to believe strongly in the value of drawing as a means of gaining important information about the world.

Ruskin has been described as an 'optical thinker' whose 'contemplation of landscape, and works of art (created) a system of thought, of logic, of arrangement, that is very different from... those who are immersed in a purely verbal culture'.[23] Robert Hewison (1976) believes that the visual dimension was his greatest strength and that in spite of the verbal bias of his education 'the picture asserted itself over the word'.[24] Sight, as he pointed out in a later Oxford lecture, was for Ruskin 'the ordering of intelligence' (22.195) and it was this which directed his teaching and became the force behind his formidable analytical skills. In this sense Ruskin's emphasis on perception places him more closely to modern psychology. Davidoff (1975) has suggested that it does not appear useful to make a distinction between 'perception defined as mere reception and cognition defined as the operation upon that which is received'.[25] Arnheim (1970) believes perception to involve complex processes and because of this he argues that the meaning of the words 'cognitive' and 'cognition' must be extended to include perception.[26] That drawing should have been described by the Schools Council Art Committee (1978) as 'an outward-looking search process and an inward looking retrieval system'[27] would have come as no surprise to Ruskin. He understood perception 'as a sort of visual thinking with association as part of, and not subsequent to, the act of seeing'.[28] His famous concept of the 'innocent eye' was not a naive view of perception, but rather an idea he developed, as a means of helping the student of drawing to overcome what contemporary psychology now refers to as the 'visual constancies' which often interfere with our perception of visual relationships.

In *The Elements of Drawing* Ruskin stated his central belief that 'the excellence of an artist... depends wholly on refinement of perception and that it is this, mainly which a master or a school can teach'. He continues:

For I am nearly convinced that, when once we see keenly enough, there is very little difficulty in drawing what we see. I believe that the sight is a more important thing than the drawing; and I would rather teach drawing that my pupils may learn to love Nature, than teach the looking at Nature that they may learn to draw (15.13).

Ian Simpson (1973) believes, like Ruskin, that 'to learn to draw you don't primarily have to learn special techniques... you have to learn to see'.[29] Equally HMI, in *Art in Secondary Education* 11–16 (1983) argue:

It is a central purpose of art education that pupils should learn to look at things to the point where the eye sees clearly and analytically. It is one of the art teacher's responsibilities to organise experiences in such a way that their pupils pay close attention to what is in front of them in contrast to merely glancing.[30]

This is precisely what Ruskin was to advocate in a series of lectures during the 1850s. In his *Address to the Students at St Martin's School of Art* on 3 April 1857, he emphasised that through drawing 'they actually obtained a power of the eye and a power of the mind wholly different from that known to any other discipline' (16.440). And in a lecture the following year, drawing is described as providing 'a power of notation and description greater in most instances than that of words.' (16.143) Also in 1858, in his *Inaugural Address at Cambridge School of Art,* he stressed the cultivation of visual experience, this time within all aspects of art and design education; '...we shall obtain no satisfactory result unless we... set ourselves to teaching... as far as we can, one and the same thing to all; namely Sight (because) to be taught to see is to gain word and thought at once' (16.179–80). He told his men at the Working Men's College 'Now remember gentlemen that I have not been trying to teach you to draw, only to *see*' (15xx).

Ruskin was convinced of the inter-relatedness of looking and drawing and believed that through an analytical approach to drawing the pupil gained greater potential for both learning and communicating. The consequences of this meant that he was directly involved in helping his pupils to see, first and foremost; for having gained visual skills 'Art enabled them to say and see what they could not otherwise say or see (and) to learn certain lessons which they could not otherwise learn' (16.439). Drawing provided a means of recording an experience of something learned; a form of visual note taking and as such it could be both expressive and highly cognitive. He suggested in the fifth volume of *Modern Painters* (1860):

If the reader will draw boughs of trees long and faithfully... he will come to see what Turner's work is, or any other right work; but not by reading, nor thinking, nor by idly looking. (7.87)

That Ruskin should (unlike the Government Art Schools), centre his teaching on the study of natural forms, is unsurprising and in fact an inevitable part of his make-up, for 'the essential love of *Nature*' (was) 'the root of all that I have usefully become and the light of all that I have rightly learned' (35.166). Secondly, the use of natural forms as a basis for study was fundamental in removing from the learner the idealised models and ornamental casts considered (then) as being essential to any education in art. Through the examination of natural forms, the pupils became free of the rigid and systematic rules which proliferated the *National Course of Instruction;* what Ruskin was later to attack as 'the dregs of corrupted knowledge which modern art-teaching, centralised by Kensington, produces' (27.605).

In addition, Ruskin was keen to introduce drawing into all aspects of the curriculum. He told Henry Cole in 1853 that children's learning could be greatly enhanced 'by putting the graphic element into other studies' (36.160). The point has been made more recently by the Art Advisers Association (1978) who claim in *Learning Through Drawing,* that 'Drawing is not so much a subject as a means whereby observation, understanding and investigations are able to develop'.[31] HMI also supports this view and *Art in Junior Education* (1978) informs us that 'teachers attach great importance to first hand observations and recording as a basic approach to all learning'.[32]

Finally, it can be seen that Ruskin's lessons at the Working Men's College were concerned with the education of sight in such a way as to draw attention to visual aesthetic qualities in the environment and thus enhance the quality of experience for each of his pupils, often dulled and hardened by repetitive labour. He illustrated the point in a lecture at the College, at the close of term:

> *Two men are walking through Clare Market, one of them came out at the other end not a bit wiser... the other notices a bit of parsley hanging over the edge of a butter woman's basket and carries away with him images of beauty which in the course of his daily work he incorporates with it for many a day. I want you to see things like these (15.xx–xxi).*

Eisner (1972) has commented that art education can vitalise people's lives, 'develop our perceptivity, and hence enable us to savour the previously insignificant'.[33] Because of this the arts can be vital in drawing our attention to the non-instrumental aspect of life which compensate for routine and the fragmentation caused by specialisation of working practices. Ruskin would have been in complete agreement and it is within this sphere that his teaching also comes closest to the aims of the Working Men's College. He told the chairman in his evidence to the *National Gallery Site Commission* in 1857; 'My efforts are directed not to making a carpenter an artist, but to making him happier as a carpenter' (13.553).

Part Four

R. L. Archer (1921) described Ruskin as being 'in some ways the greatest indirect force on education during the (nineteenth) century'.[34] In art education, however, we have become so used to certain aspects of his practical methods that his value as an educational reformer seems very underestimated. The fact that he had such limited impact on the Department of Science and Art, may appear strange, when one considers his enormous power as a critic during the second half of the century; but as David Thistlewood has pointed out, the system was 'virtually impregnable'.[35] Ruskin's influence was to be much more complex and diffused. William Morris believed Ruskin's chapter on *The Nature of Gothic* to be 'one of the very necessary and inevitable utterances of the century'[36] and embarked upon his arts and crafts revival. W. R. Lethaby, an influential educator and Principal of the Central School of Arts and Crafts (1902–11) considered that of all the masters who had been prophets to him the first was Ruskin.[37] Herbert Read argued that it was Ruskin who 'first drew attention to what might be called the educational possibilities of drawing'[38] and it was this aspect of his work which was later to be advanced by Thomas Ablett, schooled as a young man on *The Elements of Drawing*. Finally it was Ruskin's pupil at the Working Men's College, Ebenezer Cooke, who was to develop his ideas and focus art education on the nature of the child and the personal expressive possibilities of drawing, which took art education into the twentieth century.[39]

Ruskin's view of the place of art in education was both broader and more profound than the competitive, utilitarian and systematised aims of South Kensington. His approach at the College focused on the general well being of the men and aimed to furnish them with the means to begin to develop their own capacities to enjoy and appreciate the visual qualitative side of life. This concentration on the power of sight, involved a process of looking, learning and shaping experiences through drawing and the study of realised works of art. Ruskin was later to feel the task almost impossible 'when the eye has been accustomed to the frightfulness of modern city life'[40] but the recollections of his pupils tell a different story.

The last 80 years have witnessed the development of numerous rationales and methods to justify the value and place of art in education. Not surprisingly, most have lost their impetus or their significance in the wake of changing educational and social conditions, while others are being re-examined and redeployed with interesting results.[41] Ruskin's aims and teaching therefore deserve re-appraisal by art educators, for they may have a particular relevance for the changing relationship between education and society today.

Originally published in the Journal of Art & Design Education, *Volume 7: 1, 1988.*

Notes and References

1. Note: references cited in the text relate to Cook, E. T. and Wedderburn, A. (Eds.) (1903–12), *The Complete Works of John Ruskin* (Library Edition; 39 vols.) George Allen. For example (36.178) signifies Vol. 36. p. 178.
2. Bradley, J. L. (Ed.) (1984), *Ruskin: the Critical Heritage*, London: Routledge & Kegan Paul, p. 14.
3. See Macdonald, S. (1970), *The History and Philosophy of Art Education*, London: LU.P., p. 188 *et seq.*
4. *Ibid.* pp. 265–268 (Ruskin's 'lack of influence').
5. Harrison, F. (1902), *John Ruskin*, London: Macmillan, p. 84.
6. See n. 1 above. All such citations in the remainder of the text refer to this standard series of collected works.
7. Harrison, J. F. C. (1954), *A History of the Working Men's College 1854-1954*, London: Routledge & Kegan Paul, p. 67.
8. Surtees, V. (Ed.) (1979), *Reflections of a Friendship: John Ruskin's Letters to Pauline Trevelyan 1848-1866*, London: George Allen & Unwin, p. 88.
9. Quoted in Leon, D. (1949), *Ruskin the Great Victorian,* London: Routledge & Kegan Paul, p. 226.
10. Surtees, V. (Ed.) (1972), *Sublime and Instructive,* Michael Joseph, p. 11.
11. Harrison, J. F. C. (1954), n. 7, p. 59.
12. Emslie, J. P. (1904), 'Art Teaching in the College in its Early Days; II' in Llewelyn Davies, J. (Ed.), *The Working Men's College 1854-1904*, London: Macmillan, pp. 39–53.
13. Ruskin's approach has recently been described as 'the most dreary and meticulous instruction in drawing' and this appears to be at odds with accounts presented here. See Morley, J. (1983), 'Landmarks in British Art Education' in Pavey, D. (Ed.), *The Revolution in Child Art*, Harrow, Reeves, p. 1.
14. Hilton, T. (1985), *John Ruskin: the Early Years 1819-1859*, Yale U.P., p. 205.
15. Hill, G. B. (Ed.) (1897), *Letters of D. G. Rossetti to William Allingham,* Unwin, p. 98.
16. Surtees, V. (Ed.) (1981), *The Diary of Ford Madox Brown*, Yale U.P., p. 196. (16 March 1857).
17. For an interesting account of a visit to Ruskin's home by a member of the Drawing Class see Smetham, S. (Ed.) (1902), *The Letters of James Smetham,* London: Macmillan, pp. 61–66 (5 Feb 1855).
18. Collingwood, W. G. (1900), *The Life of John Ruskin*, London: Methuen, p. 154.
19. *Ibid.* pp. 153–4.
20. Surtees, 1972 (n. 10) p. 29. (19 November 1858).
21. Address 29 November 1862, reported *Daily Telegraph,* I December 1862.
22. Paul Walton deals in depth with Ruskin's training in Art. See Walton, P. (1972), *The Drawings of John Ruskin*, Oxford: Clarendon Press.
23. Hersey, G. L. (1982), 'Ruskin as Optical Thinker' in Hunt, J. D. and Holland, F. M. (Eds.), *The Ruskin Polygon*, Manchester U.P., p. 47.
24. Hewison, R. (1976), *John Ruskin: the Argument of the Eye,* London: Thames & Hudson, p. 196.
25. Davidoff, J. B. (1975), *Differences in Visual Perception: the Individual Eye,* London: Crosby Lockwood Staples, *Introduction.*
26. Arnheim, R. (1970), *Visual Thinking*, London: Faber, p. 13.
27. Schools Council Art Committee (1978), *Art* 7–11, p. 24.
28. Helsinger, E. K. (1982), *Ruskin and the Art of the Beholder,* Harvard U.P., p. 57. (Discussion of Ruskin's perceptual reforms).

29. Simpson, I. (1973), *Drawing: Seeing and Observation*, VNR, p. 10.

30. DES (1983), *Art in Secondary Education 11-16*, London: HMSO, p. 7.

31. Art Advisers' Association, NE Region (1978), *Learning through Drawing*, p. 9.

32. DES (1978), *Art in Junior Education,* London: HMSO, p. 27.

33. Eisner, E. W. (1972), *Educating Artistic Vision,* Macmillan, p. 281.

34. Archer, R. L. (1921), *Secondary Education in the C19th,* Cambridge U.P., p. 189.

35. Thistlewood, D. (1986), 'Social Significance in British Art Education 1850–1950' *Journal of Aesthetic Education*, 20: 1, pp. 71–83 (p. 75).

36. Morris, W. (1900), 'Preface' in Ruskin, J. *The Nature of Gothic,* London: George Allen, p. vii.

37. Holder, J (1984), *'Architecture, Mysticism and Myth and its Influence'* in Backmeyer, S. and Gronberg, T. (Eds.), *W. R. Lethaby 1857-1931; Architecture, Design, Education*, London: Lund Humphries, p. 63.

38. Read, H. (1943), *Education through Art,* London: Faber, p. 115.

39. Ruskin and his follower, Cooke, were seen by Victor Lowenfeld as important 'precursors of child art' and their ideas thus provided a crucial influence upon the development of his theory and philosophy. See Michael, J. A. and Morris, J. M. (1986), 'A Sequel; Selected European Influences on the Theory and Philosophy of Victor Lowenfeld'; *Studies in Art Education,* 27: 3, pp. 131–39.

40. Quoted in Benson, A. C. (1911), *Ruskin: a Study in Personality*, London: Smith, Elder & Co., p. 62.

41. An example of this is the practical work in schools based on the study of the *Marion Richardson Archive,* School of Art Education, University of Central England.

Chapter 10: Marion Richardson (1892–1946)

Bruce Holdsworth

Marion Richardson's name figures prominently and frequently in the literature of the history of art education. She is credited with having been one of the pioneers of the child art movement (though until recently this had not been substantiated with systematic research).[1] She is also well known as the inventor of the Marion Richardson *Writing and Writing Patterns,* to which her name is perhaps more readily attached than to her achievements in art education.[2] This ought not to diminish the importance of her contribution to education in art, which has been largely misunderstood until recent years, and has been in danger of being neglected altogether through lack of objective information of the circumstances surrounding her rise to fame. Some distortion of her relative importance has occurred, due mainly to the fact that her findings were not published in book form until after her death, but long before this she influenced a generation of teachers and significantly affected the New Art Teaching Movement. Her colleague at the Inspectorate of the London County Council, R. R. Tomlinson, contributed to this confusion by publishing the first accounts of the new movement, to which he had not otherwise contributed, but which would probably not have occurred without the pioneering work carried out by Marion Richardson.[3]

Early Life and Education (1892–1912)

Marion Richardson was born on the 9 October 1892 in Ashford, Kent, the second daughter in five children of Walter Marshall Richardson, a master brewer, and Ellen Dyer. According to her mother, Marion Richardson showed great powers of imagination and was fond of making up stories and inventing exciting games and was interested in literature and the arts. Her early education took place in a family schoolroom at home, followed by a small private day school; Winchester High School; Uplands School (boarding); and Milham Ford School in Oxford. She showed early promise in drawing and passed *Royal Drawing Society* examinations with relative ease. In her later life she illustrated her lectures with an 'object drawing' of a beer bottle and glass, which she had drawn when she was eleven, as an example of the type of drawing lesson which she was against. (Fig.1)

Milham Ford School, Oxford, was a girl's high school, established to meet the growing demand for middle-class secondary education for girls at the turn of the century. In 1906, the year Marion Richardson started, a new school building was opened simultaneously with a teacher-training college. Catherine Dodd was appointed joint Principal of the College and Headmistress of the School. She was

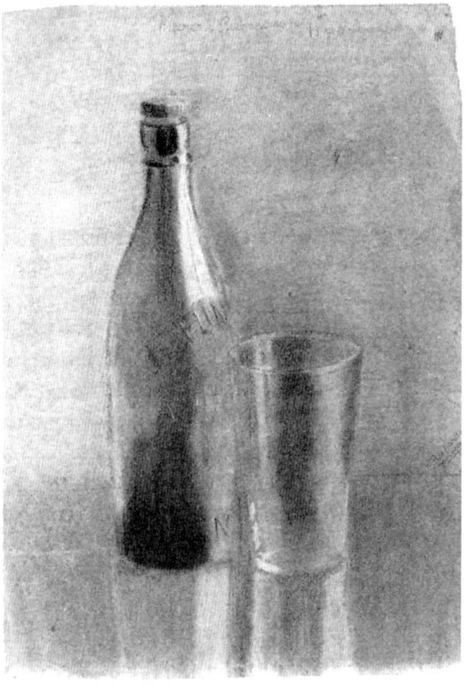

Fig. 1: Marion Richardson: Bottle and Glass drawing; aged 11. Reproduced by courtesy of the University of Central England, Birmingham. Marion Richardson Archive.

well known as one of the foremost experts on practical work in education and had written books on the principles of Johann Friedrich Herbart (1776–1841), father of scientific pedagogy. This means that Marion Richardson came into contact with progressive ideas in education when she was still at school and, as training for women teachers was far in advance of that for men at this time, this must have had some effect on the readiness with which she was later able to put her own advanced theories into practice.

The art mistress at Milham Ford, Gladys Williams, prompted Marion Richardson to sit for a teacher-training scholarship at the Birmingham Municipal School of Arts and Crafts in 1908, when she was sixteen. She passed the Oxford Senior Local Examination 'Associate of Arts' and was successful with the scholarship and reluctantly went to Birmingham. She had hoped to stay on at Milham Ford but her father had died and the change in the family's economic circumstances meant that she could not afford to overlook this opportunity.

She attended the teacher-training course at Birmingham between 1908–1912. It was here that she came into contact with two people who were to influence the course of her life and career; Robert Catterson-Smith and Margery Fry. At the end of her first year she was awarded an 'Elementary Art Certificate' by the School of Art and then went on to pass the Board of Education examinations in conventional subjects, such as: 'drawing in light and shade from a cast'; 'freehand drawing'; 'perspective'; 'geometric drawing'; all legacies of the South Kensington system. At that time Birmingham School of Art was the top art school in the country, winning more national awards and prizes than any other. Birmingham was the centre, too, of a late flowering of the Arts and Crafts movement and staff and students at the School of Art were very much involved in it. Examples of Marion Richardson's student work in jewellery, illumination and embroidery have survived and indicate high levels of craftsmanship.

Catterson-Smith, Headmaster at Birmingham, had worked with William Morris, Burne Jones and William Lethaby, and as Headmaster he was also responsible for the junior art schools, branch art schools and drawing in all the elementary and higher grade schools in Birmingham. It was this wider responsibility which led him to become interested in many different aspects of art education and to introduce a particular type of memory drawing known as 'shut-eye' drawing to teacher-training students at Birmingham.[4] His memory drawing methods were similar to, and in some respects derived from, those of Thomas Ablett. They were well known, but not widely taken up by art teachers; and Marion Richardson appears to have been his principal convert, taking one of his methods and adapting it to her own circumstances. Catterson-Smith used to show lantern slides of historic ornament and objects, which the students were asked to memorise and then draw from memory with their eyes shut before completing a finished drawing with eyes open. Marion Richardson had no access to slides or a lantern when she started teaching and so relied on descriptions or pupils' memories of things previously seen. The important point is that she began to realise that it was the strength of the pupil's mental image which seemed to give rise to the most interesting and successful art. This idea became the centre of her philosophy and eventually governed all her teaching methods.

Between April 1910 and December 1911, Marion Richardson was registered as a pupil-teacher at Moseley Art School. She was taken on to the staff as a Junior Assistant Teacher in December 1911 and left in June 1912. In her final year at Birmingham she lived at University House, Edgbaston where Margery Fry was the Warden. University House had a policy of taking women from a variety of colleges and also from the professions, a policy which derived from the University Settlement ideas of Canon Barnett. Margery Fry was active on many committees connected with education and penal reform. She provided Marion Richardson with an almost perfect model of the unmarried, professional woman at a time when female emancipation was in its formative stages. Marion Richardson never married but devoted herself completely to her work in art education. She and Margery Fry shared many interests including art, embroidery, drama and music, but it was later when Marion Richardson met Margery Fry's brother, the artist, writer and critic, Roger Fry, that their friendship developed. In the meantime Margery Fry, who was on the Staffordshire Education Committee, helped Marion Richardson secure her first teaching post as Art Mistress at Dudley Girls' High School.

Dudley Girls' High School (1912–1923)

Marion Richardson took up this appointment on the 4 June 1912, having passed the Art Class Teacher's Certificate but she left before sitting the Art Master's Certificate. Her special subjects were listed in the school staff records as 'Drawing, Embroidery, Lettering' and she worked there full-time until the summer of 1923 and then part-time as Senior Art Mistress until 1930.[5]

Dudley Girls' High School enjoyed a reputation in the Midlands for providing a good academic education but not at the expense of culture or the development of social skills. The high academic standards achieved there were due to two very good headmistresses, Miss Burke (1891–1914) and Miss Frood (1914–1941). Miss Frood found Marion Richardson particularly supportive of her own ideas, such as those for self–government, and it is significant that the 'school court', introduced by Miss Frood in 1919, was traditionally held in the art studio. It appears that after Marion Richardson came to public attention in 1917, many other educational 'experiments' were carried out, resulting in a constant stream of visitors from Great Britain and abroad including the Ministers of Education for Romania, China and Austria.

Marion Richardson appears to have led the way at Dudley Girls' High School by being particularly interested in modern methods and by developing her own system of teaching 'art' to replace the traditional subject of 'drawing'. Sometime between 1914 and 1916 she attended a course of Dalcroze Eurhythmics, which indicates her interest in modern methods, and during the same period she largely abandoned the traditional drawing syllabus, mainly object drawing, replacing it with water-colour painting which relied on the girls' own mental visualisations. She developed various methods of stimulating her pupils to ensure that they had a good mental image or 'picture' from which they could work, including a variation of Catterson-Smith's 'shut-eye' technique. The earliest surviving Dudley paintings are very small, in some cases only a few inches square, and typically represented various aspects of Dudley or illustrated a poem. The subject matter was either described by Marion Richardson or generated by the pupil, but it is important to realise that senior pupils worked directly from objects or from life for Oxford Local Examinations and there is evidence that she tried a very wide variety of techniques, media and subject matter with her pupils. The term 'generated' is used here to take account of the particularly large number of paintings known as 'Mind Pictures', many of which are entirely abstract and intended to be truthful representations of what the pupils could 'see' when they closed their eyes and concentrated on capturing a mental image.[6]

The Dudley work that has survived is remarkable in comparison with contemporary secondary school art. There is no evidence of any other secondary school in Britain producing work like this between 1912 and 1924. Although Ablett's *Royal Drawing Society* examinations encouraged picture making and working from memory, the results were largely imitative of adult work and do not compare with the abstracts, pattern-making, mind pictures and bright, colourful, childish conceptions of the Dudley work (Figs. 2, 3). Franz Cizek exhibited at an art education congress in London in 1908, but his work was not really known or imitated in Britain until it was circulated in the 1920s.[7] British artists and critics, such as Clutton Brock, one of the organisers of the Cizek exhibitions, had long been familiar with Marion Richardson's theory and practice and, as Cizek's ideas received little recognition in his own country at the time, there is good reason to believe that Marion Richardson prepared the way for the support which Cizek received in this country. Marion Richardson worked out her ideas independently of Cizek and as the leading advocate of child art in Great Britain she was called upon to open one of the first exhibitions of his pupils' work in Cambridge in 1920. Although their ideas were essentially sympathetic, she recognised the difference in results obtained and thought that his pupils produced work which was too stylised. She visited his class in Vienna in 1923 but by then she had finished working full-time at Dudley and had worked out her own fairly complete philosophy of art education based on eleven years' classroom experience.

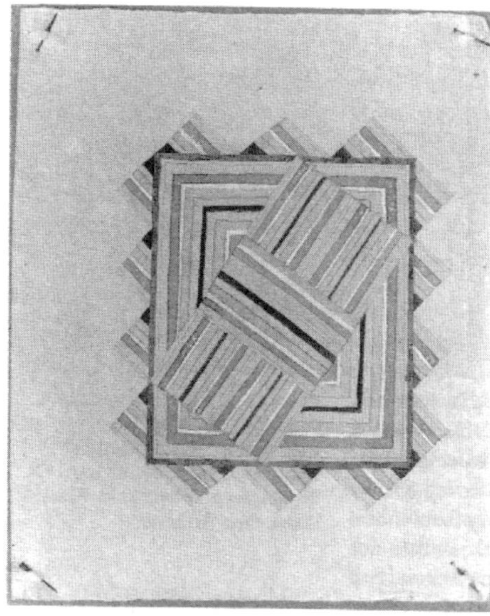

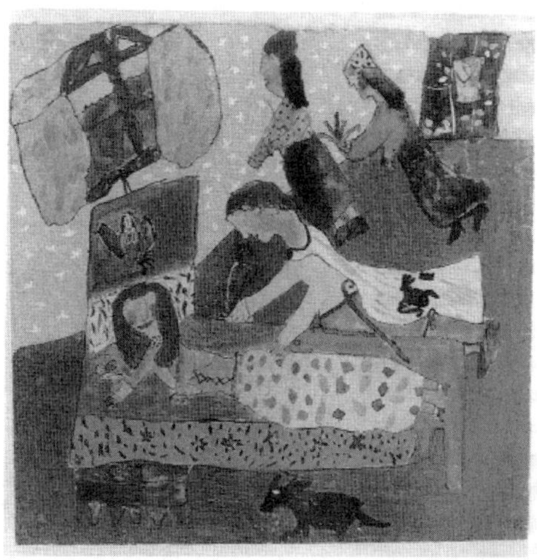

Fig. 2: Dudley Girls' High School, 'Abstract Design', watercolour. Reproduced by courtesy of the University of Central England, Birmingham. Marion Richardson Archive.
Fig. 3: Dudley Girls' High School, ' Sleeping Beauty' watercolour. Reproduced by courtesy of the University of Central England, Birmingham. Marion Richardson Archive.

The most important thing to happen to Marion Richardson in this period was her meeting with Roger Fry at the *Exhibition of Children's Drawings* held at his Omega Workshops in London in February and March 1917. She was in London being interviewed for a post for which she was unsuccessful and took the opportunity to visit Omega. Roger Fry was astonished by the Dudley work she showed him and so he included it in the exhibition and brought it to the attention of the Minister of Education, H. A. L. Fisher, who also recognised its importance. It attracted the attention of critics and received over one hundred mentions in national and international newspapers. The Omega exhibition was a milestone in art education, being the first time in Britain that children's art was exhibited in its own right and for its own qualities. Roger Fry was interested in child art for the primitive qualities it displayed and he compared it to the 'primitive'

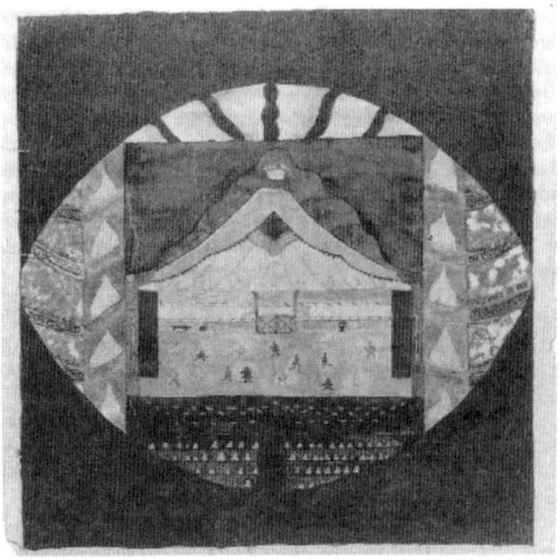

Fig. 4: Dudley Girls' High School, 'Ballet Russes' watercolour. Reproduced by courtesy of the University of Central England, Birmingham. Marion Richardson Archive.

art of other periods and cultures, including the art of the early Renaissance. He did not directly compare it with the work shown in his two famous exhibitions of Post-Impressionist paintings (1910–1913), but there is no doubt that he and Marion Richardson both considered child art to be of a similar type to Post-Impressionism.

Roget Fry helped Marion Richardson in many ways and, apart from proposing that she should be put in charge of a children's art school immediately, he introduced her to the art and artists of Bloomsbury and changed the course of her career through the influence of his ideas and contacts. He arranged for her to go backstage at Diaghilev's *Ballet Russes* to see Picasso designing for *Parade* and she followed this through by giving vivid descriptions of the *Ballet Russes* to her pupils, who produced some remarkable images. (Fig. 4)

The immediate result of her contact with Roger Fry can be seen in the extraordinary written statement she produced to accompany an exhibition of pupils' work held at Dudley Girls' High School in December 1917. It is reproduced here in full:

> *The drawings in this exhibition are all the work of children who receive no help but the encouragement to draw. They are taught that drawing is a language, which exists to speak about things that cannot be expressed in words – emotional ideas about the beauty of the world, that come to us. It is these ideas and not literal and photographic representation of appearances that the artist seeks to express, and as the children are working with this motive – the same motive that has inspired all art – their drawing must be considered as tiny works of Art. There is no fixed syllabus for the work. As far as possible each child decides what she will draw and comes to the studio with her ideas ready, using the lesson simply as a convenient opportunity for working out some idea that has come to her. There is no emphasis laid upon mere skill and no direct training of technical methods. It is felt that the force of an idea is of itself sufficient to find means of expression, and that if any such help is needed, it is better given individually when the child is ready to ask for it. The point most insisted upon is clear thinking. The children never begin to draw until they feel they have grasped the idea, until they know what they want to do and feel impelled to do it. The greatest factor in attaining this clearness is the visual power. It is towards a greater realisation of this*

power that teachers of drawing are working, but to attempt to teach visual drawing and at the same time to reject any genuine visual effort is both contradictory and dangerous. That some of these drawings are not just as we would have done them is perhaps their greatest virtue. Remembering that all art must reveal to us something of which we were not aware, we must not reject them for what seems to us queerness – queerness, which we mostly accept in primitive or foreign art – but look at them and try to receive the message they seek to convey, often simply an idea of space, colour, volume, contrast etc.[8]

All subsequent writing by Marion Richardson was essentially an elaboration of this basic philosophy, indicating that by 1917 she had arrived at a coherent and original theory of art education based on sound practice.

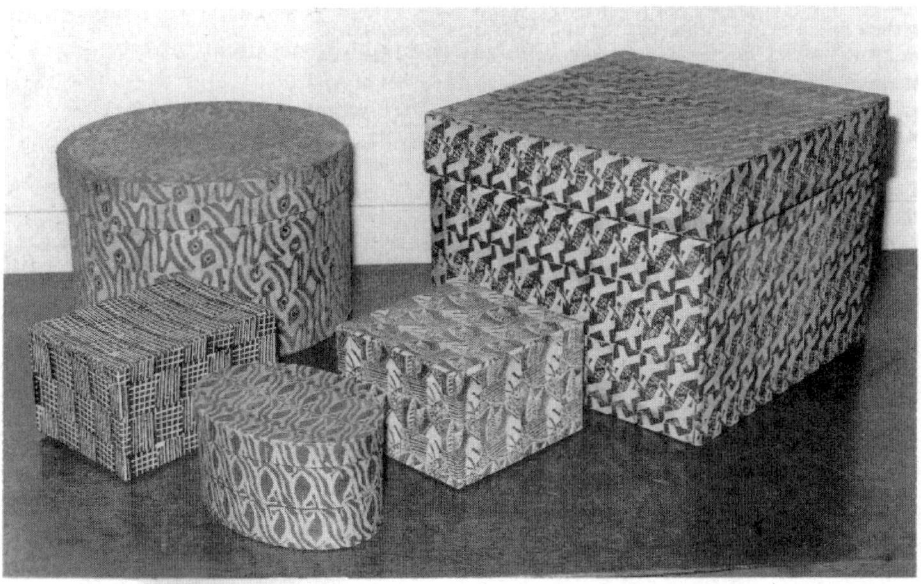

Fig. 5: Dudley Girls' High School; Block printed paper-covered boxes. Reproduced by courtesy of the University of Central England, Birmingham. Marion Richardson Archive.

The Omega Workshops, although short lived, had a profound influence on Marion Richardson. She did not follow the breakaway 'rebel' artists who became Vorticists, but extended her class work into the decorative arts in similar fashion to Omega, producing painted furniture, trays, lampshades and block-printed fabrics and papers applied to boxes etc. (Fig. 5). Roger Fry arranged for her to have an exhibition of Dudley work at Omega in 1919, in conjunction with some drawings and marionettes by Larionov. This was the very last exhibition held at Omega, because it went into liquidation in 1920, but it was the beginning of a long list of exhibitions of Dudley work held all over Great Britain and abroad. Her confidence at this time was such that she wrote an article on 'How to Teach Drawing' which was published in the *Cambridge Magazine* in August 1919.

Her interest in developing an effective handwriting scheme also dates from this period at Dudley. In 1914 she was given the additional responsibility for teaching writing to the lower school and lower fourth forms and in her usual thorough way devised a system which led to the publication of *The Dudley Writing Cards* in 1928[9] and *Writing and Writing Patterns* in 1935. She had studied calligraphy and illumination at Birmingham School of Art and shared an interest in handwriting with Roger Fry. Her system was partly based on Graily Hewitt's copy-books but she also consulted Edward Johnston who wrote an appreciation of *The Dudley Writing Cards* in the note to teachers which accompanied the sets.

By 1922 she was sufficiently well known to be invited by the Consultative Committee of the Board of Education to report on the possibility of developing Art Teaching in connection with History and Literature. In the same year she was on the Examination Committee of the Teachers' Registration Council, helping to determine the standards of attainment to be required of Registered Art Teachers.

Middle Years (1923–1930)

Within weeks of their first meeting Roger Fry had promised to help Marion Richardson secure a post as a teacher-training lecturer by using his influence with the Minister for Education. As this began to seem unlikely, she had a prospectus printed in order to take private pupils. She then began to hold private classes, while also lecturing part-time on the new graduate training course at the London Day Training College (LDTC), where the Principal, Percy Nunn, was sympathetic to her views.

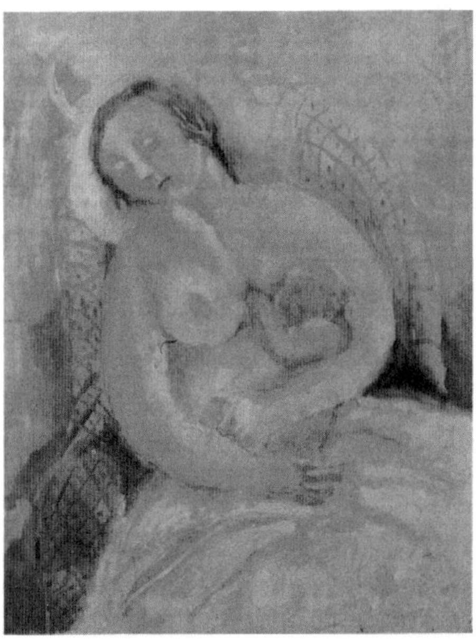

Fig. 6: 'Mother and Baby' watercolour. Reproduced by courtesy of the University of Central England, Birmingham. Marion Richardson Archive.

On Mondays she taught at Benenden, the girls' public school in Kent. On Tuesdays she supervised students on teaching practice. On Wednesday mornings she taught at Hayes Court private school in Oxford, and on Wednesday afternoons she brought in classes of elementary school children to work with her students at the LDTC. On Thursdays and Fridays she returned to Dudley Girls' High School where she carried out her duties as Senior Art Mistress and on Saturdays she held a private class at a country house in Northamptonshire. Work by pupils other than from Dudley is often more sophisticated, larger and painted with opaque colour (Fig. 6). In addition she started a class for elementary school children at an LCC school on two evenings a week. She also had other private pupils and started to build up a punishing programme of lectures all over the country and these increased in frequency until in 1939 she became too ill to continue. The following list of lectures delivered in 1929 indicates the range and type of venues:

April:	Ambleside Old Students' Association; Wiltshire Arts and Crafts Association.
July:	Two short courses for the Board of Education in Oxford.
October:	Birmingham Education Study Society.
November:	Hull Froebel Society; Conference on *New Ideals in Education,* Worcestershire; Lecture to Child Study Society.

In the Spring of 1925 she delivered the first of many lectures to LCC teachers on 'The Teaching of Drawing'. It was these lectures and her contact with teachers-in-training at the LDTC which first helped to spread her methods. Within a relatively short time she convinced a number of students, including Nan Youngman, Clarence Whaite and Clifford Ellis, of the validity of her ideas, which were now more readily understood in the light of modern art movements and the recognition afforded to Cizek. One of her students, R. J. Puttick, taught so successfully along her lines at Westminster City School that he was invited to exhibit his pupils' work with hers at the Whitworth Art Gallery in Manchester in the Spring of 1928. At this exhibition Marion Richardson summed up her approach in the following way:

> *The essence of my method is to encourage the girls to concentrate upon and give expression to mental images formed upon their own observations. I try to avoid giving them any ready-made formula for translating these visions into pictures. The most positive part of my work is to present suitable objects to the child's mind, though often the children succeed in inventing their own subjects. The study (through reproductions) of the works of great artists helps them to realise for themselves the essentials of formal design. I direct the criticisms of their own and each other's work. In this the value of an honest attempt at expression as compared with the production of an accomplished rendering is emphasised. By their working together, a common tradition and style has grown up among the girls, of a kind quite unforeseen by me.*[10]

It was at this exhibition that a number of the children's block designs were sold to manufacturers and eventually put into production. The Calico Printers' Association chose 23 designs and they were printed on 'Rossvale Rayon Crepe' and marketed as the 'Maid Marian Range'.

In the Summer of 1925, her professional standing was such that she represented the *Association of Assistant Mistresses* in Paris at a meeting of the *International Federation of Art Teachers.* She was often invited to speak at national conferences and this provides important evidence about her status within the New Education Movement.[11] The essential features of this movement have been identified as: taking account of the personality of the child; and aiming for a better society, a better world, a new era. This is a gross simplification of a movement which grew and developed over many years, but the consequence of accepting New Education principles was that the teacher was required to watch and help the growth of the child's abilities and not impose strict learning regimes. Marion Richardson's theory and practice fit easily into this concept. Her approach stands up to the criticism normally levelled against child-centred approaches, that they merely confirm the child's immaturity, because it was essentially learner-centred. The results of her methods indicate that her pupils produced carefully considered work which did not conform to normal educational requirements but went beyond them to take account of new ideas in art. Spontaneity, to her, was an element of art rather than education and she was at pains to point out that her concern was for the recognition of sincerely produced individual forms of art rather than the training of competent copyists. She took the school subject of 'drawing' away from practical training and scientific observation and linked it more firmly with new ideas about art. There is a similarity here between her idea that drawing should be linked to real art and the contemporary notion that 'drill' in the school curriculum should give way to real games.

To associate Marion Richardson with the New Art Teaching of the 1930s and 1940s is correct because this is when her influence was most directly felt, but she also belongs firmly within the New Education Movement of the previous two decades, having developed her ideas and methods at the same time as many notable pioneers of progressive education and in advance of most. Her true contemporaries then were: Maria Montessori; Margaret Macmillan; Homer Lane; Norman Macmunn; Caldwell Cook; John Dewey and Franz Cizek. This puts her in advance of Susan Isaacs; the Russells; the Elmhirsts at Dartington; and New Art Teachers such as Robin Tanner.

Marion Richardson was directly involved in the Conferences on *New Ideals in Education* and in particular the 1919 Cambridge Conference; the 1929 Worcestershire Conference and the 1930 Oxford Conference. She was also involved in the *New Education Fellowship* and spoke at the 1935 St Andrews Conference, and the Seventh World Congress held at Cheltenham in 1936. This level of involvement, at the forefront of new educational theory and practice, marks her out as a distinguished teacher within the New Education Movement and there is a noticeable and serious omission of her name in the standard history of education texts, which may be accounted for, but hardly justified, by the subject-based nature of her activities.

London County Council (1930–1946)

By April 1930, Marion Richardson's reputation in education was such that Cyril Burt asked her to read a rough draft of a report he was preparing for the Hadow Committee. In September they became colleagues when she was appointed Inspector of Art to the LCC where she had a profound influence on the teaching of art, craft, pattern-making and handwriting, particularly in infant and junior schools. Her influence was spread in many ways including: 'surgeries' for teachers, held in her office at County Hall; visits to schools; and lectures. She also ran courses for teachers, which were always oversubscribed. Applications for the 1934–1935 course, 'Art in Infant Schools', held on Wednesday evenings in January at a fee of four shillings, were refused after the number had risen to one thousand because only forty could be accommodated. She organised a number of small exhibitions and contributed to others between 1930–1938, but it was the large exhibition of children's art held at County Hall in July 1938 which attracted the most attention and is widely regarded as the point at which her work culminated and finally convinced even the most sceptical of the value of art in education. Her initiative in organising exhibitions of this type was later taken up by the British Council, through the influence of Herbert Read, and British Child Art was later toured all over the world, particularly in North and South America.

She extended the idea of handwriting and pattern making down to primary school level. The introduction of sugar paper, large brushes and powder colour for the purpose of producing writing patterns, led eventually to these materials being adopted as standard in the teaching of art in primary schools. Within a few years at the LCC she had made a dramatic difference to the type of art being produced in many London Schools. In international terms Marion Richardson was to London what Cizek was to Vienna and Arthur Lismer was to Toronto.

An important aspect of the inter-war years was the interest shown in design or 'art and industry' and the relationships between them. The effect of this movement on art education has not been properly charted but as the propaganda began to take effect it swept many educationalists on board. Marion Richardson, whose interest was in decorative design rather than product design, was involved in various ways and corresponded with some of the principal figures of the movement, including Frank Pick, Harry H. Peach, Anne Carter and Herbert Read. As early as 1928, Paul Nash sent someone from the Curwen Press along to see some of her pupils' decorative papers with a view to putting them into production. In 1930 she received a request for a memorandum from the Gorrell Committee and she was subsequently mentioned in their report.[12] She was involved with the famous *Exhibition of British Industrial Art in Relation to the Home* held at the Dorland Hall in 1933, where the Edinburgh Weavers saw some of her pupils' designs which they were anxious to purchase. In 1934 she was requested by the Council for Art and Industry to give evidence on art education in London and produced a report for them on 'The Development of Artistic Sensibility in School Children', the content of which helped towards their report *Education for the Consumer.*[13]

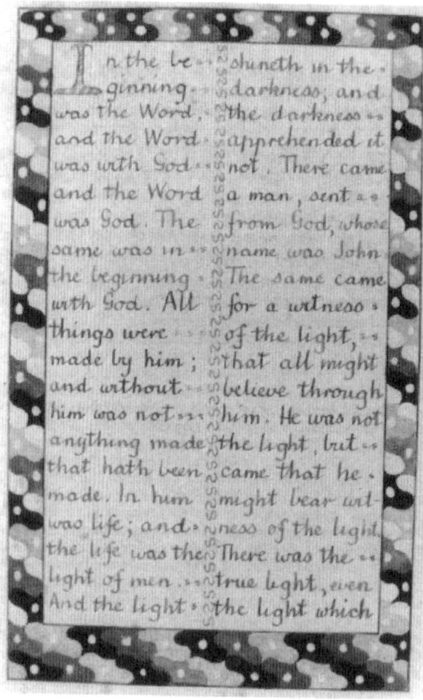

Fig. 7: Handwriting and Letter Patterns. Reproduced by courtesy of the University of Central England, Birmingham. Marion Richardson Archive.

It is not generally realised that she also played an important part in the Council for Art and Industry sponsored exhibition, *Design in Education,* held at County Hall in 1937. This was arranged as an exhibition of material for use in elementary schools, and she organised a section on 'Writing as a Form of Art' (Fig. 7), in company with Walter Gropius whose 'Mathematics' section was a display of geometrical models. The same year she delivered a lecture to the *Royal Society of Arts* which won her its silver medal. The following year, 1938, she gave a lecture to the *Design and Industries Association* on the teaching of art and design to children. This was also the year of the hugely successful exhibition at County Hall and, unfortunately, the year in which she started to show signs of illness.

When the Second World War started she was evacuated with school children to Oxford and her illness got progressively worse. She was declared unfit for duty and finished working in January 1942. She moved to Dudley in 1945 and, although seriously ill by this time, she sewed and embroidered little articles for friends and relations and wrote her book *Art and the Child,* which she finished on 11 November 1946, the day before she died.[14]

Conclusion

Marion Richardson was an early pioneer of the New Education Movement, and the theory and practice she evolved at Dudley Girls' High School between 1912–1923 subsequently influenced teachers of art, craft, design and handwriting. There were many factors involved in the development of the New Art Teaching (as identified by Tomlinson in 1934), but we can be sure that the work of Marion Richardson was one of the most important, and that she did more than any other teacher in Britain to promulgate the idea that children were capable of producing original works of art.

Her ideas are still relevant.[15] This is especially true when classroom practice is informed by a thorough study and understanding of her theory and practice. Art and design education is always capable of being enriched by the work of enlightened and influential school teachers, and we do well to study and test those that have existed in the past. Marion Richardson offers a supreme example of how we are in danger of neglecting and negating the work of our finest practising teachers, the careful study of which can help us to avoid re-inventing the wheel.

Originally published in the Journal of Art & Design Education, *Volume 7: 2, 1988.*

Notes and References

1. This became apparent when I was researching the period of English art education between the two world wars and decided that there was a need for clarification of this issue (see Holdsworth, B. (1984),'English Art Education Between the Wars' Journal of Art and Design Education, 3: 2). I have looked closely into the claims made about Marion Richardson, by researching in the Marion Richardson Archive at the former Birmingham Polytechnic; now the University of Central England in Birmingham (see Swift, J. (1985), The Marion Richardson Archive, School of Art Education, University of Central England). It is the presence of this archive and the opportunity and stimulus it offers which has led to the recent progress in research on Marion Richardson. The first substantial research to use this primary source material was conducted by D. Campbell, who carried out the initial cataloguing with the aid of a Social Science Research Grant (see Campbell, D. 'Marion Richardson: A Misunderstood Figure in Art Education', Unpublished M.Phil. CNAA thesis, University of Central England).
2. Richardson, M. (1935), Writing and Writing Patterns, University of London Press.
3. Tomlinson, R. R. (1934), Picture Making by Children, The Studio Ltd, London; and (1935), Crafts for Children, The Studio Ltd, London.
4. See Swift, J. (1978), 'Robert Catterson-Smith's Concept of Memory Drawing 1911–1920' Unpublished MA CNAA thesis, City of Birmingham Polytechnic. See also Swift, J. (1983), 'The Role of Drawing and Memory Drawing in English Art Education (1800–1980)' Unpublished Ph.D. CNAA thesis, University of Central England.
5. Dudley Girls' High School records, Dudley Public Library.
6. A detailed account of the 'mind pictures' is given by Swift, J. (1986), 'Marion Richardson and the "Mind Picture"' Canadian Review of Art Education Research, 13.
7. Hancock, J. C. (1984), 'Franz Cizek; A Consideration of his Philosophy, Methods and Results' MA CNAA thesis, University of Central England.
8. Handwritten statement; Marion Richardson Archive, University of Central England.
9. Richardson, M. (1928), The Dudley Writing Cards, London: G. Bell & Sons.
10. Introduction to catalogue Exhibition of Drawings and Designs by Children, Whitworth Art Gallery, Manchester, Spring 1928.
11. This movement has been identified by Selleck and others as a late nineteenth and early twentieth century reaction against the rigid educational methods which had set in following the

'payment by results' system and the Revised Code (see Selleck, R. J. W. (1968), The New Education, London: Pitman.) The New Education started with the abolition of the Standards in the 1890s and was helped along by the reorganisation of local educational administration and the establishment of the LEA's in 1902.

12. HMSO (1932), Art and Industry (The Gorrell Report).

13. HMSO (1935), Education for the Consumer (Art in Elementary and Secondary School Education).

14. Richardson, M. (1948), *Art and the Child*, University of London Press. Death Certificate records death as: (a) Myocardial Failure; (b) Rheumatoid Arthritis; (c) Anaemia.

15. (a) Cieslik, K. D. (1985), 'Marion Richardson: A Curriculum Study'. (The effectiveness of the teaching techniques of Marion Richardson on pupils with learning difficulties.) DES/Manchester Education Committee/City of Birmingham Polytechnic Teacher Fellowship.

    (b) Hart, E. V. (1984), 'Marion Richardson: A New Curriculum Study.' DES/Manchester Education Committee/City of Birmingham Polytechnic Teacher Fellowship.

    (c) Keene, J. (1986), 'Marion Richardson: Her Approach to Handwriting.' DES/Hertfordshire Education Authority/City of Birmingham Polytechnic Teacher Fellowship.

    (d) Kinch, B. (1985), 'Curriculum Project on the Work of Marion Richardson.' DES/City of Birmingham Polytechnic Teacher Fellowship.

A Condensed Marion Richardson Chronology

1892 Born, Marion Elaine Richardson, 9 October, Ashford, Kent.

1904 Winchester High (Junior) School.

1906 Uplands School.

1906 Milham Ford School, Oxford.

1908 Birmingham School of Arts and Crafts.

1910 Pupil-teacher at Moseley School of Art.

1911 Met Margery Fry at University House. Junior Assistant Teacher at Moseley School of Art.

1912 Dudley Girls' High School.

1917 Met Roger Fry at Omega Workshops, *Exhibition of Children's Art.*

1919 Exhibition at Omega Workshops. Saw Russian Ballet. Article in *Cambridge Magazine. New Ideals in Education* Conference, Cambridge.

1920 Opened Cizek Exhibition in Cambridge.

1922 On Sub-Committee of Board of Education Consultative Committee. On Examining Committee of Teachers' Registration Council. Article in *Woman's Leader.*

1923 Visited Russia and Cizek in Vienna. Finished full-time work at Dudley and moved to London to stay with Roger Fry and Margery Fry. Started private classes and part-time teaching.

1924 Started lecturing at the London Day Training College. Exhibition at the Independent Galleries.

1925 Delegate of Association of Assistant Mistresses, Paris.

1927 Exhibitions at Independent Galleries and LDTC.

1928 *Dudley Writing Cards* published. Exhibitions at the Whitworth Art Gallery, Manchester; Claridge Gallery, London; Heals, London. *New Ideals in Education* Conference, Worcestershire.

1930 *New Ideals in Education* Conference, Oxford. Appointed Inspector of Art for the LCC Memorandum for the Gorrell Committee.

1933 Exhibitions; *British Industrial Art in Relation to the Home,* Dorland Hall; County Hall.

1934 Evidence to Council for Art and Industry. Visited Canada and USA.

1935 *Writing and Writing Patterns* published. *New Education Fellowship* Conference, St Andrews. Silver Jubilee Exhibition, County Hall.

1936 *New Education Fellowship* Seventh World Congress, Cheltenham *1937 Design in Education* Exhibition. *RSA* lecture and silver medal

1938 Lecture to *DIA. Exhibition of Children's Art,* County Hall.

1939 *Jubilee Exhibition* at County Hall. Evacuated to Oxford.

1941 British Council Exhibitions.

1942 Finished work at the LCC.

1946 Marion Richardson died aged 54.

1948 *Art and the Child* published. *Marion Richardson Memorial Exhibition.*

All photographs kindly produced by Frank Power.

Chapter 11: Herbert Read: a Critical Appreciation at the Centenary of his Birth

David Thistlewood

Introduction

Herbert Read was a poet devoted to the evocation of vivid pictorial imagery, especially of his native northern English countryside. He was also an internationally respected historian of ceramics and stained glass, and was strongly committed to the modern revitalisation of industrial design. He was a literary critic, contributing important studies of the English Romantic poets Wordsworth, Coleridge and Shelley. Twice decorated for bravery in the First World War, he subsequently became a pacifist and theoretical anarchist. His unconventional politics did not prevent his being honoured with a knighthood, nor his belonging to the British cultural establishment as signified in honorary professorships, prestigious lectureships and ambassadorial duties for such organisations as the British Council. But in spite of this diversity of achievement he is best remembered for two things: art historians acknowledge him as an important critic of, and apologist for, the avant-garde art of his lifetime – particularly English and European Modernism;[1] and art educationists recall him as a profound explicator and defender of children's creativity – he was, of course, a very active Chairman and President of the Society for Education in Art, one of the antecedent organisations of the NSEAD, for 22 years.

His interests in art education, though obvious in his earlier aesthetic theorizing, did not develop fully until he was approaching his fiftieth year. They emerged from his interests in theories and practices illuminating the position of the avant-garde within the socio-political flux. The subject of child art was at first of subsidiary importance: arguments about a 'pre-logical' essence within avant-garde creativity could be supported with reference to properties apparent in both primitive art and the imagery of children. However, he became deeply interested in children's drawings and paintings after selecting works for an exhibition of British art that would tour allied and neutral countries during the Second World War. As it was considered too risky to transport across the Atlantic works of established importance to the national heritage, it was proposed that children's drawings and paintings should be sent instead.

Read, in making his collection, was unexpectedly moved by the expressive power and emotional content of some of the younger artists' works. This experience prompted his special attention to their cultural value, and his engagement of the theory of children's creativity with a seriousness matching his devotion to the avant-garde. This work both changed fundamentally his own life's work throughout his remaining 25 years and provided art education with a rationale of unprecedented lucidity and persuasiveness. Key books and pamphlets resulted: *Education through Art;*[2] *The Education of Free Men;*[3] *Culture and Education in a World Order;*[4] *The Grass Roots of Art;*[5] and (published posthumously) *Redemption of the Robot.*[6]

As these titles suggest, Read elaborated a socio-cultural dimension of creative education, offering the notion of greater international understanding and cohesiveness rooted in principles of developing the fully-balanced personality through art education. Child art was the driving force of this philosophy: the heroic task of education was to prevent the young child from losing access to whatever ancient, ingrained, cultural wisdom he or she was able to manifest in symbolisation. Read's last years were devoted to the proclamation of this philosophy throughout the world, especially in the proceedings of the International Society for Education through Art, which he was instrumental in establishing under the auspices of UNESCO. He was responsible for planting British conceptions of art education in new landscapes: Brazil,[7] Japan, China and (only weeks before his death, and when the illness that was its cause was critical) Cuba.

Philosophical Anarchism

Read was the son of a tenant farmer in north Yorkshire, and his first perception of the world was of an utterly stable, conservative, rural community. In 1903, however, when he was ten, his father died and his family was dispossessed of its tenancy. His mother entered domestic service, he being boarded at an orphanage school in Halifax before leaving, at the earliest opportunity, to be a bank clerk in Leeds. The obvious facts of industrial poverty around him challenged inherited political prejudices, and by the time he entered Leeds University in 1912 to study economics (after having matriculated at evening classes) he was a ready participant in socialist debates.

He began to read *The New Age,* among the leading journals of socialist politics and aesthetics of its day. He became a regular contributor to this paper throughout a period in which it was a vehicle for promoting socialist alternatives to Fabianism, a movement dedicated to opposing capitalism by debate and force of argument rather than precipitate action. Read himself differed with the Fabians not so much on questions of revolution as of materialism. In pursuit of improving wages and conditions, and increasing workers' share of goods, the Fabians appeared willing to surrender fundamental socialist principles, notably the aesthetic and spiritual goals of arts and crafts reformers such as William Morris. For Read aesthetic pleasure and spiritual satisfaction in work were paramount.

In Read's earliest childhood memories, even the most severely exploited workers had experienced the satisfactions of working with the land, with growth and harvest and with animal husbandry, and even the meanest tasks had been acknowledged periodically in thanksgivings, seasonal festivities and other kinds of common celebration. His images of work were of hard toil cheerfully endured in the countryside, of industrial processes centred upon forge or smithy, and of urban employment housed in small-scale machine sheds – an imagery very similar to that of the theoretical anarchist Piotr Kropotkin, whose writings he admired.

Read's early contribution to socio-political thought, published in the relatively obscure periodical *The Guildsman* in 1917, was to propose a theory of economic groupings and networks that would have fused both localised and internationalised interests. Rural industries would have run on anarchistic principles, while the world's urban centres would have formed such an interlocked system of economic mutual dependence as to have made any future international conflict – such as the war he had recently fought in – impossible. He saw trades unions and industrial federations as prototype economic groups which, with only a little more purpose, could be the regulators of an international economy; and like the Marxists he could foresee the withering of the State, though not into extinction but to a size commensurate with its remaining responsibilities, virtually all of which, to Read, would have been cultural.

Read's political beliefs had roots in these convictions – another war is unthinkable; the State has no economic purpose; and the ideal form of government is one which guarantees utmost equality while preserving individual freedoms, including the right of an individual to become detached from those community interests into which he or she had been accidentally projected by birth. This is precisely what had happened to Read as a result of his father's premature death, his own dislocation from the locality of his birth, and his having found a role outside the agricultural community. His position was summarised in his critical appreciation of Julien Benda's book *La Trahison des Clercs*[8] in which a series of propositions were found to be so strikingly familiar that they came as self-revelations.

All real human existence is the existence of an individual, either of an individual person or of a common interest group, and is competitive and necessarily aggressive. The 'clerc' or disinterested person of learning is one who protests against a morality of aggression by proclaiming ideal values revealed in contemplation of matters abstract, universal and infinite. Civilised humanity is made possible by the coexistence and synthesis of aggressive expediency and disinterested philosophy. A world observing only a code of practical necessity would be barbarous; one which practiced only a code of ideals, would cease to exist. Real existence admits the gradual softening of aggression with idealism.

Read (having left the Army with the rank of Captain, having worked for a brief time as a government civil servant at the Treasury, and then having transferred his employment within the Civil Service to an Assistant Keepership of Ceramics at the Victoria and Albert Museum) naturally identified with the dislocated individual who, while leading an ostensibly unproductive life, had the special purpose of divining abstract principles for the benefit of the wider community in an age of idealism following, and counteracting, a period of great international aggression. At this time in his life, like his friend T. S. Eliot, and the classicist T. E. Hulme, whose collected works he had edited,[9] Read considered the goals of aesthetic contemplation to be formal precision, harmony and elegant proportion – principles which, he firmly believed, when evident in literature, art and conduct, offered the world the prospect of an international medium of understanding.

This was in the 1920s. In the following decade he also advocated the very opposite of formal precision, harmony and elegant proportion, urging society's artists and art theorists to cultivate the irrational and the imprecise. This new dimension was stimulated by Read's discovery of the celebration of the irrational creative act in Surrealism,[10] besides his own liberation from the Civil Service – first in order to be Professor of Fine Art at Edinburgh University (1931–1932) and subsequently to be Editor of *The Burlington Magazine* (1933–1939). But a prime contributory factor also was his perception of changes taking place in European politics, in particular the rise of aggressive German nationalism. He saw it as no coincidence that this nationalism attempted to eradicate avant-garde art of both Abstract and Surrealist tendencies. It seemed obvious to Read that Communism and Fascism were about to contest for domination of Europe, and that even if Britain were not directly involved individuals at least would be obliged to take sides. Though he recognised the repressive State capitalism that was the Russian reality,[11] Read was prepared to countenance Communism for he saw in it an essence which promised respect for disinterested ideals.

He flirted with philosophical Communism, but was finally dissuaded from close association with this movement because of its antipathy towards all realities of art except the one it had contrived in Social Realism. He was appalled to discover that Communism in Russia, like Fascism in Germany,[12] had stamped out avant-garde art; and his conclusion was that contemporary art had to become active rather than contemplative, partisan rather than disinterested, and subliminal rather than super-evident. In other words, artists and theorists had to adopt a militancy of a sort that was, in the 1930s, most apparent in Surrealism; contemporary aesthetics had to assume less easily victimised forms than those that had fallen victim to Stalinist and Hitlerian doctrines. The most prominent themes of the book he wrote in the heat of this belief were that the greatest art of the past had belonged to communal societies,[13] and that the modern artist, conscious of an ability to transform the world by his or her visions of a new reality, had to become a more consistent Communist than those, so-called, who would compromise with the aesthetic conventions of a last phase of capitalism.[14]

He hesitated to use the term 'anarchism' to describe his preferred culture and politics because of its undesirable connotations of violence. But he came to believe that he had no choice because other concepts were even more tainted. Communism, in its Russian form, opposed individual creativity while shoring up the State and its bureaucracies. Fabianism was unredeemably materialistic. And Socialism was either soulless or soaked in nostalgic mock-mediaevalism. In spite of the fact that he knew he would thus forfeit any serious consideration of his views in Britain,[15] he took the concept 'anarchism' to be the most appropriate encapsulation of his beliefs because it embraced principles of individual freedom, self-determination, and a social framework of common interest groupings, to which he himself added the idea of an avant-garde, agitating on behalf of free creativity.[16]

The fundamental changes in intellectual direction which affected Read at around his fortieth year, persuading him to identify with theoretical anarchism[17] and also to recognise the apparently contradictory claims of Abstraction and Surrealism in avant-garde art, also prompted his critical revision of the formative stages of his own philosophical development. Read recalled that his earliest contact with art had been with avant-garde painting. He had been an utterly conventional nineteen-year-old (conservative, Christian and with bourgeois aspirations) when he had encountered works by Paul Gauguin, Vincent van Gogh, Paul Klee and, particularly, Wassily Kandinsky – in the house where his mother had become housekeeper – and these had so shocked and fascinated him that he had been driven to an equally shocking and subversive literature for explanations. He had read Bergson and Nietzsche, Hegel, Marx and Kropotkin, discovering explanations linking the aesthetic and the sociopolitical. This experience sowed the seeds of those moral and spiritual convictions that would become fully realised in early middle age, and his retrospection on this fact confirmed for him the authority of the aesthetic imperative.

The explanations he had found in philosophy were, he believed, weaker versions of truths perceptible in their most potent forms in the works of art themselves. This initiated a number of subsequently consistent beliefs: human concepts, of all kinds whatsoever, originate *aesthetically* by virtue of insight, and only subsequently percolate through philosophy and other forms of interpretation and use, eventually to become effective upon general life and conduct. Society needs special individuals – members of avant-garde groups – possessing heightened sensibilities necessary for engaging such truths or realities. Ordinary people, too, require some awareness of this process of origination and dissemination. In the short term this was to be provided by Read and others like him – intermediaries between society and its most creative artists. In the longer term, however, interpretation would be largely superfluous, because by virtue of reformed educational practices everyone, in some special way, would be an artist, and comprehension of the work of avant-gardes would be so much the more direct.

As for the avant-gardes themselves: their authentic creativity, though invariably individual in conception, would not be the *property* of individuals. It would be effected by individuals who happened (Read would have said involuntarily) to be the sensitive registers of an evolving intelligence comprising the whole social body. His vision of society required the special creativity of certain accomplished individuals, and also the special creativity latent within everyone, because it would only be by extraordinary means that new aesthetic perceptions might be won on behalf of society as a whole, as a vital aspect of a constant, necessary process of social renewal and reinvigoration.

His concept of the avant-garde was therefore not élitist: it simply referred to the extraordinary insight required to give shape to some value or truth newly perceived or perceived anew. And it referred to a cohort functioning as if it had no choice in the matter, for an occupation demanding constant nervous activity, and erratic fluctuation between achievement and despair, would surely have been the conscious choice of very few. It became Read's vocation to speak for such necessary 'outsiders', those exerting perceptive shaping influence upon the stream of ordinary events they could never join or rejoin, and to attempt to influence some co-ordination of their creative originality. It became a consequent objective to raise the consciousness of ordinary people by means of education through art; and his amused realisation that this was considered subversive (while encouragement of *really* subversive avant-garde art was merely regarded as eccentric) reinforced his inclination to call himself an anarchist.

The Prevailing Condition of Art Education

In what sense did Read's educational beliefs threaten conventional practices? When Read began to take an interest in educational philosophy in the mid-1930s, art education in Great Britain had been stabilised around certain conventional principles for over 50 years. In spite of decentralised authority in matters of curriculum, with responsibility for subject content resting with individual headteachers, the maintenance of standards was effectively in the hands of professional bodies such as the National Society of Art Masters (NSAM) and – to a much lesser degree – the Art Teachers' Guild (ATG). The NSAM was dedicated to the preservation of drawing as an *academic discipline,* and possession of its certificates indicated a teacher's competence both in classical draughtsmanship and in design allied to the industrial arts. The interests of the ATG centred on the specific educational needs of young children; but, largely confined to infant application, they were thus of little threat to a system of drawing education that began seriously when pupils were old enough to apply intellectual rigour to their work.[18]

There was a tacit distinction between the 'higher' discipline of teaching drawing and design and the 'lower' discipline of teaching art. The former was associated with national economic purposes and aspired to academic respectability; the latter connoted 'play' and rather modest learning. The NSAM encouraged its members to pursue high levels of technical accomplishment as measured by its own examination system – the true descendant of a Victorian system of achievement recognition in which the most demanding exercises required months of unremitting attention to the copying, shading and rendering of prescribed images circulated by the Victoria and Albert Museum.[19] The ATG, on the other hand, was much more concerned with tactical approaches necessary for encouraging an essential creativity – an 'originating' activity – in children not specifically destined for an aesthetic way of life. The ATG's referents therefore included theories of child-centred creativity, and it became its prime purpose to propagate the ideas of such as Ebenezer Cooke and Franz Cizek, whose arguments centred on the proposition that art was an aspect of human development, the absence of which impaired mental growth and social fitness. Before the 1930s such beliefs were regarded as peripheral to the main educational tasks of teaching drawing and design, and their attendant practices were considered at best *preparatory* to this mission.

For the values embedded in the NSAM – what may be termed the *classic thesis* of twentieth-century art education – had been confirmed in recommendations for this discipline following the Education Act of 1918. These recommendations affected not only Great Britain but its Dominions and all other countries of Anglo-centric culture. They were the NSAM's initiative, and they comprised an emphasis on drawing (conventional and observational) and design (the realisation of artefacts through practical involvement with materials), the twin features of a specifically modern, industrially-strategic education. The great contemporary enterprise was industrial commercial competition with Germany and France, and it is salutary to note that a universal education in art was its unquestioned cornerstone.

Drawing education was harnessed to the needs of industry and thus directly to conceptions of the *national* wellbeing. *Individual*-centred values could be accommodated to this scheme only if confined to the education of the young child. This was tacitly regarded as the ATG's province: throughout the 1920s and early 1930s this organisation had persevered with a defence of free, spontaneous creativity as both obviously present in the drawings and paintings of young children, and also desirable in continuation beyond adolescence – that is, beyond the stage in an individual's development when 'unstructured' creativity was deemed normally to cease.

Marion Richardson[20] was the champion of this proposal, and her work with young, adolescent and teenage pupils was regarded as proof that inherent, spontaneous creative aptitudes could be protracted beyond their stage of supposed decline. Her approach was based upon stimulation of the pupil's imagination with unconventional teaching, evoking vivid mental images through verbal discourse and cultivation of pictorial memory.[21] Richardson enjoyed the support of theorists such as Roger Fry, who compared the work of her children to that of expressionist avant-garde artists. Such comparisons dignified 'child art' as being in some sense a 'natural' or 'proper' form of creativity – lost in conventional education, and regained only with the greatest difficulty by those few adult artists sufficiently motivated to eliminate intellectual processes from their art-making. This emphasis on individualism, especially in the 1930s when it emerged as an equally well-argued alternative to the conventional, may be regarded as the *romantic antithesis* of twentieth-century art education.

What was thus established by the time Read took an intense interest in the field were (a) an overtly subject-centred system in operation, comprising a 'progression' from individualist art in the earliest years of education, via conventional art and design in the later years, to continuing education and training in tandem with craft trades and industries, and (b) a growing body of theory and practice supporting the proposal that it was precisely the intervention of conventional teaching that extinguished spontaneous creativity in and beyond adolescence.

Read's Philosophy of Education Through Art

Read's interest in child art was at first peripheral to his interpretation of the significance of the avant-garde. In an early engagement of the subject he suggested that more could be learned of the essential nature of art from its origins in the primitive, and its continued rehearsal in childhood imagery, than from its intellectual elaboration in great periods of culture – an elaboration conventionalised in formal education. Children, he wrote, do not distinguish between the ideal (the conventionalised) and the *real.* Child art was to be regarded as an intensification of children's elementary perceptions of the reality of the world around them, which he considered also a paramount purpose of the avant-garde.

However, in this discussion there is no evidence that Read supported the notion of a necessary *continuity* of child and mature creativity. Their common feature he recognised as 'play', which in the adult realm was 'a limited activity:'

> *...confined to special individuals who have special faculties – not of feeling or of thought-but of expression, of objectification.*[22]

In other words, authentic creativity in adults is confined to individuals of particular, pre-logical disposition. This was not, for the time being, to countenance the possibility that all members of the adult community might aspire equally to creative fulfilment.

Instead Read at first seemed to endorse the legitimacy of one kind of educational provision for children who would become 'artists' and another for future artisans and all the rest. It is not difficult to detect Benda's influence in suggestions that society required some external shaping guidance provided by disinterested visionaries, but that there had to be safeguards against a proliferation of visionaries too great to be supported by productive labour. Read argued precisely this case in the first edition of his book *Art and Society*,[23] maintaining that a consequent responsibility of art teachers would be to distinguish between the education of positive, creative capabilities in the few who would be initiators, and the encouragement of taste, discrimination and appreciation in the many who would be consumers. This view accommodated the Freudian conception of the artist as a potential neurotic who had chanced upon ways of evading this fate by expressing what would have been repressed phantasy in plastic form.

One of the most original features of Read's philosophy in its perfected state was the extension of this principle to embrace everyone. The artist is no longer to be regarded as unusual in his or her potential neurosis: modern humanity in general suffers this propensity. In *Education through Art,* published in 1943 (only six years after *Art and Society*) everyone, that is, every child, is said to be a potential neurotic capable of being saved from this prospect if early, largely inborn, creative abilities were not repressed by conventional education. *Everyone* is *an artist of some kind whose special abilities, even if almost insignificant, must be encouraged as contributing to an infinite richness of collective life.* Read's newly-expressed view of an essential *continuity* of child and adult creativity in everyone represented a *synthesis* of the two opposed models of twentieth-century art education that had predominated until this point.

What prompted this change of outlook was Read's direct (more than theoretical) encounter with the work of the very young. In response to his own initiative,[24] he was invited to advise the British Council on a collection of children's art for wartime exhibition overseas. There are two versions of the cause of the profound effect this had upon him, but what is not in doubt is that Read's sudden exposure to great quantities of children's art (at virtually the mid-point of his productive life) persuaded him that here was a socio-aesthetic phenomenon of unparalleled importance. In a memorial tribute shortly after Read's death, written by Alexander Barclay Russell, it is recorded that he, with some difficulty, persuaded Read that the paintings of one of his young pupils were reminiscent of the work of Rouault. Read is said to have recognised an affinity, and thereafter to have taken children's art with the utmost seriousness.[25]

However, Read himself records that in the course of selecting exhibits he came across an image, drawn by a five-year-old girl, which she called *Snake around the World and a Boat.*[26] He was deeply moved, he said, upon immediately recognising this image as a 'mandala', an ancient symbol of psychic unity, universally found in prehistoric and primitive art and in all the principal cultures of history. The child, of course, could not attach meaning to what she had done; but Read, aware for some time of what until now had been merely an interesting hypothesis of Carl Gustav Jung's, was shocked to find phenomenal evidence of archetypal imagery. He then discovered an astonishing consistency in children's art of symbols Jung had associated with community stability, and he also found them replete in the paintings and sculptures of the adult avant-garde.

The most significant of these images, to Read, was the 'mandala', invariably a unified shape, perhaps in the form of a flower or some other fourfold arrangement, with a distinct centre, the appearance of an unfolding, and a gathering perimeter. Especially in Eastern philosophy, though also for example in Christian iconography, these images had been held to symbolise collective thought and mutual belonging. Other archetypes which gave Read shocks of recognition were the tendency to fabricate a 'dark shadow' from aspects of a personality opposed to those personified in the self; and the tendency to protest against isolation, individuation and independence by creating mother images, earth forms and other symbols of dependence.

All of these – a fixing upon abstract unities; a collation of personality traits in externalised forms; the celebration of maternity; an acknowledgement of belonging to the land – all of these projections-beyond-self, Read thought, were fundamentally anarchistic. Manifest in the work of the avant-garde, their purpose was to guide the collective unconscious into normal patterns of aspiration and behaviour and away from those sinister alternatives (mass hysteria, nationalistic pride, dumb subservience to the State) to which the unnatural mode of modern life had left people prone. This remedial function, however, would wither into obsolescence if the self-same imagery, evident in child art generally, could be protracted into adulthood for everyone.

Read's encounter with the archetypal content of child art demanded explication. It was this research, conducted at the University of London in 1941–1942, that resulted in his seminal work *Education through Art,* the central premises of which were:

> *that the general purpose of education is to foster the growth of what is individual in each human being, at the same time harmonising the individuality thus educed with the organic unity of the social group to which the individual belongs.*[27]

The 'organic principle', signifying normal, unhampered development of individual creativity, and a corresponding development of society through collective creative enterprise, was thus adopted as both generator and evaluative principle.

This book provided art education with a rationale, a defence and an optimistic programme. It comprised definitions of authenticity in art and art-making; offered explanations of the materialising of images from the imagination; compared typologies discernible in the literature of psychology and in the study of children's drawings and paintings; and proposed that the *variety* evident within such typologies supported the principle that everyone could be regarded as a special kind of artist. Realisation of this principle obliged Read to revise the relevant passages of future editions of *Art and Society*.[28]

In *Education through Art,* then, the 'organic' principle was deployed in defining 'art' which – reasonably interpreted as 'good form' – could be illuminated by scientific analogy. Good form is perceptible in all manner of natural organisms at microscopic, normal and macroscopic scales, and exhibits such attributes as structural order, elegance, harmony, economy, and dynamic equilibrium – as revealed to Read by the scientific philosophy of D'Arcy Wentworth Thompson.[29]

Objectified in art-making, such properties evince balance, symmetry and rhythm, thus suggesting the comparability of growth in nature and composition in art. But for Read their applicability was not confined to objective art (that is, an art of purely formal relationships). The subjective also respects these principles to the degree that it is *externalised* (objectified) feeling, intuition or emotion; and, Read speculated, the subjective may also tend to formal relationships even when *internalised,* for fantasy and dreaming may be instigated by pathological complexes akin to force systems, and be subject to intrinsic dramatic unities and patterns of organization.[30]

He therefore maintained that a comparability of nature and art extends across the whole range of creative faculties that produce and appreciate art. He presented a digest of psychological research demonstrating the inherent complexity of the human mind especially in its great variety of 'forces', 'impulses' or 'drives', and he suggested correlations between mental types recognised by psychologists, their characteristic impulses, and the sorts of imagery these impulses might manifest.[31] Enough of a consensus was evident for Read to generalise on the basis of his undoubtedly profound knowledge of the avant-garde creative processes he had studied at length – of contemporary artists in great number;[32] of the Surrealists;[33] and of English artists and Europeans working in Britain – particularly Henry Moore, Barbara Hepworth, Ben Nicholson, Paul Nash and Naum Gabo – studies of whom he published retrospectively.[34] He therefore proposed that a distinction of avant-garde creativity as between (1) realism, (2) superrealism, (3) expressionism and (4) constructivism offered a comprehensive categorisation of all evident modes, and that these correlated directly with the psychological functions of (1) thinking, (2) feeling, (3) sensation and (4) intuition.

He was particularly interested in the idea of an impulse-driven emergence of imagery from the subconscious into conscious attention by the reflex coordination of mental, physical and perceptual faculties. Conjoining Freudian and Jungian philosophy, he wrote of the 'calling-up' of images – images with primordial significance – from hidden depths of the mind. This formed theoretical connections between the artist's command of eidetic visualisation (mental evocation or recall of images in vivid detail) and an archetypal significance (deep-seated social and cultural symbolism) that could be divined in the images so evoked. It also associated sociocultural symbolism with modes of creativity that rejected conventional, long-implemented methods of art education, concerned as they were with replication of *given* realities rather than evocation of the *new*.

Ultimately, however, *Education through Art* was received as proof that a number of distinct types of child artist could be identified in education, and a varied diet offered them that would both strengthen their natural affinities and credit their unique achievements. In his study of children's images Read discovered eight distinct categories, all transcending age or stage development. He suggested they corresponded to the four composite categories of mature creativity 'realism: thinking'; 'superrealism: feeling'; 'expressionism: sensation'; and 'constructivism: intuition' – if each of these were considered in both introverted and extroverted modes.[35]

By this means Read constructed a coordinate system that would account for the characteristics of all apparent tendencies in child art. Moreover, this categoric division related directly to tendencies perceptible in the works of mature avant-gardes. The pursuit of authentic avant-garde creativity, Read had long maintained, was so emotionally and nervously demanding that it was the conscious choice of very few. In the adult's realm it was an *obsessional* activity, while paradoxically in the child's realm it manifested the effortlessness of inherited reflex behaviours. This suggested a *normality* of creative identification shared between all children and those adults who would strive to regain pre-logical sensibility. It also suggested a fundamental *abnormality* in what had been considered 'normal' in conventional education, namely the intervention of logical, intellect-dependent education at around the age of ten. If education were to go with the grain of the biological imperative, ways needed to be found of encouraging the perfection and protraction of pre-logical creative states.

Read did not offer a curriculum but a theoretical defence of the genuine and true. His claims for genuineness and truth were based on the overwhelming evidence of characteristics revealed in his study of child art. But they were founded also in speculative extrapolation of a kind that was most welcome during the Second World War (when his ideas received first publication), in the period of reconstruction (when they were recognised in the 1944 Education Act), and in succeeding decades dominated by cold war politics. This extrapolation focused on the apparent fact that authentic creativity was an inherent human necessity. The question was why was it so necessary as to be universally present (though in eight complementary modes) in all children, and potentially present in the citizens they were to become?

Read discovered the answer in social psychology, at the same time confirming his predilection for anarchism and his recognition of profundity in Jung's conception of the archetype. The biological necessity has two aspects – to call up imagery from the subconscious and to externalise it in communicable form – the second of which is *served* by the originating activity and is therefore the more important. He argued that this is not an outpouring for its own sake, nor is it evidence of children conversing with, and confirming, their own individual subconscious experience: it is essentially '*an overture demanding response from others*'.[36] It is thus to be regarded as an integrating activity:

> *a spontaneous reaching-out to the external world, at first tentative, but capable of becoming the main factor in the adjustment of the individual to society.*[37]

This not only establishes art – an authentic, non-intellectualised art – as of profound significance in education, it downgrades all other subjects in the curriculum that are intended to develop *individuation,* or rather maintains that they too may serve *integration* if taught with artistic focus.

The Agencies of 'Education through Art'

When published, Read's philosophy gave new meaning to the work of many thousands of art teachers. Instead of merely assisting technical expertise, recreational skill and consumer discrimination, their role would be to take command of the larger curriculum, and help innate creative abilities survive in an uncongenial world for the sake of individual wellbeing and also for the health of a collective social harmony. The potential for success was evident in Read's observation that children quite naturally give forth imagery which maintains contact with the deepest levels of social experience, and with times when social cohesion was the normal order.

A corollary, which armed the art teachers and explains the enormous, immediate and continued, success of his book was that defects of modern life – injustice, immorality, harsh competition, even war – had roots in prevailing systems of education and, specifically, in an emphasising of intellectual development to the exclusion of everything else, visited upon children from around the age of ten. Because of this the infant with inborn access to ancient, collective experience became a rootless ten-year-old and a centre of self-interest. What the authorities considered to be liberal education was nothing more than systematic repression, the elimination of which would give rise to recovery of individual creative fulfilment, mutual communication and collective social health.

These combined objectives and ambitions disseminated rapidly, but outside Read's direct control – he was not a teacher. While this took place he readdressed his other great purpose, encouragement of the avant-garde, which he could engage directly because of its finer focus. It was of temporary, but no less vital, importance as he saw that avant-garde enterprise had to retain its effectiveness until such times as its forms of creativity would cease to be exceptional. This was the objective which as its first President, he projected into the Institute of Contemporary Arts (ICA) when it was established in London in 1947. The ICA's founding purpose was both propagandist and educational. It brought accomplished artists into contact with those who, as a result, became the next generation of accomplished artists. Ordinary members could tap current creative research at source and effect its dissemination throughout the wider community. It was not a place where art was made, but where the most tentative beginnings of its translation into other forms of thought and action – by exposition, argument and debate – took place.

In effect it was an echo of Read's own formative experience when, as a young man, the shock of unprecedented abstract images had sent him rushing to philosophy. But now the philosophical context had considerably altered: Jung and D. W. Thompson had influenced the present Zeitgeist,[38] and theories of collective mind and organic formation were in the air. Artists, by whose efforts the organisation of society was to be incrementally changed, needed to be alive to such philosophy, the full range of aesthetic principles which had nurtured it, and its ramifications for a cross-section of human understanding. Thus the ICA embraced a comprehensive spectrum of avant-garde art, including Abstraction, Surrealism, and every shade or tendency between them;[39] and it also provided a forum for advanced scientific philosophy, as well as the latest researches in sociology, anthropology and other disciplines. It was in Read's special sense an anarchist cell, an organic community dedicated to the constant revision and reinvigoration of its essential values, and to the integration of diverse interests meeting in the common sphere of art.

But while Read took direct action in relation to the avant-garde, his general educational philosophy – spread by means of his lecture tours but principally through his writings – affected practices throughout the world. *Education through Art* was translated into over 30 languages and is still regarded as a seminal text in countries as diverse as Egypt, Brazil and Japan. Dissemination relied upon remote conviction, but in Britain was assisted by the popularisation of Read's ideas through cheap pamphlets. In one of these[40] he acknowledged his belonging to a tradition first given authoritative shape by Plato, simplified Platonic theory for popular consumption, sketched out a strategy for building an authentic communal culture by perfecting parent-child, teacher-child and individual-group relationships, and argued against the curbing of schools' freedom to determine curricula appropriate to localised circumstances.

Yet there was also within Read's scope a form of direct influence on national and supranational institutions. From 1946 until his death in 1968 he was President of the Society for Education in Art (SEA), the renamed ATG, in which capacity he had a platform for addressing UNESCO. He was extremely welcoming of policies expressed at UNESCO's launching conference in 1946 – policies devoted to the cultivation of worldwide understanding through education, and the elimination of international conflict at the point of its normal origination, mutual ignorance – but he was nevertheless critical of an automatic reliance on conventional modes of education, and a perceived confusion of culture with learning, education with propaganda.

In a lecture at the Museum of Modern Art, New York (timed to coincide with a sitting of the United Nations) he delivered a devastating critique of attempts to prevent war with card-indexes and documentary films.[41] He argued that UNESCO's desired moral revolution could not be secured by arguments addressed to minds corrupted with individuated intellectualisation: a moral revolution required the total reorientation of the human personality, which could only be secured by integrative education. On the basis of such representation Read, with others, succeeded in establishing the International Society for Education through Art (InSEA) as an executive arm of UNESCO in 1954.

No doubt the most compelling argument he proposed to UNESCO was that art provides the best prospect of an international medium of cultural exchange and understanding, for the otherwise-comparable internationalism of science is always to be confounded by national interests. While almost all other enterprises are intended to address the removal of barriers – of sovereignty, custom, language or trade – the visual arts know no such barriers. They constitute:

> *a language of symbols that communicates a meaning without hindrance from country to country across the centuries.*[42]

This posthumously published assertion has continued to be the cornerstone of InSEA philosophy until the present day. But it has required of officialdom a remarkable investment in faith, for what Read proposed was not a means of transforming states of mind by propaganda.

Education through art is in effect a reverse propaganda, for it begins with the felt truth which is then expressed as symbol – the feeling finds its equivalent in a plastic image.[43] Images originate in collective experience and create correspondences in shared realities: the social bond is rehearsed and reinforced. That a virtual metaphysics should frame a supranational programme is evidence of its conviction and sincerity.

So we must begin with small things, in diverse ways, helping one another, discovering one's own peace of mind, waiting for the understanding that flashes from one peaceful mind to another. In that way the separate cells will take shape, will be joined to one another, will manifest new forms of social organisation and new types of art. From that multiplicity and diversity, that dynamic interplay and emulation, a new culture may arise, and mankind be united as never before in the consciousness of a common destiny.[44]

Originally published in the Journal of Art & Design Education, *Volume 12: 2, 1993.*

Footnote

This is a modified version of a contribution on Herbert Read to the publication: Tedesco, J. C. & Morsy, Z. (Eds.), *Thinkers of Education,* Paris, UNESCO, a collection of critical appreciations of the world's great educationalists and educational philosophers.

Notes and References

1. See Thistlewood, D. (1984), *Herbert Read: Formlessness and Form; an Introduction to his Aesthetics,* London: Routledge & Kegan Paul.
2. Read, H. (1943), *Education through Art*, London: Faber & Faber.
3. Read, H. (1944), *The Education of Free Men*, London: Freedom Press.
4. Read, H. (1948), *Culture and Education in a World Order*, New York: Museum of Modern Art.
5. Read, H. (1955), *The Grass Roots of Art,* London: Faber & Faber.
6. Read, H. (1970), *Redemption of the Robot,* London: Faber & Faber.
7. See Pedrosa, S. G. (1993), 'The Influence of English Art Education upon Brazilian Art Education from 1941', unpublished Ph.D. thesis, University of Central England, Birmingham, esp. pp. 139-49, 370 *et seq.*
8. Benda, J. (1928), *La Trahison des Clercs;* translated by Richard Aldington as *The Great Betrayal,* London: Routledge.
9. Hulme, T. E. (1924), *Speculations,* edited by Herbert Read, London: Kegan Paul.
10. See Read, H. (Ed.) (1936), *Surrealism,* London: Faber & Faber.
11. Read, H. (1937), *Art and Society,* London: Heinemann, pp. 266–73.
12. Read (along with Kenneth Clark, Cyril Norwood, Pablo Picasso, Michael Sadler, Julian Huxley and H. G. Wells) was a member of the organising committee that brought the so-called *'Degenerate' German Art* exhibition to London in 1938. Intended by the German authorities as a propaganda against approved culture and ethnicity, this exhibition was in fact substantially responsible for stimulating paradigms of Modernism that helped defend and explicate its various forms.
13. *Ibid.* n. 11, esp. pp. 1–73.
14. *Ibid.* esp. pp. 321–76.
15. Read, H. (1940), *Annals of Innocence and Experience*, London: Faber & Faber, p. 136.
16. See Read, H. (1938), *Poetry and Anarchism,* London: Faber & Faber; Read, H. (1954), *Anarchy and Order*, London: Faber & Faber; and Read, H. (1968), *The Cult of Sincerity,* London: Faber & Faber, pp. 76–93.
17. Woodcock, G. (1972), *Herbert Read: the Stream and the Source,* London: Faber & Faber.
18. See Thistlewood, D. (1988), 'The early history of the NSEAD; the Society of Art Masters (1888–1909) and the National Society of Art Masters (1909–1944)' *Journal of Art and Design Education,* 7: 1, pp. 37–64. (See Chapter 7 of this book). See also Thistlewood, D. (1989), 'The

formation of the NSEAD: a dialectical advance for British art and design education' *Journal of Art and Design Education*, 8: 2, pp. 135–152.

19. See Macdonald, S. (1970), *The History and Philosophy of Art Education,* London: London University Press.

20. See Richardson, M. (1948), *Art and the Child*, London: London University Press.

21. Macdonald (n. 19) pp. 320–354.

22. Read, H. (1933), *Art Now,* London: Faber & Faber, p. 47.

23. *Op. cit.* (1937), pp. 221–23.

24. 'On the suggestion of the well known art critic Mr. Herbert Read, the British Council is considering the possibility of organising an Exhibition of Adolescent Art, on the lines of the one held last spring at the St Martin's School. The proposal would be to send the collection to America and the Dominions for a series of exhibitions in various important centres... Mr. Barclay Russell... is also being invited to serve...' Letter dated 24 October 1940 from Mr Alfred A. Longden, Secretary of the Fine Arts Committee of the British Council, to the Secretary of the Art Teachers Guild. (NSEAD archives). In the event, two exhibitions were organised – one for North America and the other for South America.

25. Barclay Russell, A. (1968–69), 'Sir Herbert Read', in: *Athene: Sir Herbert Read Memorial Issue,* 14: 1, pp. 4–11, p. 8. Barclay Russell maintains that the St Martin's school initiative was his, that he persuaded the British Council to commission Read to select the exhibits, and that Read's 'conversion' took place during extended discussions with Barclay Russell prior to Read's agreeing to accept the British Council's invitation. It is not inconceivable, therefore that Read was first primed by the Rouault phenomenon and later moved profoundly by the mandala phenomenon.

26. Read (n. 2) p. 187. See also Read: *The Cult of Sincerity* (n. 16) pp. 44–5.

27. Read (n. 2) p. 8.

28. Read, H. (1945), *Art and Society* (2nd Edn.), London: Faber & Faber, p. 107.

29. Thompson, D. W. (1942), *On Growth and Form*, Cambridge: Cambridge University Press. See Read (n. 2) pp. 18–19.

30. Read (n. 2) p. 32.

31. *Ibid.* p. 28.

32. Read (11.22).

33. Read (n. l0).

34. Read, H. (l952), *The Philosophy of Modern Art*, London: Faber & Faber.

35. Read (n. 2) p. 145.

36. Read (n. 2) p. 164, quoting Suttie, I. D. (1935), *The Origins of Love and Hate,* London: London University Press.

37. Read (n. 2) pp. 164–165.

38. See Thistlewod, D. (1982), 'Organic art and the popularisation of a scientific philosophy' *British Journal of Aesthetics,* 22: 4; pp. 311–32l.

39. See Thistlewod, D. (1989), 'The Museum of Modem Art, New York, and the London Institute of Contemporary Arts: a common philosophy of modem art' *British Journal of Aesthetics,* 29: 4, pp. 316–328.

40. Read (n. 3).

41. Read (n. 4).

42. Read (n. 6) pp. 233–254.

43. Read (n. 5) pp. 88–89.

44. Read (n. 4) p. 15.

Chapter 12: Basic Design and the Pedagogy of Richard Hamilton

Richard Yeomans

A Society for Education through Art (SEA) conference on 'Adolescent Expression in Art and Craft' held at Bretton Hall in 1956 highlighted some of the immense divisions in the art educational world brought about by the advent of the so-called 'Basic Design' movement.[1] The contributions at the conference, and the attitudes expressed by Harry Thubron, Tom Hudson and Maurice de Sausmarez, represented a radical challenge which cut against the grain of many cherished educational values and assumptions. The divisions at the conference were complex and it would be wrong simply to describe it as a clash between progressive and reactionary forces, because many of those who opposed the forthright views of Harry Thubron and Tom Hudson were sensitive and enlightened teachers. In many ways, as Herbert Read pointed out in the final discussion, the very assumptions underlying the title of the conference, 'Adolescent Expression in Art and Craft' were challenged. Intuition and expression, which had formed the bedrock of much liberal art educational thinking, were brought into question and found wanting as the sole basis for the future demands of art education. The roles of the traditional crafts were equally scrutinised and their relevance and compatability to the world of science and technology examined. Many of the expressed values which dominated the first two days of the conference, particularly the child centred model with its emphasis on expression, feeling, inner development and nurture, seemed blasted by a cold air of rational modernism. Barclay Russell spoke of intuition as the origin of all expression in art and rejected 'conscious logical processes of mind' as playing any part in the act of creation.[2] Veronica Zabel spoke in almost mystical terms of the work of her girls 'who, like beauty itself remain mysterious and (fortunately perhaps) beyond all explaining'.[3]

In contrast, Harry Thubron projected a hard modernism arguing that art should address the modern world of science and technology and jettison any woolliness of thought which sustained the 'romantic isolation of the artist'. He argued that while the role of the painter was central, he must not occupy an isolated position and should be in touch with and open to the wider world of design. Thubron emphasised 'increased professionalism' and the preparation of students for the 'rigours' of their calling. He suggested that pupils in secondary schools should be allowed to work creatively with tools and advanced machinery, and from the evidence of the work which Thubron had done with the pupils of New Earswick Secondary Modern School near York, there was a decisive shift away from traditional crafts towards new materials and a Constructivist mode of thinking.

Thubron stated that he was developing an experimental approach to art teaching which frequently employed the exploration of material as a starting point and which was also concerned with the investigation of a visual language that was complementary to the figurative tradition. Unlike Victor Pasmore, Thubron did not state that his work was concerned with objective abstract values, but formal concerns with colour and shape were indicated as the starting point of much of his teaching. More significantly, and in opposition to previously-stated views, he went on to say that many adolescents needed a rational basis on which to build and develop, having 'outgrown the emotive and expressionist forms so admirably developed by Marion Richardson'.[4] He then stated that 'the emotive expressive age ends at seven or thereabouts, and must be followed by a more intellectual conception'. Although the rational and intellectual aspects of creativity were stressed, Thubron argued that it was only within a more rational and experimental framework that the role of the intuition could be freed.

Maurice de Sausmarez argued that there was an imbalance in much art teaching and that all the faculties, including the intellect should be developed:

> *There is in art theory today a thinly disguised conspiracy against intelligence, resulting from an arbitrary splitting of consciousness into intuition and intellect as though they were mutually exclusive, instead of inseparable... the denigration of intelligence has serious consequences in art education, showing fully at adolescence.*[5]

He went on to suggest that the crisis in confidence which besets adolescents is the result of their acquired logical and critical faculties casting doubt on their ability to measure up to their perception of adult standards. Those very logical and critical faculties needed to be developed and harnessed with intuition in order to allow the adolescent to break through the impasse and reach adulthood. Victor Pasmore, Harry Thubron, Tom Hudson and Maurice de Sausmarez were consistent in suggesting that free expression had played a vital role in fostering creativity in the primary school, but all agreed that at the adolescent and adult stages, a more objective and rational approach was necessary.

The following year another SEA conference was convened, with an accompanying exhibition at the Royal Festival Hall, entitled 'Basic Form'. This consisted of work by students of Victor and Wendy Pasmore, Harry Thubron and Tom Hudson. The publicity statement proclaimed that:

> *The development of a new process of art teaching on purely emotional and intuitive levels has already been established in infant schools with successful results. However, the need for extension on the rational plane of the adolescent and adult is now necessary.*[6]

It was this extension on the rational and intellectual plane, putting art education to the service of the mind, which most characterised the pedagogy of Richard Hamilton.

Richard Hamilton's first attempts to introduce radical changes in art educational thinking had occurred at the Central School of Arts and Crafts where a number of major figures, including Eduardo Paolozzi, William Turnbull, Victor Pasmore, Alan Davie, Patrick Heron, Nigel Henderson and several members of the newly formed and influential Independent Group were teaching part-time. Radical educational changes were taking place there, but it was on an ad hoc basis and the nature of the part-time teaching prevented a clear unified educational philosophy from emerging. It was not until Victor Pasmore and Richard Hamilton joined forces at Newcastle University in 1954 that a new, programmed course was possible. Even so, there were great differences, and it is remarkable that any degree of consensus and collaboration was possible between two artists who were advancing opposed positions in respect of abstraction and figuration in their own work. Pasmore's teaching was totally concerned with formal and abstract values and he was primarily interested in establishing some objective basis for abstract art. He frequently referred to his course as an abstract foundation course. Nevertheless, Pasmore recognised that Hamilton had already established new thinking in his teaching within the Design School of the Department of Fine Art, and brought him in, along with Geoffrey Dudley of the Sculpture School, to broaden the scope of the emerging course. When Pasmore left Newcastle in 1961, Hamilton took over the foundation course and transformed and extended it from the dominantly abstract base which Pasmore had established. With the exception of joint exhibitions, such as 'The Developing Process' held at the Institute of Contemporary Arts in 1959, Hamilton was not involved in collaborative projects. His contribution to Basic Design thinking was distinctly his own, but like many of the others it sprang mainly from his own creative interests and commitments. However, there were certain shared attitudes which link the group.

The Basic Design movement was as diverse as the people involved, but two essential points which emerge from the Bretton Hall conference need to be considered in relation to Richard Hamilton's position. One was the necessity for a more rational and objective approach to art teaching, and the other was the need to embrace and affirm the modern world along with its science and technology. On the issue of objectivity in teaching, Richard Hamilton was to take an uncompromising and extreme position in his total rejection of self-expression. In an interview with Richard Willing, Hamilton discussed the work of Tomas Maldonado at the *Hochschule für Gestaltung* at Ulm, and said that what interested him most about the school was the rational method of the pedagogy and the exclusion of self-expression. For Hamilton, the adult student was beyond the need of self-expression, and its nurturing in higher education was a misapplication of Montessori in the adult realm.

In the same interview he stated that the teacher must eradicate preconception, and the worst preconception of all was the notion that art was only something you feel, rather than something you think about. The whole thrust of Hamilton's teaching was towards training the mind and teaching students to think. He described his approach as deductive, and concerned with:

> *...the development of practical disciplines which will promote orderly logical modes of thought – the ability to analyse action already taken, to make deductions about a future course of action and to draw conclusions from the final product which projects a further series of self-directed acts.*[7]

The approach was analytical, looking at various internal processes and procedures in an open-ended and experimental manner which precluded any predetermined outcome. He felt that too many art schools were propagating styles, like the Euston Road style, and deplored any teaching which offered ready made formulas. Hamilton's view was that you could analyse the 'grammar' and 'syntax' of art, but the onus was on the student ultimately to decide how he would use it and what he would say with it.

Such terms as the 'grammar', 'syntax' and 'vocabulary' of art, much employed by those involved in Basic Design teaching, have to be accepted as working metaphors, indicating that there are underlying forms and structures which are susceptible to analysis. The formal elements, as the course evolved, broadly fit into the categories of 'point', 'line', 'shape', 'shape relationship', 'positive and negative', 'area division', 'space filling', 'surface developments' and 'colour'. These were investigated in two and three dimensions, and as the course changed under Hamilton, other categories were added including, 'perception and illusion', 'transformation and projection', 'sign and situation', 'image', and 'the analytical project'.

The groundwork for the study of formal elements had been laid by Victor Pasmore, and when Richard Hamilton assumed responsibility for the Foundation Course in 1961, much of this content was retained. The main difference between the teaching of Pasmore and Hamilton, with regard to formal analysis, was that Pasmore asked his students to investigate forms independently and dissociated from the natural world. Pasmore felt that the student should take his cue from the palette, from the autonomy of the marks created rather than from observed phenomena, whereas Hamilton encouraged a balance between observation, invention and free composition. A line could be observed from the convolutions of string (Fig. 1), or the twist of wire, or from the contours of the life model, as well as being composed in an abstract, architectural or melodic way. The exploration of point groupings would begin in a very elemental way, observing how one point placed off centre on a square may destabilise space and prompt a further action which in turn will create another relationship. As the points accumulate on the surface, new directions and axes are formed which create lines (Fig. 2), and as the density increases, shapes and masses occur.

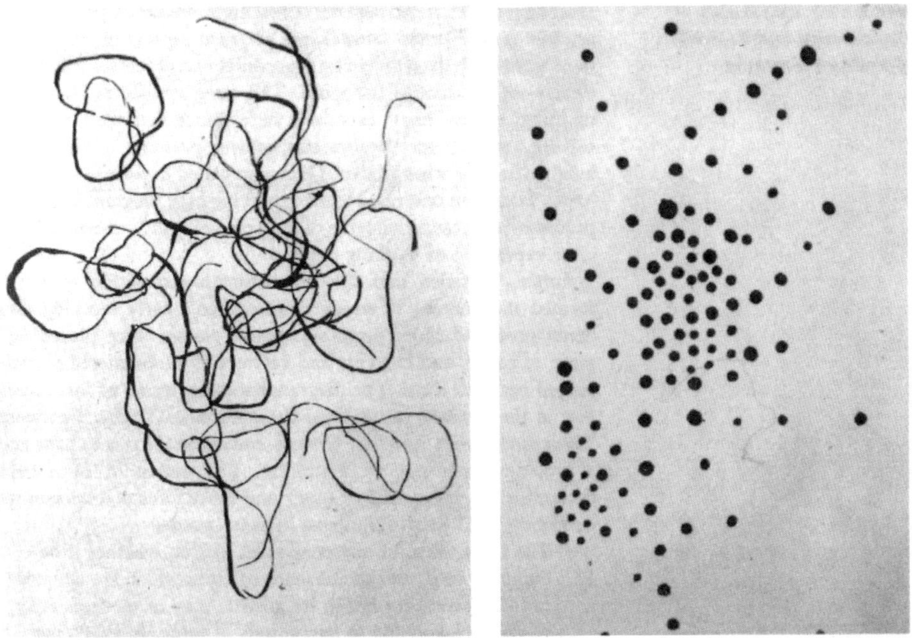

Figs. 1 and 2.

It was very much an exercise concerned with going back to first principles, investigating the simple art of mark making. In 1950, Hamilton began a number of paintings including *Induction* and *Chromatic Spiral* which were concerned with these very factors, and most of his teaching can only be understood within the context of his own creativity and those ideals and influences which came to bear on it. Another example in the point grouping exercises concerned the element of chance, where students would trace and plot configurations based on the throw of drawing pins, matchsticks, darts and dice, or mark the number of times that a given letter appeared in a piece of newsprint. These researches into the role of chance in art stem very much from Hamilton's interests in Dada and Surrealism and the work of Marcel Duchamp in particular. Duchamp's chance procedures in *The Large Glass,* such as the nine cannon shots produced by paint-dipped matchsticks fired from a toy cannon, or the subjection of absolute forms and measurements, like the metre, or the squares of gauze, to the vagaries of wind and air currents, provided the context for many of these ideas.

Marcel Duchamp, who argued that 'art should be put to the service of the mind',[8] is central to any understanding of Hamilton's own work and teaching, and explains the cerebral nature of his approach. Both artists manifest an intellectual rigour in their work, and both stand out against formalist modernism. In the fifties, when the avant-garde in Britain was strongly linked to abstraction, Hamilton presented something of a challenge by pointing towards literary, historical, epic, mythological, legendary and anecdotal possibilities, which had long been disparaged and denigrated in the visual arts. Duchamp and Hamilton not only presented a literary and intellectual art, but both rejected sensual and physical aspects of art, wishing their work to be determined by procedures and processes which were clearly the product of the mind. The same applied to Hamilton's teaching where many exercises were concerned with problem-solving, which specifically suppressed personal style, touch, handwriting, or what Marcel Duchamp called *la patte* - the artist's 'paw'. Hamilton described a good drawing as a 'diagram of thought processes' suggesting a degree of impersonality in its execution and a clear exposition of working method.

Points, particles, and the diagrammatic exposition of forces, formed the content of much of Hamilton's early teaching. Students produced 'flow diagrams', where shapes were placed on a piece of paper, and currents and vortices of unobstructed particles surged between them. The diagrammatic exposition of force manifest in these works stems from the naturalist D'Arcy Wentworth Thompson whose book *On Growth and Form*[9] was to have such a profound influence on Hamilton. The notion of form being determined by the action of outer and inner force and tension was described by D'Arcy Thompson in these words:

> *The form, then, of any portion of matter, whether it be living or dead, and the changes of form which are apparent in the movements and in its growth, may in all cases alike, be described as due to the actions of force. In short, the form of an object is a 'diagram of forces', in this sense, at least, that from it we can deduce the forces that are acting or have acted upon it...*[10]

The causative relationship between form and function, and the inherent beauty of nature's processes, revealed in D'Arcy Thompson, was to provide a model for artist and teacher. In his introduction to *On Growth and Form* D'Arcy Thompson suggested that the immediate concern of the naturalist is to consider the causes, effects and mechanism of nature, and postpone consideration of universal truth, or teleological preoccupation with final causes. It is a mode of thinking which puts preconception to one side, concentrates on the analysis of process and activity and seeks to penetrate the inner structure of the natural world. *On Growth and Form* was first published in 1917 and it is no coincidence that his perception of the natural world as a dynamic and changing entity should find its parallels in the atomised world of Seurat and the open, dynamic spatial continuums of Cubism and Futurism.

The most explicit example of this in Hamilton's Foundation Course can be seen in a number of exercises concerning ideas about transformation and projection. The source of these ideas can be found in the celebrated chapter in D'Arcy Thompson entitled, 'On the Theory of Transformation, or the Comparison of Related Forms'. Here D'Arcy Thompson put forward a method of co-ordinates, by means of which certain variations of a particular type of organism, such as a skull, could be related by grid deformation (Fig. 3). In so doing, the regular grid underwent a process of transformation in order to fit the shape of the related form, taking account of changes of proportion, length, breadth, axis and direction. It was the alteration and deformation of the Cartesian grids which defined in precise, and often dramatic terms, the changes and subtle shifts of emphasis from one form to another. Perhaps the importance of these diagrams of transformation for the artist and art student was the way they demonstrated the relativity of form. Rather than defining form, the grids mapped the change of form, thus paralleling in scientific terms those artists and movements, such as Monet, Degas, Muybridge, Marey, Cubism, Futurism and Duchamp, that had been preoccupied with delineating the processes of change.

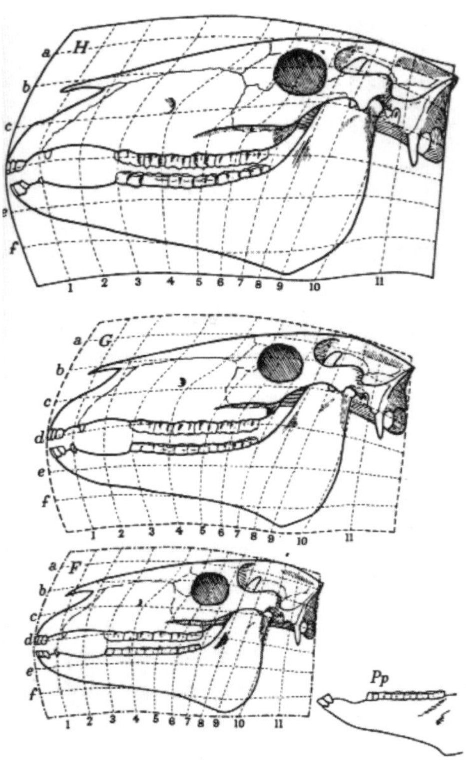

Fig. 3: Transformation of Skull of Hyracotherium, *in THOMPSON, D.W:* On Growth and Form *(1917) 1962; Reproduced by courtesy of Cambridge. U. P.*

The visual realisation of some of these ideas in Hamilton's Foundation Course did not always match the profundity of the source and this can be said for other aspects of the course. Sometimes the idea was explored in purely abstract terms as, for example, where a circle may transform into a square in a fairly systematic way. This links with Hamilton's interests in the chronophotography of Muybridge and Marey, and with the work of the perceptual psychologist J. J. Gibson, who in his book *The Perception of the Visual World*,[11] described our vision as a continuous reception of form through a series of projections, transformations and deformations. The theme of transformation and projection was extended into ideas concerning perspective and shadow projection. Many of these ideas had been explored in Hamilton's painting of the early fifties in such works as *After Muybridge* and *re Nude*. Ideas concerning perspective, shadows, and notions of the projection of two, three and four-dimensional forms are also found in Marcel Duchamp. These ideas were applied in the life room where grids were projected onto the model which paradoxically both revealed and destroyed the form. Other explorations of this idea might simply have observed the deformation of stripes on a football jersey, or sequential drawings of objects undergoing change, like crumpled milk cartons, or the ubiquitous crushed Coke can referred to by Alan Simpson in the *Journal of Art & Design Education*, 6: 3, 1987.

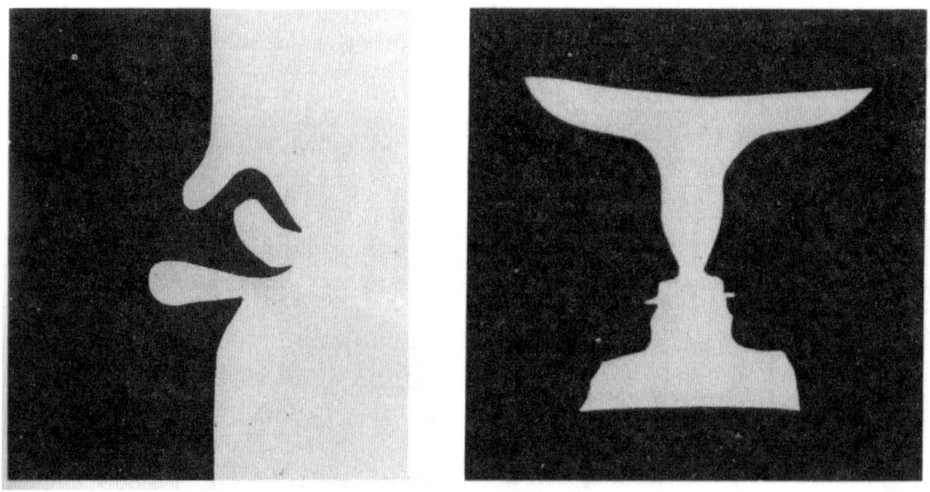

Figs. 4 and 5.

In his own work and teaching Hamilton had been concerned not only with what we observe in the natural and man-made world, but with how we perceive it. In his own thinking and within the wider context of the Independent Group, he had studied the work of the Gestalt psychologists. Edgar Rubin's 'Claw' (Fig. 4) had appeared in the tableau created by Hamilton for the exhibition *This is Tomorrow* held at the Whitechapel Gallery in 1956, where a part of the imagery had been concerned with perception. Gestalt psychologists like Rudolph Arnheim had contributed to the publication *Aspects of Form*[12] which was the outcome of the symposium held in association with Hamilton's *Growth and Form* exhibition at the ICA in 1951. Rubin's 'Claw' and the more celebrated image of the 'Vase-Face' (Fig. 5) are demonstrations of ambiguities in visual perception, and the whole problem of figure and ground and the equation of positive and negative images formed the basis of an important Foundation Course exercise.

The positive-negative exercises were essentially pictorial problems concerned with the balance of shapes in such a way that no form took precedence or dominated the field. These were design exercises where the problems were essentially compositional and could be usefully applied to screen printing and repeat patterns (Fig. 6). The emphasis was on how we read pattern, but there was a conceptual dimension to the positive-negative exercises which related to Duchamp's notion that objects and forms can be signified by their opposite or negative manifestations. Duchamp's work was also concerned with optics, perceptual conundrums and visual ambiguities concerned with perception and illusion. Duchamp and the Gestalt psychologists made their contributions to Hamilton's thinking, but probably the man whose observations squared most with Hamilton's experience was the American perceptual psychologist J. J. Gibson, author of the book already mentioned.

Gibson, who had researched the problems of depth and motion perspective during the war, when he was engaged on the problems of landing aircraft on aircraft carriers, provided a lucid account of the dynamics of visual perception, explaining how we perceive the world through an infinite multiplicity of projections received by the constant scanning movements of the eye. If the constitution of the world is essentially dynamic, Gibson explained, so are the mechanics of our perception of that world. The influence of Gibson on Richard Hamilton's own painting can be seen in 'Trainsition IIII' painted in 1954. This picture is about motion perspective and is almost a diagrammatic exposition of some of the phenomena dealt with in chapter seven of Gibson's book. It describes the sensation of travelling on a train and the experience of differing rates of velocity observed between foreground and background. Gibson's observations provide the context for some of the ideas Hamilton introduced in that section of the Foundation Course dealing with perception and illusion. Figure 7, for example, is very similar to some of Gibson's diagrams dealing with the gradient of textural elements. Most exercises were investigations of depth perception and colour advance and recession. Diagrams were produced in which forms presented in linear

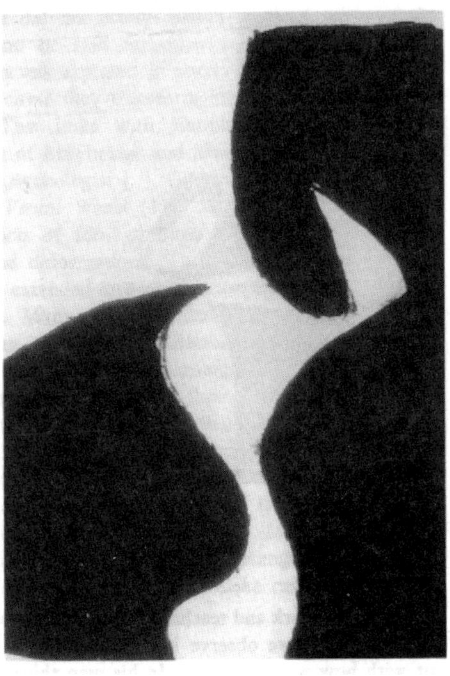

Fig. 6.

perspective were contradicted by the advance and recession of applied warm and cold colours. As all colours have tonal values, students considered the problems of whether colour denotes depth by virtue of hue, intensity, tonality, or by a combination of several of these factors. The dominant preoccupation with ambiguity and contradiction was in some respects an extension of the positive-negative idea and a recognition that the strongest visual images are at root paradoxical.

These perceptual problems overlapped with the colour project where warm, cold, complementary and discordant factors were studied. Most students were required to make a colour wheel and Hamilton would deal with perception and optics.

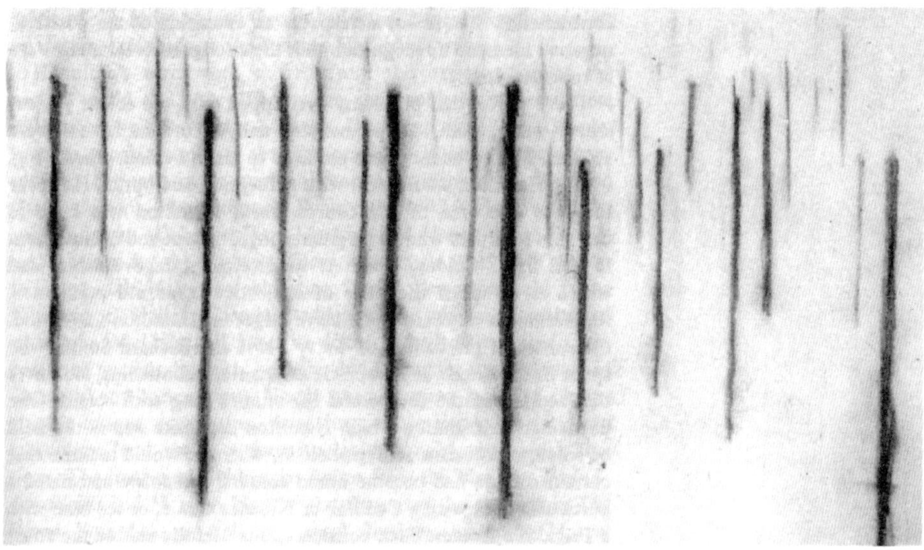

Fig. 7.

However this was one area of the course which Hamilton was keen to delegate to artists who had a greater involvement and commitment to the field. Colour, which is intellectually ungovernable, and which is so much the prey of subjective taste and preference, represented a wayward and elusive target for Hamilton's attention. Colourists of the calibre of Terry Frost and Richard Smith, who spent brief periods at Newcastle on visiting fellowships, took over that section of the course and the studios sang with colour. One particular contribution that Hamilton did make was in the field of colour association and symbolism, where he would indicate that certain colours had become brand colours, and so we associated a particular pink with a Cadillac or Kleenex tissue, or ice-blue with a Frigidaire freezer. Such considerations usefully shifted the study of colour from the abstract and optical domain to the realm of object and artefact. In similar vein, Hamilton's semiological interests prompted a series of exercises on signs and symbols which helped to bridge the gap between abstract form and the figurative world.

Although much of Hamilton's course relates to his own interests and creative concerns, he did as far as possible distance his own work from his teaching. Invariably the examples which were put to students were outside the realm of art, often in the field of science and technology. Hamilton's first links with the scientific world occurred when he was a student at the Slade, when he collaborated with a group of leading scientists including J. D. Bernal, Jacob Bronowski, Peter Medawar, Joseph Needham and C. H. Waddington, for the preparation of the '*Growth and Form*' exhibition held at the ICA in 1951. Bringing art and science together, and widening the content of art had been a major preoccupation of the Independent Group. William Turnbull described the situation at the Slade where the content of sculpture was narrowly perceived as the human figure, reclining, seated, standing or on horseback.[13] He and Eduardo Paolozzi attempted to show that sculpture could be about landscape, or draw its inspiration from technology, astronomy, microscopy, literature and a host of other things. The Independent Group which discussed such disparate topics as advertising, science fiction, information theory, helicopter engineering, popular music, *Tom and Jerry,* and logical positivism, were concerned with art coming to terms with the modern world, as well as scattering all kinds of subject possibilities for the artist. The Independent Group's affirmation of the modern world was in sharp contrast to the mystical, introverted spirit of much Neo-Romantic art of the time. In many respects the contrast between Neo-Romantic introversion and sensibility, and the outward-going spirit of the Independent Group reflected those differences in art educational thinking at the Bretton Hall conference.

Hamilton's own work shifted from the investigation of the natural world of D'Arcy Thompson, and problems of perception, influenced by Muybridge, Marey, Duchamp and J. J. Gibson, towards considerations of the man-made world and contemporary society. The man-made world of machines, inspired by Siegfried Giedion's book *Mechanisation Takes Command*[14] provided the subject for the exhibition *Man, Machine and Motion* which Hamilton designed for the Hatton Gallery, Newcastle in 1955. This was followed in 1956 by the exhibition *This is Tomorrow* held at the Whitechapel Gallery, London, where in his tableau, constructed with John McHale and John Voelcker, Hamilton itemised categories of current interest, broadly divided under the headings of 'imagery' and 'perception'. Under imagery were included photographic images, advertising, journalism, television, styling and sex symbolism, and under perception, colour, light and visual illusions. The images of Robbie the Robot from the film *The Forbidden Planet* and Marilyn Monroe standing over the air vent in *The Seven Year Itch,* as well as optical illusions, including Marcel Duchamp's 'Rotoreliefs', prophetically spelt out the content of future Pop and Op Art, as well as indicating a range of ideas which would influence the content of his own work and the developing foundation course.

The impact of this imagery from the wider world can be seen in the 'image' projects in the Foundation Course where we observe a distinct move from formal to figurative concerns. Image was broadly divided between 'invented' and 'selected' images. 'Invented' imagery consisted of head images made of collage and assemblage, and the idea almost certainly stemmed from imagery explored by Nigel Henderson, Eduardo Paolozzi, and to some extent Picasso. Hamilton was interested in the way in which any roughly spherical or oval shape, once anchored to a base, immediately assumes a head identity in our perception. Head images made up of collage taken from colour magazines suggested all manner of visual punning and metaphor. Collage was no longer concerned with qualities of colour and texture, but with the free association of ideas in the Dada and Surrealist mould. Because of the nature of much of the source material in colour magazines, these images do reflect the Pop world which indirectly fostered them. It is only with regard to this part of the course, that one can determine the Pop influence of Richard Hamilton, and this was due more to the nature of the source material than any specific Pop ideas which he was communicating. Hamilton was not interested in imposing Pop images on his students. The three-dimensional realisation of these ideas demonstrate a firmer root in Dada and Surrealism, rather than Pop. (Fig. 8)

'Selected' images were mainly concerned with the idea of the transformation of form by a process of selection and enlargement. This originally began as an extension of collage investigation beyond the confines of the limited scale of colour magazines. A number of students would prevail on a local advertising agency and

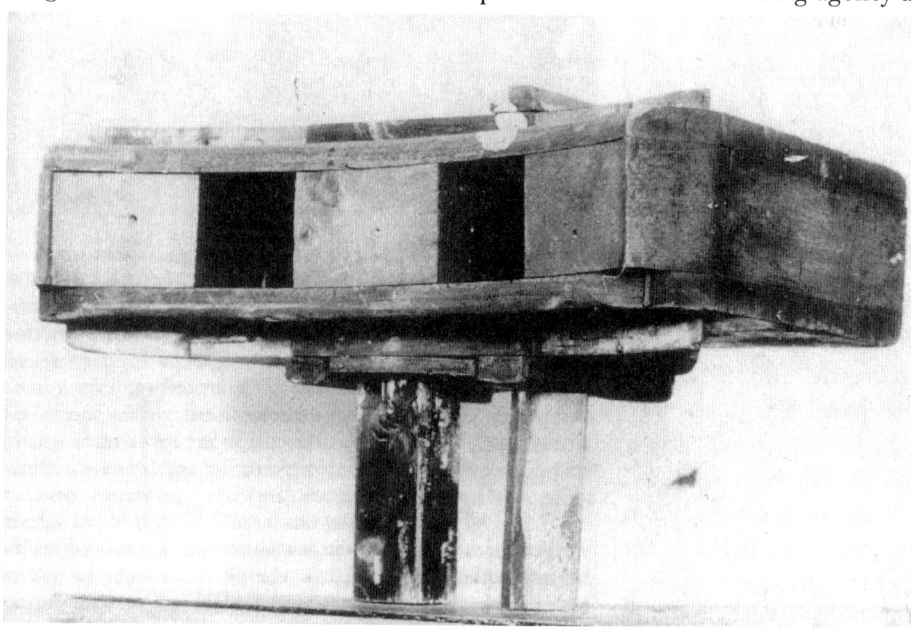

Fig. 8.

bring in large fragments of billboard posters which dramatically transformed the studio environment. The changed context of these huge fragments of billboard imagery in the confined studio space, produced a disquieting effect on the spectator, where food adverts, in particular, assumed a menacing and sinister aspect. Many common objects blown up to such a scale lost their identity completely. Enlargement revealed the inner landscape of the object and the character of the marks which constituted the image. The *pointillist* nature of dots which make up the image brings us full circle back to the point exercises, and other researches which Hamilton was making into the grainy marks which make up a photographic image and how we infer meaning from elementary visual data. From a few indeterminate grainy marks we infer meaningful patterns and images, thus endorsing the Gestalt theory of the brain's capacity to seize the pattern and grasp the whole. In such a manner, Hamilton was able to extend this exercise into the field of perception.

The final term of the Foundation Course was given over to analytical drawing, painting and sculpture, which normally took the form of object analysis. The students were asked to select an object which had a particular meaning and interest for them. The notion of object was applied liberally, to such categories as the cricket match, cuckoo clocks, artificial limbs, toothpaste tubes, lemon squeezers and Charlie Chaplin's trousers. Most of the analytical drawings which survive reflect a certain preference for a clear mechanistic and diagrammatic approach in the Duchampian and Picabian manner, exemplifying Hamilton's injunction that a good drawing should be a 'diagram of thought processes' (Fig. 9). Stephen Buckley chose oranges (which were initially analysed from billboard images revealing their inner structure) and then made drawings investigating the surface texture of peel and the incomplete marks left by the rubber Jaffa stamps. He collected the tissue wrapping papers and explored the advertising, presentation, packaging and processing of the product (Fig. 10). Buckley states that it was the analytical project which gave him some sense of identity and achievement, and it is true that the analytical work did afford scope for some prominent realisation of large scale paintings and sculptures.[15] The throwaway, process-dominant attitude which prevailed in the rest of the course did not apply to the analytical work. It can also be observed that the course which began with predominantly abstract concerns, climaxed with realisations of objects which were very much a part of the everyday visual world. So it was that Hamilton tried to expose his students to a range of visual possibilities which served the interests of the potential abstract or figurative artist.

This summary of certain aspects of Richard Hamilton's Foundation Course is of necessity highly selective, indicating just a few of the ideas and influences which came to bear on it, and there are many important features of the course which I have not mentioned. Other people contributed to the teaching, including Ian Stephenson, who played a critical role in explaining the new thinking during the

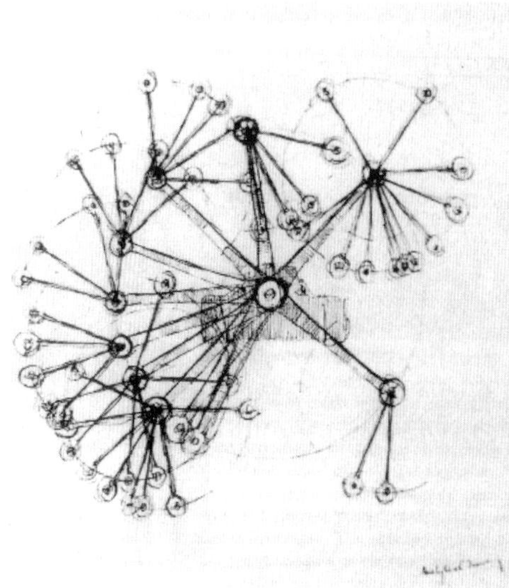

Fig. 9.

formative stage of Pasmore's course, and Rita Donagh and Matt Rugg, as well as visiting fellows like Terry Frost, Richard Smith, Joe Tilson and Eduardo Paolozzi, made distinctive contributions to Hamilton's course. It was a course which by its very nature was constantly changing, or to use Victor Pasmore's term, a 'developing process'. It reflected essentially the creative concerns and commitments of those artists involved and in many respects it mirrored the abstract and figurative researches of an avant-garde of the fifties and sixties. There was a real sense of being at the sharp end of modernism and this was reinforced by Hamilton's knowledge of contemporary art in America, which prompted enterprising students like Mark Lancaster to go to America and visit Andy Warhol and Jasper Johns.

What happened at Newcastle was never intended as a prescription for art education in Britain, and Richard Hamilton was the first to condemn the application of Basic Design thinking to the newly emerging foundation courses of the post-Coldstream era. He deplored the enforcement of teaching methods which had hitherto represented a personal and genuine creative relationship between teacher and student. In many ways it was Victor Pasmore, through his influential position on the Coldstream committee, who was responsible for the wider dissemination of Basic Design thinking throughout the country. Pasmore's move to abstraction in the post-war years had been like a religious conversion, and likewise he propagated his new educational thinking with a missionary zeal and conviction which was quite irresistible. The wholesale spread of Basic Design methods inevitably created a new academicism when it was severed from its creative roots and the whole movement, to some degree, fell into disrepute.

However, the question remains as to how much of this art educational thinking should merely be consigned to the history of the fifties and sixties, and how much of it has enduring value. I would argue that some kind of formal study of line, shape, colour and so forth is central to any art training and it is up to each generation to reinterpret this in its own way. At the time, the selective way in which these formal elements were studied at Newcastle seemed very avant-garde, but there is little that is ever new in art education. Certain features of the course are timeless and link with art educational practice which goes back to the eighteenth and nineteenth-centuries. Some of the line exercises could have come straight from Ruskin's *Elements of Drawing,* and it is worth noting that it was Ruskin who promoted the idea of taking a line for a walk long before Paul Klee.[16] Some of the shape making exercises such as cube and cylinder building relate in spirit to the eighteenth and nineteenth-century practice of drawing solid geometric bodies. Perhaps the most enduring aspect of formal study is colour, which in certain principles, such as the analysis of complementary colours and discords, has changed little since Goethe and Chevreul. Much of the content of the Newcastle course will remain a constant source of interest although changing contexts will determine the method of teaching.

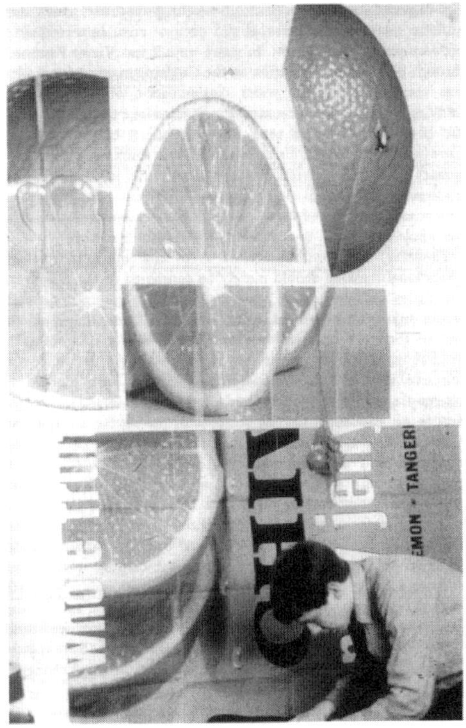

Fig. 10.

Hamilton's Foundation Course was not just concerned with formal analysis; and what distinguished this course was the experimental manner in which the students were encouraged to work. Basic Design courses represented a distinct shift from technique-based courses, towards a more open-ended experimental approach which encouraged a critical attitude of mind. This drive towards experimentation was spearheaded by artists, like Victor Pasmore, who regarded their teaching as a natural extension of their studio researches. The studios were laboratories and the spirit in which the teaching was carried out was more important than the content. Walter Gropius, who firmly established the principle of putting leading artists in the workshops and studios, stated that what defined the Bauhaus was its 'atmosphere', and for that reason the Bauhaus could never be replicated. So it was with the early Basic Design courses and for the same reason they cannot be repeated or replicated. What should be ensured is that we try to foster similar experimental attitudes and critical minds and, above all, maintain the practice of having creative committed artists working alongside their students.

Originally published in the Journal of Art & Design Education, *Volume 7: 2, 1988.*

Notes and References

1. Following the publication of Maurice de Sausmarez's book *Basic Design: the dynamics of visual form* the term 'Basic Design', like 'Impressionism' has become common currency, and for this reason I use it with some reservations. Victor Pasmore emphatically rejects the term preferring to describe his course as a 'developing process' thus emphasising its dynamic and changing

nature. The term 'Basic Design' was never used at Newcastle where the course was called the foundation course or basic course, or occasional reference was made to basic form studies.

2. Barclay Russell, A. *The Language of Adolescent Expression.* Summarised in the conference report, National Arts Education Archive, Bretton Hall BHBRPL00037.

3. Zabel, V. *Adolescent and Post-Adolescent Art, Op. cit.* n. 2.

4. Thubron, H. *An Experiment in Basic Art Education, Op. cit.* n. 2.

5. De Sausmarez, M. *The Next Phase, Op. cit.* n. 2.

6. Hudson, T., Pasmore, V., Pasmore, W., Thubron, H. *A Pedagogical Approach to Basic Form in the Visual Arts,* Royal Festival Hall, 26 April 1957.

7. Hamilton, R. (1961),'About art teaching, basically' *Motif* 8, Winter 1961.

8. Duchamp, M. (1976), 'The Trouble with Art this Century' in Sanouillet, W. and Peterson, E. (Eds.), *The Essential Writings of Marcel Duchamp*, Thames and Hudson, p. 126.

9. Thompson, D. W. (1961), *On Growth and Form*, Cambridge University Press.

10. *Op. cit.* n. 9, p. 12.

11. Gibson, J. J. (1950), *The Perception of the Visual World*, Houghton Mifflin.

12. Whyte, L. (1951), *Aspects of Form,* Lund Humphries.

13. William Turnbull. Interviewed by the writer, Camden, January1984.

14. Gideon, S. (1955), *Mechanisation Takes Command*, Oxford University Press.

15. Livingstone, M. (1985), *Stephen Buckley: Many Angles,* Oxford University Press/Liverpool University Press, p. 18.

16. Mccarthy, F. (1972), *All Things Bright and Beautiful,* Allen and Unwin, p. 111.

Chapter 13: Who is to do this Great Work for Canada? South Kensington in Ontario

Graeme Chalmers

Introduction

Although other British art masters came to North America, Walter Smith, as Supervisor of Drawing in Boston schools and State Director of Art Education in Massachusetts, has been heralded as the person most responsible for bringing South Kensington's rigid system of art education across the Atlantic.[1] But this role may have been usurped by Egerton Ryerson. As Chief Superintendent of Education for Upper Canada, Ryerson had travelled in the United Kingdom and Europe and was familiar with developments at South Kensington following the Great Exhibition of 1851. In 1857 Ryerson arranged for a Mr Bentley to be paid his South Kensington Certificate allowance while teaching drawing at the Government Model School in Toronto. He established an educational museum in Toronto:

> *...founded after the example of what is being done by the Imperial Government as part of the system of popular education... training the minds and forming the taste and character of the people.*[2]

In his 1859 report, Ryerson praised as 'exerting a very salutary influence' the South Kensington system that was imparting instruction in drawing to the British working classes. He went on to state that a large portion of the contents of the Toronto-based Educational Museum (all the requisite plaster casts of the South Kensington System) had been purchased 'with a view to the School of Art, which has not yet been established'.[3] While this does not deny either Smith's considerable role in the introduction of a systemised approach to the teaching of drawing in Canadian schools in the 1880s[4] or that South Kensington textbooks were used as early as the 1860s in Nova Scotia, it does point to a significantly different, wide-scale implementation of what was happening in Britain. The South Kensington System has been defined by a number of writers.[5] Minihan has stated that:

> *No beguiling dreams of high art distracted [the South Kensington Art Masters] from their daily tasks. They were practical men working to include art in the national elementary school curriculum and to educate the taste of artisans and consumers alike in the interests of British industry and trade.*[6]

I have chosen to structure this paper around the characterisation of theDepartment of Science and Art at South Kensington provided by Walter Smith on one of his visits to Canada:

Led by that great man, Prince Albert the Good, the consort of our beloved Queen, the nation went to work to remedy past deficiencies, to provide for a national system of education in elementary art and science, and to sustain the civilisation of the country at its weakest point. Every child was to be taught how to draw; every boy or girl was to have a chance; every stray genius was to be carefully husbanded; every mechanic to be given the choice of whether he would spend his evenings profitably in a school of art and science, or waste it at street corners or even in more pernicious surroundings. And the masterpieces of the world's concourse were purchased and kept in London, as nest eggs for future use.[7]

On a visit to Montreal in 1882 Smith gave a lecture on 'Technical Education: Its Position in a Public System of Education' in the Mechanics' Hall. The meeting was sponsored by the Council of Arts and Manufactures of the Province of Quebec, and, according to the *Montreal Gazette,* was very well attended. Smith described the 'development' of the Science and Art Department headquartered at South Kensington and of its system of art instruction. He issued the following challenge:

Who is to do this great work for Canada? We have seen the formation of a Canadian Royal Academy. When is the Science and Art Department of Canada to come? Who shall do for the Dominion what Prince Albert did for Great Britain?[8]

Smith argued that the establishment of South Kensington-like art education should be a Dominion-led rather than provincial initiative. He suggested that the Governor-General, the Marquis of Lorne, 'might thus profitably follow in his great father's footsteps'.[9] The Marquis's wife, Princess Louise, had briefly been a South Kensington student. Eventually the Dominion government did establish a Royal Commission to consider art schools and art related to industry outside Canada, but the Commission did not report until 1913.

Education being a provincial concern in Canada, it was the various provinces that developed South Kensington-like systems of art instruction in industrial drawing and practical art. Later nineteenth-century art education in Ontario was a system of social control that had its origins not only overseas at South Kensington, but also at home in the increasingly centralised 'educational state'.[10] Art education was controlled by a centralised education bureaucracy and also by the governing classes, who, as boards of trade and individual manufacturers awarded prizes for conventional, industrially related art work. Although art was also taught as a refined accomplishment, especially to 'ladies', it was rarely taught as a liberating force in the world, and when it was this was always a cause for conflict between those proposing it and the 'System.' Although Goodson and Dowbiggin[11] are concerned with later technical education in Ontario and do not mention South Kensington, their notions of institutional discipline and the perpetuation and legitimation of social differences among classes through particular types of schooling can certainly be found in approaches taken to art education in nineteenth-century Ontario.[12]

Existing Histories of Art Education in Ontario

Very little work has been done on the history of art education in Ontario. The earliest was May's self-congratulatory account of the development of Ontario's systematic course of training in industrial drawing and practical art.[13] There is a brief centennial history of the Ontario College of Art.[14] Two chapters in Gaitskell's doctoral dissertation and his subsequent book[15] as well as a dissertation by Tait[16] were, like Saunders's comparative history of United States and Canadian art education,[17] largely descriptive and presentist in orientation.

Because nineteenth-century art education was very different to that being proposed by their contemporaries, such as Lowenfeld, these writers gave Ontario's South Kensington-like drawing curriculum minimal space but considerable condemnation. The best interpretive history of art education in Ontario is undoubtedly Wood's 'The hidden curriculum of Ontario school art, 1904–1940'.[18] Her study begins where this paper concludes. Although apparently unaware of Wood's work, Clark[19] studied art as an emergent school subject in Ontario. He too begins with 1904 when 'drawing' in Ontario schools was renamed 'art'. Clark relies extensively on Blackwell's Tacon Lecture[20] which provides teachers with a useful chronology of Ontario's art educational events, policies, and personalities. With the exception of Stirling's[21] study of art institutions in Ontario and Quebec from 1876 to 1914 there has not been a substantial piece of work done on art education in nineteenth century Ontario.

The Key Personalities

In Canada Egerton Ryerson's contribution to the Ontario educational system is well known and well documented. I will concentrate more on the Sir Henry Cole of this story; another practical man who was never distracted from his daily tasks by high art and who worked valiantly to educate the taste of artisans and consumers alike in the interests of Ontario industry and trade. This was a man of whom it was said:

> *It is only once or so in a generation that there arises a man like him, endowed for the pursuit and mastery of so many subjects; and Pope has said, 'One science only will one genius fit, so vast is art, so narrow human wit;' but Dr May is perfectly at home as a practitioner of medicine, as a lecturer upon science and mechanics, in grouping and analysing in the department of natural history, or in the artistic arrangement of a museum or exhibition hall. He has a genius for organisation.*[22]

Samuel Passmore May was born in Truro, Cornwall in 1828. He received a private school education, but this was not confined to the classics, and included science and natural history.[23] Two years after the Great Exhibition, and the same year that a government art school was established in Truro, this 'genius for organisation' emigrated to Quebec where his first employment was with the Literary and Historical Society. He was responsible for rearranging the collection and preparing a scientific catalogue. This he apparently did with the efficiency that came to characterise the South Kensington approach; an approach under which art masters were to be rewarded according to the passes their students achieved in national examinations. Rose states:

> *He [May] completed the work in seven weeks and received a written testimonial and bonus, making a remuneration of ten pounds per week.*[24]

It would seem that such a fact could have been provided by none other than May himself who was fond of blowing his own trumpet. His reports to the Minister of Education would frequently contain numerous testimonials provided by others, including one from the Queen's secretary! When he was Commissioner of Education for the 1886 Indian and Colonial Exhibition in London he had sent Queen Victoria some work from Ontario art schools. He was in charge of the Ontario educational exhibit at the 1893 World's Fair in Chicago and reported that 'the touches of a master hand' were evident in Ontario's presentation![25]

May was Superintendent of Ontario Art Schools, Mechanics' Institutes and Public Libraries from 1880 until 1905. He began work for the Education Department under Ryerson as clerk in charge of the educational depository and library. He was also responsible for Ryerson's Educational Museum and for a number of exhibitions. In addition to London and Chicago mentioned above, he organised an educational exhibit in Kingston in 1856, the Canadian contribution to the Philadelphia Centennial Exhibition in 1876, and in 1878 he was appointed Secretary for the Dominion at the Paris Exposition, for which he was inducted into the French Legion of Honour. But 'C.L.H.' was not the only credential to appear after May's signature. In 1858 he went to Victoria College, Cobourg, Ontario as curator of the museum and lecturer in pharmacy and microscopy. He was awarded an MD in 1863. Except for a brief period of military service against the Fenians near the United States border he does not appear to have worked as a physician, although he certainly found the title 'doctor' advantageous in the authoritative regulation and administration of Ontario's centralised copy of the South Kensington Art Department.

A bureaucrat to the core, there is no denying that May was stubborn and single-minded. As in England, between the Royal Academy and the South Kensington System, conflict existed between the Ontario fine arts establishment and this key personality in the Education Department. For example, the artist Lucius O'Brien, first president of the Royal Canadian Academy, resigned from the Council of the Ontario School of Art because he believed 'the teachers [were] hampered and the efficiency of teaching impaired by injudicious arrangements and restrictions' imposed by May and the Department.[26] This resulted in the Ontario Society of Artists appointing a subcommittee to study the School's deteriorating relationship with Dr May and his myriad of rules and regulations. The committee rallied around O'Brien and reported that:

> *...had the representative of the Government [Dr May] possessed such knowledge of Art and Art Education as to qualify him for the control of the school [then] this arrangement might not have been prejudicial.*

It was therefore inadvisable that the Ontario Society of Artists should continue to act with him in any capacity.[27] This did not deter S. P. May. He simply took over the school.

Contributing to the Economy and Remedying Deficiencies in the Public Taste and in Manufactured Articles

Dr May was a forceful advocate for 'practical' art education. In his report for 1884 he included a lengthy history of the South Kensington System and drew parallels with Canada. Throughout his career he preached a doctrine of salvation for all through practical, industrially oriented, art education, and this report was no different:

> *[Art] concerns the advancement of the rich as well as the poor; it exercises an influence for culture and refinement, and when applied to the commonest product of labour, it increases its value.*

The working classes had a right to art because it 'is not the privilege of a class, but is individual and universal'.[28] He then, using figures from the 1881 Dominion Census, presented an argument documenting art's necessity in the working man's [*sic*] education.

In a fashion similar to South Kensington reports, May counted 84 Canadian industries employing over 50,000 persons that he believed had some need for art instruction. These ranged from agricultural implements to wool cloth making. The common worker, he argued, could derive prosperity from an export-oriented economy. But the objects to be exported had to be well designed. Throughout his reports May often quoted figures to show that Canada was importing more than it was exporting. This, he felt, could be rectified by art education, particularly:

If our pupils can execute beautiful designs... the articles we manufacture will have more value, and, what is still of more importance, will act as a check against the importation of articles similar to those manufactured in this country.[29]

Art education achieved these objectives only in the popular rhetoric of the time.

There was considerable sympathy for May's ideas. Even the dispute with the Ontario Society of Artists, referred to above, was perhaps more with the man than the mission. Radford, a member of the Ontario Society of Artists, still felt able to echo Walter Smith and other South Kensingtonians in claiming that:

All civilised nations require the necessity of art education, because the commercial value of many manufactured articles is based upon their artistic merit. So it is a matter of vital importance that the best method of educating people in art should be followed. If artistic wares are not found at home, purchasers will not fail to seek for them elsewhere. When Canada produces these wares up to the standard of her competitors, in finish, form and workmanship, her manufactures will be placed on an equal footing in the markets of the world with other nations ...At present, unfortunately, the imports of artistic ware are increasing, and they will continue to do so until the art applied in the designing and manufacture of them equals that of foreign countries. From all standpoints, ethical and economic art education is a vital need.[30]

May was certainly able to convince the reporters and editors of the time that the system of art education that he had put in place, and was minutely regulating, really was 'remedying deficiencies in the public taste'. Toronto's *Globe,* perhaps printing something submitted by May himself, reported thus on the annual exhibition of work submitted for Departmental certificates:

On Saturday night about 3,000 mechanics and workmen with their wives and families were present, the walls and screens were lit up with the electric light which, together with the enlivening strains of music and the happy smiling faces, fanned a fairy-like scene long to be remembered by those present, and proved that a taste for the beautiful has been developed amongst all classes of our society.[31]

The following year, in an article entitled 'Industrial art: the progress it is making in Ontario,' *The Globe* was still singing the praises of the 'System':

The importance of this branch of instruction is impossible to overestimate. It has done much – it is doing much – to give to the daily life of our citizens a grace and finish that aesthetic reformers long deplored the absence of in the older countries of the world. It unlocks the door to a multitude of educating perceptions from which the people have been kept estranged, and it imbues with a sense of refinement the households of the land. We see in little objects, conceived in true artistic spirit and eloquent of the dis-

tinguishing tone of modern culture, the awakening to a new artistic life. It is this kind of education that has taught the Philistine public, against which the late Matthew Arnold inveighed so bitterly, a true appreciation of the beauty of form as well as the beauty of colour. Its influence has been in the direction of sweetness and light.[32]

Drawing Manuals and a Graded System

A provincial system of education in elementary art in which every child was to be taught how to draw

A national system of instruction in drawing, progressing in graduated stages, was at the heart of the South Kensington system. Although drawing in common schools, in what was to become the Province of Ontario, was prescribed by Ryerson as early as 1856, the annual reports indicate that the number of students who actually studied drawing never quite reached the number who were learning to read. However by 1890 nearly all elementary school pupils, and nearly all first year high school pupils were learning to draw in Ontario's schools.[33]

As in Britain, authorised drawing texts were used. One of Walter Smith's texts was published in Toronto.[34] This was replaced by copy books prepared by local normal school drawing masters: McFaul's *Public School Drawing Course* consisting of six books[35] and Casselman's three-book *The High School Drawing Course*.[36] By the 1890s copy book drawing manuals were used in all but the first year of the elementary school. In reproducing South Kensington models and concepts the Ontario authors reflected the views of current educators such as William T. Harris who believed that the textbook was the centre of curriculum and should reflect 'what has been tested and found essential to civilisation'.[37] Younger children did blackboard drawing exercises related to their first reader.

Drawing was an important part of teacher education and all elementary school student teachers were introduced to drawing in the normal and model schools. Through additional summer courses and evening study they were expected to obtain initially a 'Grade B' and then a Primary Art Certificate.

Examinations and Prizes

Every boy or girl was to have a chance and every stray genius carefully husbanded

In Ontario, as in Britain, an elaborate system of Education Department examinations was developed. The system included certificates in primary, advanced, and mechanical drawing as well as industrial art. The drawing and art examinations could be entered by students in public and private secondary schools as well as in the mechanics' institutes, teacher-training sites such as model and normal schools, and schools of art. By 1890, in Ontario, drawing was taught in all the publicly supported elementary schools, art schools in six towns, twenty-one mechanics institutes, twenty-five high schools, and seven private, mostly 'ladies', colleges. As *The Globe* stated in 1890:

The figures are the best illustrations that can be given of the rapid advance that has been made. In the year 1882 the number of certificates granted in the primary art course was 106, last year the number was 3,508. There were forty certificates in the advanced course granted in 1883, the first year of the establishment of the classes, last year there were 222. In the mechanical drawing course there were eleven issued in 1883, and last year eighty-two.[38]

The stray geniuses were carefully nurtured and controlled by the extensive award of the prizes and medals of the Education Department, as well as those of individuals, companies, and groups such as the Canadian Manufacturers' Association. Onward, upward, and outward; the 'system' even extended into the western Province of Manitoba. In 1889 Landsdowne College in Portage la Prairie applied for affiliation. May stated that 'pupils in Manitoba now have the *privilege*' [May's emphasis] of competing for the Art certificates awarded by the Ontario Education Department.[39]

The Art Education of Artisans

Every mechanic was given the choice of whether to spend evenings profitably or waste them at street corners or even in more pernicious surroundings

Between 1835 and 1882 86 mechanics' institutes were established throughout what became Ontario. These institutions provided meeting rooms, reading rooms and libraries. They also conducted evening classes for persons twelve years of age and older. The subjects taught tended to be writing and bookkeeping, English grammar, arithmetic and drawing.

Artisans were particularly welcome in the art schools established in the bigger towns and cities. They filled most of the evening classes. In 1888 the Toronto Art School opened a special west end branch and reported at the end of the year that:

...because it was... in the centre of the artisan population, [it] has done a large and useful work, and its success fully justifies the decision to open a school among the working classes, and also points the direction to which government assistance should go in reaching the classes most deserving in practical Industrial Art work.[40]

In order to be assured of government grants the art schools had to work hard at recruiting working class students. The Brockville school lamented[41] that the local carriage company began operations too late in the season for the employees to enrol, but, the construction of the Provincial Asylum was expected to bring many young artisans to Brockville and hopefully also to the art school.

As already stated, May liked to pat himself on the back and his report for 1888 is no exception. It records the impressions of 'a visiting Englishman' who was inspecting technical education in North America:

The... School of Art in Toronto is an institution supported by the Legislature of the Province for the purpose of imparting special instruction, embracing subjects in science and art teaching suitable to mechanics, and bearing on their employment. There are evening classes adapted to working men. This excellent school is the commencement of an institution similar in object and appliances to our South Kensington. Although in its infancy, the instruction given is evidently valued by the various trades of the city. Out of 121 students last year, one half were engaged in trades and manufactures; the remainder studying as teachers. The instruction is confined to drawing in every branch, and designing. I was particularly struck with the manifest relation between the work done in the school and industrial pursuits.[42]

May felt that one drawback to the complete success of industrial art education in Ontario was the opposition and jealousy of the foremen in factories:

...to the attendance of their workmen at the Evening Classes for Mechanical and Industrial Drawing, fearing that ordinary workmen may thus become equal or superior to themselves.[43]

The Art Education of Girls and Women

The 'accomplishments' curriculum and the South Kensington system

Among the recipients of medals and diplomas awarded for art work submitted to such events as the Colonial Exhibition of 1886 it is easy to find Ontario's church-related ladies colleges. Students at these institutions often submitted 'beautiful paintings in oils and watercolours' to provincial exhibitions.[44] Art needlework was taught at three of the provincial art schools (Hamilton, Ottawa, St Thomas), but students paid higher fees as no government grants could be used to pay the instructors. The chair of the board of the St Thomas Art School unsuccessfully appealed for government funds by stating that:

The beauty of this work is that it tells directly on the home life, in ornamenting and beautifying the home, bringing the young under its influence and implanting taste for the arts.[45]

But May had other ideas. He saw 'industrial' art as particularly valuable for women who were not 'ladies'. He would have approved of *The Globe's* review of the work of 'ladies' who painted on china as a leisure pursuit because it went on to restate one of his favourite themes:

By the way painting on china has become quite an industry. ...There are two factories in existence employing about forty people, and these are mostly pupils of the [London, Ontario] Art School. The industry has assumed such magnitude that the manufactures in England have begun to look upon it with some amount of apprehension, for it has already made its effect felt upon their trade.[46]

Although the Countess of Aberdeen had a special gold medal struck to present to the 'ladies of Loretto Abbey' in Toronto for their fine exhibit of china painting that was shown at the National Council of Women's meeting in Ottawa in 1898, Dr May, as an invited speaker, had impressive figures at hand to convince the women present that art education for girls and women had other dimensions! For ten of the thirteen previous years the highest provincial medal for drawing had been awarded to a woman. Out of the thirteen medals awarded for the Primary Art Course (the initial teacher's certificate), ten had again been won by women. Ten out of fifteen medals for industrial drawing had been awarded to women, and out of twenty-eight special prizes presented by manufacturers, twenty were won by women and girls. Nearly half of the initial teachers' certificates, and close to 75 of the advanced and industrial art certificates were taken by women![47]

This of course did not mean that these women obtained positions as designers, or even that they wanted such positions. Although removed from 'lady-like' pursuits the certificates themselves did confer a notion of accomplishment. There are isolated instances of women who either wanted or needed work (such as that of a Miss Stewart who gained all Ontario certificates while studying at the Brockville Art School, won a fellowship to the Philadelphia Women's School of Design, and returned to Brantford) but were unable to find employment. This was not necessarily related to gender as the chair of the board of the Brockville Art School reported in 1897:

> *...we can only regret that the manufacturers in our own vicinity do not seem it expedient to employ designers [of either gender] for the goods they manufactures, but borrow designs of foreign origin.*[48]

This causes us to ask whether the system ever really achieved its objectives in Ontario? Thistlewood argues that South Kensington did not achieve its objectives in Britain but instead became a self-perpetuating bureaucracy with graduates of both sexes returning to initiate the next generation.[49] Miss Stewart eventually taught in Brockville.

The Certification of Teachers

Special certificates in art began in 1882, and once the Department of Education had assumed the management of the Ontario School of Art it wasted no time in circularising teachers in the provincially supported schools informing them that free industrial drawing classes would be conducted the following summer. Twelve lessons each in freehand drawing, practical geometry, linear perspective, model drawing, and blackboard drawing were given. Examinations were held in August and a supplementary examination was given in the fall for a grade B certificate entitling successful candidates to teach industrial drawing in Ontario's schools. That this qualification was directly compared with South Kensington's most basic certificate is abundantly evident in the various reports of the Minister of Education. It appears that the most difficult subjects were model and blackboard drawing.

A grade A certificate was required to teach drawing in high schools, county model schools involved in teacher training, mechanics' institutes, and the provincial art schools. This certificate required that candidates pass examinations in each of ten subjects: shading from flat examples, outline drawing from the round (casts and nature), shading from the round, drawing from flowers and objects of natural history, advanced perspective, descriptive geometry and topographical drawing, drawing from dictation, machine drawing, building construction, and industrial design. After 1886 the grade B certificate was re-labelled as the Primary Art Course, and the grade A certificate was split into the Advanced Art Course and the Mechanical Drawing Course. The largest number of Primary Art Course certificates was awarded in 1896 when the full teacher's certificate was awarded to 341 candidates and 6,543 individual subject certificates were issued to students in a variety of educational institutions.

A Central Art School and Dependent Branch Schools

Characteristic of the South Kensington system was the notion of one art school, that is the 'head' school at South Kensington, being more important than the branch schools. Under the auspices of the Department of Science and Art the 'head' school controlled the curriculum and examination system for all the affiliated schools and was itself more of a 'post-graduate' school for the advanced training of art masters and mistresses. Similarly, once the Ontario Department of Education assumed control of the Ontario School of Art in 1882, the following institutions were affiliated with it, taught the same curriculum, gave the same examinations, awarded similar certificates and, with one or two exceptions, also competed for the same departmental medals and prizes: Western School of Art, London; Ottawa School of Art and Design; Alma College, St Thomas; Albert College, Belleville; Wykeham Hall, Toronto; and the Mechanics' Institutes (although initially only Kincardine, Orangeville and Strathroy entered candidates for examination). The Ontario School of Art was discontinued in 1886 and reconstituted as the Toronto School of Art. However, although this diminished the notion of a head school, it did not lessen the control of the Department of Education over the art schools and affiliated examination centres. They were all under the inspection of the department, meaning Dr May, and a new Act and regulations assured that a slightly revised, centrally administered[50] certificate examination system (primary, advanced and mechanical) continued into the twentieth century.

The Ontario School of Art, founded by the Ontario Society of Artists, began, with 25 students, on 30 October 1876. The society was assisted by a provincial government grant. At the beginning the unpaid director, T. Mower Martin, and his colleagues seemed to have no difficulty in endorsing South Kensington-like aims and purposes. Initially there was good co-operation with the Education Department that lent a number of plaster casts from the museum. But soon there were problems with funding and there was pressure to have the school become a more integral part of the provincial educational system. The artists were also beginning to question the emphasis on industrial art. This culminated with the school being taken over by the Education Department and moved to the department buildings.

Although the board recommended 'a first class trained teacher from South Kensington',[51] Samuel Passmore May became Superintendent. The Ontario Society of Artists retained an interest in the non-financial matters of the school, but the Education Department's interests in drawing, industrial art, and teacher training were emphasised. As a 'head school' May felt that:

> *Its objects can be made beneficial to the whole Province in reaching with its excellent teaching a large number of the teachers in training at the Normal School, and evidencing this by a special certificate, as well as by fitting them and others to supply the want now felt by many of the Mechanics' Institutes for competent instructors by evening classes in such drawing or machine designs and other objects to the many who are now seeking such instruction.*[52]

As Fleming and Taylor, the centennial historians of the Ontario College of Art, state:

> *The school became integrated into the provincial educational system with examinations, a board of examiners, three types of certificates, and an abundance of rules.*[53]

Thus the Ontario Society of Artists severed its connection with the art school in 1884. The management was assumed entirely by the Education Department and an unfettered Ontario Government School of Art briefly emerged until it was decided to administer the whole system from headquarters. The school in Toronto became simply the Toronto Art School with a branch school in the west end of the city, and from 1890 until 1912 was known as the Central Ontario School of Art and Design. Although this last named school was again 'in affiliation with the Ontario Society of Artists'[54] the Society's interests were largely restricted to the annual exhibition. The prospectus until well into the twentieth century was to state:

> *The purpose of the School is not to turn out only picture painters or sculptors, the main object of its promoters and guardians is, and has been, to meet the need for designers for manufactures in which decoration is essential.*[55]

The Western Ontario School of Art and Design was established in the Mechanics' Institute Building in London in 1878. It prided itself on both containing 'over 400 drawing models, including plaster casts and various sections of machinery' and having an instructor from South Kensington itself; S. Kelso Davidson, who went on to become the first art master at the Normal School in London.[56] The board, consisting of two colonels, a QC, a member of the provincial legislature, a member of the Royal Canadian Academy, and seven other 'gentlemen' benevolently supported teaching that 'is of that practical character which aids the pupils in becoming more fit for their several trades and occupations'.[57]

The School of Art and Design in Ottawa was affiliated with the Ontario Government School of Art in 1883. The school had its beginnings in the Art Association of Ottawa, founded in 1879. A school of art began in Kingston in 1884, and one in Hamilton in 1885 with Ida N. Banting as the senior instructor. The trustees at Hamilton were anxious to secure the services of a 'fully qualified headmaster'.[58] This resulted in the appointment of S. John Ireland, whose South Kensington credentials were touted in nearly every annual report from then on (e.g. late bursaried student and Assistant Art Master at South Kensington, late principal of art schools at Barrow, Barnstaple and Ilfracombe, England, late Lecturer and Deputy Professor, King's College, London, England and at present Examiner for the City of London and Birkbeck Colleges).

The Brockville and Stratford art schools enrolled their first students in 1886, although Stratford did not continue for more than a year or two as a government affiliated art school. The principal at Brockville, R. H. Whale, who held all the Ontario certificates, went on to become a South Kensington student.[59] By the time the Ontario College of Art assumed its present name in 1912 the other provincial art schools had disappeared. Their activities were absorbed into a developing system of secondary education.[60]

The Educational Museum

At South Kensington, as Walter Smith stated 'the masterpieces of the world... were purchased and kept in London as nest eggs for future use'.[61] This collection became the core of the Victoria and Albert Museum. Not until the Ontario School of Art was taken over by the Education Department were the purposes of Ryerson's Educational Museum finally fulfilled. As May stated in 1882:

> *Hitherto the complete and valuable collection of the Education Department in sculpture, paintings, architectural and other designs, engravings and models, have not been utilised as fully for practical art studies as they are capable of being made.*[62]

The contents of the museum are discussed in several of Ryerson's reports.[63] In addition to housing a growing collection, the museum was also used to exhibit student work from throughout the 'system'. Periodically work from the South Kensington parent was exhibited as special exemplars for Canadian students.

Conclusion

Just as Ontario admired Britain's South Kensington system of practical art education, Britain, in turn admired what happened in Canada. In writing about the Colonial Exhibition in 1886, May stated that:

> *The press gave most flattering notices, and said that the efforts of the Government [of Ontario] in promoting Industrial Art in Art Schools are calculated even to a greater degree than the exhibit of pictures from Canadian artists to open the eyes of the British public to the artistic progress of Canada in recent years.*[64]

But change was in the art educational winds blowing from both the United States and Britain.[65] In 1901, May, then over 70 years old, visited art schools and public schools in Buffalo, New York and Philadelphia. He was impressed, and upon his return to Canada announced that in the American schools:

> *no drawing books are used, their work is done on Manila paper for all grades of drawing, white paper for brush work in colours, and grey paper for work in charcoal and coloured chalk.*[66]

In the same year Albert H. Leake was appointed Director of the Manual Training Schools for Ontario and by 1904 was also reporting on art instruction in the schools. Leake's 1906 report,[67] coming as it did after legislation that changed 'drawing' to 'art' in Ontario schools, contained many photographs of craftwork and other three-dimensional art work. The system was waning and with the exception of libraries and cultural institutions May's job had disappeared. He resigned on 1 November 1905.

Although not wishing to overemphasise a similarity between Harris and May, Cremin's words about American educator William T. Harris could be equally applied to S. Passmore May:

> *His emphasis [was] on order rather than freedom, on work rather than play, on effort rather than interest, on prescription rather than election, on regularity, silence and industry that preserve and save our civil order.*[68]

The legacies are several. Whether or not it actually made any difference in the nineteenth century, art educators still link the supposed need for design education in schools with both improving the public taste and economic prosperity. In Ontario, long after 'drawing' became 'art' there were still strong notions of central control which included a provincial supervisor of art. Unlike other provinces where specialist certificates had been designed, taught, and awarded by university faculties of education, this biggest replication of South Kensington outside of Britain lingers on. In Ontario specialist teaching credentials continue to be linked with the provincial Ministry of Education, than with more autonomous agencies, and graduate studies in art education are underdeveloped in comparison with other Canadian provinces. But more importantly than this, art educators everywhere still have difficulty seeing and implementing art education as a potent social force for the disempowered. Instead we cling to a few narrow controlling objectives, to exemplars from one dominant culture, and to simple non-solutions to difficult educational dilemmas.

Originally published in the Journal of Art & Design Education, *Volume 12: 2, 1993.*

Notes and References

1. Soucy provides a useful discussion of the dominant position given to Smith in many North American art education histories. See Soucy, D. (1990), 'A history of art education histories' in Soucy, D. & Stankiewicz, M. A. (Eds.), *Framing the Past: Essays on Art Education*, pp. 3–31, Reston VA, National Art Education Association. I wish to thank Professor Soucy for his helpful comments on an earlier draft of this paper. See also Clarke, I. E. (1885), *Art and Industry.* Part 1, *Drawing in Public Schools,* US Senate Report, 46th Congress, 2nd Session, Vol. 7 (Washington, Government Printing Office); Clarke, I. E. (1892), *Art and Industry.* Part 2, *Industrial and Manual Training in Public Schools,* US Senate Report, 46th Congress, 2nd Session, Vol. 7 (Washington, Government Printing Office); Green, H. B. (1966), 'Walter Smith: the forgotten man' *Art Education*, 19: 1, pp. 3–9; Macdonald, S. (1970), *The History and Philosophy of Art Education*, New York: American Elsevier.
2. Chief Superintendent of Education (1860), *Annual Report of the Normal, Model, Grammar and Common Schools in Upper Canada*, Quebec: Thompson & Co. and Toronto, Legislative Assembly, p. 14.
3. *Ibid.*
4. See Chalmers, F. G. (1985), 'South Kensington and the colonies II: the influence of Walter Smith in Canada' in Wilson, B. & Hoffa, H. (Eds.), *The History of Art Education: Proceedings from the Penn. State Conference*, pp. 108–112. Reston VA, National Art Education Association.
5. E.g. Macdonald (n. l). See also Thistlewood, D. (1986), 'Social significance in British art education 1850–1950' *Journal of Aesthetic Education*, 20: 1, pp. 71–83.
6. Minihan, J. (1977), *The Nationalisation of Culture*, London: Hamish Hamilton, p. 96.
7. Smith, W. (1883), *Technical Education and Industrial Drawing in Public Schools: Reports and Notes of Addresses Delivered at Montreal and Quebec*, Montreal, Council of Arts & Manufactures, pp. 16–17.
8. *Ibid.* p. 19.
9. *Ibid.*
10. Curtis, B. (1988), *Building the Educational State: Canada West,* 1836–1871, London, Ontario: Falmer Press, Althouse Press.
11. Goodson, 1. & Dowbiggin, I. R. (1991), 'Vocational education and school reform: The case of the London (Canada) technical school' *History of Education Review*, 20: 1, pp. 39–60.
12. One of several incidents that could be used to illustrate this point concerns l'Institut Canadien-Francais, a cultural organisation located in Ottawa. The Institute fostered debate on issues of political economy, presented lectures on history, discussions and experiments in science, and literary and artistic entertainments. As the recipient of an annual provincial grant the Institute was subject to annual inspection. During his inspection of 1880 Dr May met with the officers and directors and recommended that evening classes be established for French Canadian artisans. Although very different in tone and flavour from the usual beaux arts offerings of the Institute by 1881 they were offering courses in '*dessin d'apres modele, dessin d'apres nature, dessin d'architecture, dessin de macanique, et dessin de geometrie*'. Report (1882–1883), *Report of*

the Minister of Education with Statistics and Appendices, Ontario, Toronto: Legislative Assembly, p. 264.

13. Report (1885), *Report of the Minister of Education with Statistics and Appendices,* Ontario, Toronto: Legislative Assembly, pp. 232–250.
14. Fleming, M. L. & Taylor, J. R. (1976), *100 Years: Evolution of the Ontario College of Art*, Toronto: Council of the Ontario College of Art,
15. Gaitskell, C. D. (1947), 'Art education in the Province of Ontario', Ph.D. thesis, University of Toronto; Gaitskell, C. D. (1948), *Art Education in the Province of Ontario*, Toronto: Ryerson Press.
16. Tait, G. E. (1957), 'The history of art education in the elementary schools of Ontario', thesis, University of Toronto.
17. Saunders, R. J. (1954), 'The parallel development of art education in Canada and the United States, with emphasis on the history of art education in Canada', MA thesis, Pennsylvania State University.
18. Wood, B. A. (1986), 'The hidden curriculum of Ontario school art, 1904–1940' *Ontario History*, 78: 4, pp. 351–369.
19. Clark, R. A. (1991), 'Art as an emergent school subject: perspectives and a proposal from Ontario' *Studies in Art Education*, 32: 2, pp. 220–229.
20. Blackwell, R. (1989), 'The visual artist in general education in Ontario: whither and especially whence' *Journal of the Ontario Society for Education through Art*, 18, pp. 17–30.
21. Stirling, J. C. (1991), 'Development of art institutions in Quebec and Ontario (1876–1914) and the South Kensington influence', Ph.D. thesis, University of Edinburgh.
22. Rose, G. M. (Ed.) (1886), *A Cyclopedia of Canadian Biography Being Chiefly Men of the Time*, Toronto: Rose Publishing Co., pp. 655–656.
23. *Ibid.* p. 654.
24. *Ibid.*
25. Report (1893–1894), *Report of the Minister of Education with Statistics and Appendices*, Ontario, Toronto: Legislative Assembly, p. 322.
26. Ontario Society of Artists (1884), Minute Book, 4 March.
27. *Ibid.* 11 March.
28. Report (1885) (n. 13).
29. Report (1887–1891), *Report of the Minister of Education with Statistics and Appendices*, Ontario, Toronto: Legislative Assembly, pp. 240–241.
30. Radford, J. A. (1894), 'Canadian art schools, artists and art' *The Magazine of Politics, Science, Art and Literature,* 2, pp. 462–466, p. 466.
31. (1889), 'Amateur art: annual exhibition of provincial art schools' *The Globe*, 45, 4 June, p. 4.
32. (1890), 'Industrial art: the progress it is making in Ontario' *The Globe*, 46, 21 June, p. 3.
33. Report (1887–1891) (n. 29), p. 240.
34. Smith, W. (1883), *Teachers' Manual for Freehand Drawing in Primary Schools*, Toronto & Winnipeg: W. J. Gage.
35. Mcfaul, J. H. (1892), *The Public School Drawing Course*, Toronto: Canada Publishing Co.
36. Casselman, A. C. (1894), *The High School Drawing Course*, Toronto: Canada Publishing Co.
37. Harris, W. T. (1880), 'Textbooks and their uses' *Education*, 1. p. 9.
38. *Globe* (n. 32) p. 3.
39. (1890) Report (1887–1891) (n. 29).
40. *Ibid.* p. 282.

41. Report (1893–1894) (n. 25), p. 276.
42. (1889) Report (1887–1891) (n. 29), p. 211.
43. (1888) Report (1887–1891) (n. 29), p. 212.
44. *Globe* (n. 32), p. 3.
45. Report (1893–1894) (n. 25), p. 256.
46. *Globe* (n. 32), p. 3.
47. (1898) Provincial exhibition of industrial art, *The Globe*, 54, 11 June, pp. 1–2.
48. Report (1897), *Report of the Minister of Education with Statistics and Appendices*, Ontario, Toronto: Legislative Assembly, p. 337.
49. Thistlewood (n. 5).
50. As in Britain, compliance carried tangible rewards and by the 1890s, under May's supervision, Ontario art school grants were supplemented according to the number of students who had been successful in the previous year's certificate examinations.
51. Report (1882–1883) (n. 12), p. 265.
52. *Ibid.*
53. Fleming & Taylor (n. 14), pp.11–12.
54. *Ibid.* p. 14.
55. Prospectus of the Central Ontario School of Art & Industrial Design (1909–1910). In the prospectuses for 1905–1906 and 1909–1910 'Industrial' was inserted in the Central School's title.
56. Report (1882–1883) (n. 12), p. 261.
57. *Ibid.* p. 262.
58. (1887) Report (1887–1891) (n. 29), p. 147.
59. Report (1887–1891) (n. 29).
60. Harris, R. S. (1967), *Quiet Evolution: A Study of the Educational System of Ontario*, Toronto: University of Toronto Press. See also Goodson & Dowbiggin, (n. 11).
61. Smith (n. 7), p. 17.
62. (1882) Report (1882–1883) (n. 12), p. 266.
63. (1860) Chief Superintendent of Education (n. 2).
64. (1888) Report (1887–1891) (n. 29), p. 215.
65. For a discussion of change in early twentieth century art education in another Canadian province see Rogers, A. W. (1987), W. P. Weston, 'Educator and artist: the development of British ideas in the art curriculum of BC public schools', Ph.D. thesis, University of British Columbia. To further understand the nature and social significance of this change, particularly the new winds blowing from Britain, see Thistlewood (n. 5).
66. Report (I902), *Report of the Minister of Education with Statistics and Appendices*, Ontario, Toronto: Legislative Assembly, p. 203.
67. Report (I907), *Report of the Minister of Education with Statistics and Appendices*, Ontario, Toronto: Legislative Assembly.
68. Cremin, L. (1961), *The Transformation of the School*, New York: Vintage Books, p. 200.

Chapter 14: European Modernist Art into Japanese School Art: the Free Drawing Movement in the 1920s

Akio Okazaki

Introduction

In the field of education in Japan, there has been a great deal of European art education literature which has been translated or introduced into Japanese. In the 1870s, for example, two British textbooks by Burn were translated into Japanese by Togai Kwakami. One is the *Illustrated London Drawing Book* (1852), and the other *Self-aid Cyclopedia for Self-taught Students* (1863). Both were edited into one volume, and published in 1871. This Japanese edition, *Seiga Shinan* (Guide to Western Pictures)[1] was recommended by the Ministry of Education in Japan (established on 18 July 1871) for use at the elementary level, in accordance with the regulations of the first modern comprehensive educational ordinance (issued on 8 September 1872).[2] Rosenfield describes Togai:

> *Togai's knowledge of European art was based on Dutch texts of considerable age, well removed from the aesthetic issues that were affecting contemporary European art. This situation was not really changed even in the later 1860s when more up-to-date French and English books were imported. Among these was a drawing manual by Robert Scott Burn, a British writer who specialized in instructions for self-teaching of artistic and mechanical subjects. Togai translated it under the title* Seiga Shinan (Guide to Western Pictures)*, and it was published in 1871.*[3]

Comparing original texts with the Japanese edition, Kaneko indicates that the translation of Burn's books can be seen as almost accurate, though with some additions and modifications of figures according to the translator's own interpretation.[4]

Another example of British influence on Japanese art education in the 1870s can be found in a Japanese textbook, *Shogaku Hutsu Gagakubon* (Drawing for use in Elementary Schools) by Miyamoto, which was published by the Ministry of Education in 1878.[5] This textbook includes pictures that were reprinted from Walter Smith's *Teacher's Manual of Free-Hand Drawing and Designing and Guide to Self-Instruction.*[6] The influence of 'the South Kensington System' of art education was not limited to American, Canadian, and Brazilian art education,[7] it also extended to Japan through Miyamoto's textbook.

Apart from the translations of key textbooks, subsequent European influences are demonstrated by several Japanese art educators who made survey trips to the Western world in the earlier decades of the last century. Among them was Akira Shirahama (1866–1927). He arrived in Boston on 6 April 1904, entered the Massachusetts Normal Art School in May and graduated 22 June 1905. He left Boston on 25 August of that year and arrived in London on 6 September. He visited France and Germany before returning to Japan on 21 March 1907. In the same year, the Normal Course of Drawing was established at the Tokyo Fine Arts School with the special purpose of training teachers for secondary schools, and Shirahama was appointed chairman of the course. Shirahama trained many normal school art teachers and teachers of art at the secondary level for twenty years until his death.[8] After coming back to Japan, he devoted himself to developing more modernised drawing curricula.

The turn of the twentieth century was a remarkable period for building the Japanese compulsory education system. For example, in 1887 elementary school attendance reached only 45 per cent. By 1897 it was 66 per cent, and jumped to 97 per cent by 1907. Drawing became a required subject in grades three to eight. At that time, the Ministry of Education defined the purposes of drawing in the elementary educational ordinance, as 'to cultivate in children the faculty of perceiving clearly and drawing correctly ordinary objects, and to foster the sense of the beautiful'.[9]

Corresponding to the extension of elementary school attendance, the Ministry of Education desired to have a comprehensive textbook of drawing that was not a mere copybook but a systematically organised text, including such content as drawing, painting, colour theory, composition, decoration and design. The Ministry, therefore, issued new drawing books for each elementary grade called *Shintei Gacho* (New Textbooks of Drawing) in 1910. This set of drawing textbooks was the first modernised series in the history of modern art education in Japan. The content and organisation of the curriculum in the textbooks were developed under Shirahama's direction.[10] Thus the modern Japanese art education system was established around the year 1910.

In the 1920s, Shirahama was criticised by certain art educators such as Kanae Yamamoto, the leading advocate of the Free Drawing Movement in schools during the later half of the Taisho Era (1912–1926) in Japan. He claimed Shirahama was responsible for the remnants of 'copyism' and the lack of expressive value in the new textbook of drawing. He began the Free Drawing Movement in December 1918.

Background

The Taisho Era (1912–1926) in modern Japanese history is the period of Taisho Democracy. Politics were concerned with the rapid rising of parliamentary power and party leadership. Culturally, there was a broad range of liberalizing tendencies and the swing of the pendulum back to enthusiastic borrowing from the West. The tendency towards democratic style depended not only on the expansion of the Japanese economy during World War One, but on the Japanese enthusiasm for liberal Western concepts. Japanese people were indeed responding to the victory of the major Western democracies such as Britain, France, and the United States, and the defeat of the more autocratic nations such as Germany and the Austro-Hungarian Empire, in their image of the ideal Western democracy.[11]

Western writers on modern Japanese history in general show that the democratic movement in the Taisho Era of Japan caught the imagination of the country. They also describe how these political, social, cultural, and educational innovations took place at that time.[12] In his 1919 article 'Liberalism in Japan', Dewey reported the climate of the period:

> *One heard the word frequently from the mouths of Japanese fellow travellers as one crossed the Pacific: De-mo-kras-ie... Autocracy out of fashion, democratic styles were in... The change of fashion was a fact, was indeed a large part of the situation. But it operated mainly to depress the prestige of the reactionary bureaucrats and to increase that of the liberals so that men were willing, and even glad, to listen to them.*[13]

Beasley, a British writer on modern history of Japan, refers to the second decade of the century in Japan as 'the Liberal Twenties'.[14] Under the global democratic movement, the new wave of liberalising ideas and ways from the West gave impetus to political changes. All adult males gained the franchise in the mid 1920s.[15] Eckroade (1979) identifies the relationship between innovation in the political system and schooling in the 1920s in Japan.[16] Konayashi (1976) points out the growing interest in democratic education among Japanese educators.[17]

The democratic orientation in education resulted in a new movement of education in the 1920s. Sugiyama describes the movement as an:

> *Early 20th century educational movement emphasising the individuality and initiative of the student in opposition to the standardised education of state controlled school system as it has existed since the early Meiji (1868–1912). The principles and methods espoused by the Japanese movement were those of the European and American progressive education movement that arose in the late 19th and early 20th centuries.*[18]

The free expression or self-expression movement in Japanese arts and aesthetic education also began in response to the liberalising tendencies in education at the time. By 1920 elementary and secondary school curricula included drawing, singing, and manual arts. In addition, students received lessons in literary composition or writing within the Japanese language education programme. 'In art[s] education, a movement that included free composition developed to promote self-expression by school children'.[19]

This movement aimed at promoting children's self-expression in school subjects related to the arts. In children's literary composition, for example, this movement emphasised the children's free expression and the educative value of composition based on their experience. It also aimed to free children from the strictly standardized language curriculum prescribed by the Ministry of Education. Children wrote in response to their life and world. Teachers encouraged students to express their individual ideas freely through the arts.[20]

> *Emphasis on free expression was not limited to literary composition, but spread also to music, art and school drama exemplified in the children's song movement and the free drawing movement at the end of the second decade of this century. From such stimuli developed a movement for education through art.*[21]

We call this movement for education through art *Geijutsu Kyoiku Undo* (Arts Education Movement).[22]

The Free Drawing Movement

The Free Drawing Movement *(Jiyuga Undo* in Japanese) in the 1920s is a historic event in the development of modern Japanese art education. As already stated, Kanae Yamamoto (1882–1946) was its originator. As a young man he had trained as an engraver of Western style line-blocks for book and magazine illustrations. He also graduated from Tokyo Fine Arts School in 1906, and later spent several years (1912–1916) in Europe.[23] On the way back to Japan, he had an opportunity to attend an exhibition of children's paintings in Moscow. The children's free expression in the exhibition impressed him, and on his return to Japan he proposed the idea of free expression in drawing education to Japanese art educators.[24]

Yamamoto's book of 1921 expressed his idea of the *Jiyuga* (free drawing).[25] Yukawa later summarised Yamamoto's great contribution to the innovation of theory and practice in Japanese art education:

> *After his return to Japan he advocated the idea that the teaching of 'Drawing' should develop the creative, aesthetic ability of each individual child. For this purpose he suggested that the child should be released from copying textbooks and be placed in nature, which he should be encouraged to draw as he felt. He told Japanese teachers that they should believe in the natural aesthetic potentiality that would be inherent in every child. ... The idea of 'JIYUGA' aroused an echo from young teachers, in spite of the opposition raised by conservative art teachers and educational authorities.*

Copying textbooks was rejected by many teachers, and children were seen everywhere – in fields, forests and towns – drawing directly from nature.[26]

Why did Japanese elementary classroom teachers soon accept Yamamoto's advocacy of free drawing? The answer to this question relates to both the positive and negative aspects of the national textbooks for drawing used in public primary schools. The Ministry of Education established *Shintei Gacho* (New Textbooks of Drawing) in 1910, and required that they serve as the only national textbooks until 1931. They reflect the instructional, or practical, means of teaching art. They considered children's developmental psychology, and included design methodology as part of the contents of a drawing programme. Teachers' manuals for each grade prescribed special teaching methods in each lesson plan. However, there remained the over-emphasis on a strict instructional approach to teaching art. The textbooks ignored the expressive aspect of art while they contained copyist or imitative drawing.[27]

Japanese elementary school classroom teachers neglected the positive aspects of the Japanese textbooks, and took the easy way of having their students copy from illustrations in the textbooks. Yukawa (1964) describes how the negative aspect of the textbooks was used:

This new series of textbooks was characterised by diversified contents, suggesting that the child copy, sketch, depict from memory, as well as make patterns and learn simple pictorial drawing. In these various activities it was suggested that pencils (both lead and colour), brushes and watercolours might be used according to the interests and needs of children of different grades. When these textbooks were put into actual use, however, many schoolteachers were not prepared to utilise them properly; the textbooks were used by children as a mere collection of pictures to copy. The idea conceived in the textbooks was little realised in classrooms.[28]

Yamamoto was the first one to point out publicly the continuation of copy work and the lack of expressive value in the new drawing textbooks. He believed that the purpose of drawing in education was for children to express themselves freely in artistic activities. His philosophy of art education provided another way for elementary school teachers to teach drawing. Those who were critical of the *Shintei Gacho* were willing to agree with his proposal. Yamamoto's free drawing movement brought several innovations. It denigrated copying from illustrations. It taught both teachers and their students the use of natural objects, out of doors, as the primary source of expression. Influenced by their environment, students produced drawings and paintings with spontaneity and with minimal instruction. European modernist art, especially French Impressionism, became an exemplar for this sort of school art practice. Dependence on the official national textbooks declined from 3.5 million distributed in 1921 to 2 million in 1926, while the distribution of teachers' editions declined from 75 thousand to zero in the same period.[29]

Counterbalance to a State-Controlled Policy

Yamamoto's movement only lasted for a decade but it clearly was appropriate for its time. He contributed to the decline of what Elliot Eisner has called the 'external mode' of curriculum development, which 'occurs in locations outside of the context in which the materials are to be used', and which 'takes form most often in textbooks'. Instead, Yamamoto provided art teachers with an alternative approach – the 'internal mode of curriculum development' (as Eisner has proposed) – where 'art teachers have a professional responsibility to develop programmes for the students they teach'.[30]

The free drawing movement, by providing a counterbalance to the state-controlled centralisation of art education, had the effect of depressing the prestige of reactionary bureaucrats, and increasing the prestige of liberals.[31] There have since been many such 'counterbalances';[32] accounts of which offer an alternative to the official history developed by the Ministry of Education. The free drawing movement is thus the root of a modern tradition of holding state-controlled art education in check.

Some American art educators are interested in adopting such practices.[33] Others, however, perceive that Japanese educational systems 'proceed vertically from a central power base'[34] and this worries them.[35] The balancing of governmental and non-governmental systems, which now has a seventy-year history, is not always obvious. In responding to American views in 1985, I wrote:

> *The Japanese style of setting national standards by guidelines and counterbalances to centralisation by nongovernmental art educators, however, is ambivalent. We have profitable feedback systems for discarding old art education practices and introducing new ones though we also have dangerous forces that cause the Ministry to overemphasise one particular ideology. Our energies and inventiveness for future art education can be harmed, and our counterbalance can be destroyed.*[36]

In short, the free drawing movement in the 1920s gave elementary school classroom teachers the freedom to develop their own curricula for the students they teach. It made Japanese art educators perceive the necessity of using their energies and inventiveness for future art education through the 'internal mode' of curriculum development in art education. It can be praised as the first counterbalance to state-controlled policy of art education in the history of modern Japanese art education.

Conclusion: Figure-Ground Relationship

The Free Drawing Movement also changed attitudes of Japanese art educators from the limited view of industrial drawing toward the more modernised concept of art as individual expression. Gradually there appeared the new conception of art, and the old view of drawing for industrial use disappeared.

Yamamoto used the Japanese term *Jiyu* (free) to equate children's freedom with the individualism of artists.[37] His efforts to replace the old concept of drawing with the new one, art, met with success. Both Japanese artists and art educators responded to works by Manet, Gauguin, Van Gogh, Renoir, Matisse, Cézanne, and Rodin. At that time Japanese art magazines provided information about European Impressionism and Post-Impressionism. Young Japanese artists returned to Japan after their study in Europe, and they produced their works of art in the style of modernism. 'The point about Renoir, Matisse, Cézanne, Van Gogh, and Gauguin,' says Kawakita (1974), 'was not so much a matter of the variations in their artistic styles as the insistence of all upon individualistic expression'. Kawakita concludes: 'the individualism of these artists agreed with the newest trends in thought and literature'.[38]

With Yamamoto, Japanese art educators believed that any copied drawing was harmful to children. They recognised that the art teacher should encourage his or her children to create their own style or mode of artistic expression. They gave students the freedom to express themselves. Yamamoto recommended that teachers should encourage children to express their impressions out-of-doors like the French Impressionists. Such methodology continues to the present and gains in popularity. 'At the zoo and in the parks in Japan one can see swarms of children with their teachers painting and drawing'.[39]

Brent Wilson, after his lecture to Japanese art educators at a national conference on art education in March 1989, asked whether Cizek or other European teachers had influenced the movement towards creative expression in Japanese art education.[40] The answer is that there was no such apparent influence during the first half of the century. We recognise Cizek as the father of child art through the Japanese edition of Herbert Read's *Education through Art,* available in 1953. Read mentioned Cizek twice and also listed Viola's works (1936, 1942) in his bibliography.[41] Japanese art educators thus read Viola's texts, and were introduced to Cizek's ideas, during the 1950s. For example, Shimoda illustrated Cizek's view of child art in 1959,[42] though the Japanese edition of Viola's *Child Art* did not become available until 1976.

It was Yamamoto who was the father of child art in Japan, as Cizek was elsewhere. Indeed, he was the first modernist in Japanese art education. His ideas were extended in the 1950s by those he had helped towards an understanding of modernism 30 years earlier. They began the 'creative art education movement', of which Shimoda has written that it 'advocates letting pupils develop their creative power by releasing them from repressions and also by featuring their free expression'.[43]

Japanese art educators translated such books as *Education through Art* (1943) by Read, *Children as Artists* (1947) by Tomlinson, and *Art and the Child* (1948) by Richardson. These were available in the 1950s,[44] and Japanese art educators could use them to support the creative art education movement. Such British sources helped them see their mission to reconstruct art education more clearly. They were able to reflect British ideas upon their own goals and methods because of their background of responding to the historic free drawing movement of the 1920s.

Just as Japanese art had influenced Impressionism and Post Impressionism,[45] the idea of European modernism influenced Japanese artists and art educators. European artists had turned to Japan to find something that European art had lacked. In a similar way, Japanese artists and art educators later turned to Europe to find those elements missing from their current practices. The story of the introduction of European modernism into Japanese school art practice therefore is reminiscent of what Eisner calls 'the idea that requires contrast in order to... have figure-ground relationship'.[46] It is a prime field for cross-cultural research in art and art education.

Originally published in the Journal of Art & Design Education, *Volume 10: 2, 1991.*

Notes and References

1. *Seiga Shinan* [Guide to Western Pictures] (1871). Tokyo, Ministry of Education. (T. Kwakami, trans. and ed.). Togai Kwakami is one of the early scholars of Western painting. He established a private art studio and school for the study of Western-style painting, ((1983), *Kodansha Encyclopedia of Japan*, vol. 4, Herts: International Book Distributors Ltd, p. 181). He instructed many Japanese who later became early leading masters of Western-style painting.
2. Okazaki, A. (1984), 'An overview of the influence of American art education literature on the development of Japanese art education' *Journal of Multi-cultural and Cross-cultural Research in Art Education*, 2: 1, pp. 82–95.
3. Rosenfield, J. M. (1971), 'Western-style painting in the early Meiji period and its crisis' in Shiverly, D. H. (Ed.), *Tradition and Modernization in Japanese Culture*, pp. 181–219. Princeton, NJ, Princeton University Press.
4. Kaneko, K. (1981), Meiji shoki no honyaku zuga kyokasho to sono genpon no kenkyu [On the translations of drawing books in the early Meiji era], *Ibaragi Daigaku Kyoiku Gakubu Kenkyu Kiyo* (Bulletin of the Faculty of Education, Ibaragi University), No. 30, pp. 19–34.
5. Miyamoto, S. (1978), *Shogaku Hutsu Gagakubon* (Drawing for use in Elementary Schools). Tokyo, Ministry of Education.
6. Smith, W. S. (1873), *Teacher's Manual of Free-Hand Drawing and Designing and Guide* to *Self-Instruction*, Boston: James R. Osgood & Co (reprinted in 1876, Boston, L. Prang & Co.).
7. See Macdonald, S. (1970), *The History and Philosophy of Art Education*, London: University of London Press, pp. 253–262; Chalmers, F. G. (1985), 'South Kensington and the colonies: David Blair of New Zealand and Canada' *Studies in Art Education*, 26, pp. 69–74; and Barbosa, A. M. (1984), 'Walter Smith's influence in Brazil and the efforts by Brazilian liberals to overcome the concept of art as an elitist activity' *Journal of Art & Design Education*, 3, pp. 233–246.

8. Kaneko, K. (1978), Zoku nihon no kindai bijutsu kyoiku shi (9) [A history of modern Japanese art education, Part 9), *Biiku Bunka* [Magazine for Art Education], 28: 7, pp. 42–45.

9. Kikuchi, B. D. (1907), *Japanese Education*, London: John Murray, p. 186.

10. Okazaki, A. (1985a), 'American influence on the history of Japanese art education: the case of Akira Shirahama' in Wilson, B. & Hoffa, H. (Eds.), *The History of Art Education: Proceedings from the Penn State conference,* pp. 59–66. Reston, VA, National Art Education Association of America.

11. Reischauer, E. O. (1981), *Japan: The Story of a Nation* (3rd edn.), Tokyo: Charles E. Tuttle Co, pp. 171–172.

12. For example, Beasley, W. G. (1982), *The Modern History of Japan* (third revised edn.), Tokyo: Charles E. Tuttle Co.

13. Dewey, J. (1919, 4 October), 'Liberalism in Japan: 1, the intellectual preparation' *The Dial*, 67, pp. 283–285.

14. Beasley, n. 12, p. 214.

15. Reischauer, E. O. (1964), *Japan: Past and present* (revised third edn.), Tokyo: Charles E. Tuttle Co, p. 93.

16. Eckroade, G. A. (1979), 'Political socialization and schooling: American views of Japanese educational politics from 1872 to 1952', Ph.D. thesis, The University of Maryland. (University Microfilms No. 80–12656).

17. Kobayashi, T. (1976), *Society, Schools and Progress in Japan*, Oxford: Pergamon Press, p. 30.

18. Sugiyama, A. (1983), Shin kyoiku undo, in *Kodansha Encyclopedia of Japan* (volume 7), p. 121. Hemel Hempstead, International Book Distributors Ltd.

19. Japanese National Institute for Educational Research (1978), Modernization of education in Japan (special issue), *Research Bulletin of the National Institute for Educational Research*, 17, p. 7.

20. *Ibid.* p. 65.

21. *Ibid.*

22. Ueno H. (1981), *Geijutsu Kyoiku Undo no Kenkyu* [Study of the Arts Education Movement], Tokyo: Kazama Shobo.

23. Sullivan, M. (1965), *Chinese and Japanese Art* (The Book of Art, Volume 9), New York: Grolier Inc., p. 145.

24. Okazaki, A. n. 2, pp. 86–87.

25. Yamamoto, K. (1921), *Jiyuga Kyoiku* [Education through Free Drawing], Tokyo: Arusu Co.

26. Yukawa, N. (1965), Art education of Japan (0. Muro trans.) *Kyoiku Bijutsu* [Art in Education], Special Issue, pp. 9–16.

27. Okazaki, A. n. 10, p. 64.

28. Yukawa, N. n. 26, p. 10.

29. Kaneko, K. (1979), Zoku nihon no kindai bijutsu kyoiku shi (13) [A history of modern Japanese art education, Part 13], *Biiku Bunka* [Magazine for Art Education], 29: 1, pp. 42–45.

30. Eisner, E. W. (1984), 'Alternative approaches to curriculum development in art education' *Studies in Art Education*, 25, pp. 259–264.

31. Dewey, J. n. 13, p. 283.

32. See Dobbs, S. M. (1983), 'Japan trail '83: American art education odyssey to the Orient' *Studies in Art Education*, 36: 6, pp. 4–11.

33. For example, Foster, M. S. (1975), 'Materials for teaching art in Japan: Textbooks and posters for the elementary grades' *Art Teacher*, 5: 2, pp. 23–26; and Wachowiak, F. (1985), *Emphasis Art: A Qualitative Art Program for Elementary and Middle Schools* (4th edn.), New York: Harper & Row.

34. Ott, R. W. & Hurwitz, A. L. (1984), 'Introduction: international art education' in Ott, R. W. & Hurwitz, A. L. (Eds.), *Art Education: An International Perspective,* pp. 1–8, University Park, PA, The Pennsylvania State University Press.

35. See Carson, J. (1981), 'What American art educators can learn from the Japanese' *Art Education*, 34: 6, pp. 42–44, 46; and Dobbs, n. 32.

36. Okazaki, A. (1985b), 'What American art educators learned from the Japanese: A response to Carson and Dobbs' *Art Education*, 38: 4, pp. 6–10.

37. Yamamoto, K. n. 25.

38. Kawakita, M. (1974), *Modern Currents in Japanese Art* (C.S. Terry, trans.), New York: John Weatherhill, p. 96.

39. Carson, J. n. 35, p. 43.

40. Wilson, B. (1989), Amerika to nihon niokeru modanisumu no bijutsu kyoiku [Modernists' art education in America and Japan: seasons of shaped beliefs and prophecies for the postmodern era] (M. Nagamachi, trans.), *Aato Edyukeishon* [Japanese Journal of Art Education], 1: 3, pp. 7-18.

41. Read, H. (1943), *Education through Art* (2nd edn.), London: Faber and Faber, pp. 204, 209, 312.

42. Shimoda, S. (1959), *E ni Miru Kodomo no Shinri* [Psychology of Children's Painting], Tokyo: Toto Syobo.

43. Shimoda, S. (1959), 'Internationalism and nationalism in art education from the standpoint of Japan' in *FEA Congress Report: Xth Congress of the International Federation for Education through Art,* pp. 229–231, Ravensburg, Ono Maier.

44. Japanese edition of *Education through Art* was available in 1953 under the title *Geizjutsu niyoru Kyoiku;* Japanese edition of *Children as Artists* was available in 1951 under the title *Geijutsuka tositeno Kodomotachi;* and Japanese edition of *Art and the Child* was available in 1958 under the title *Ai no Bijutsu Kyoushi.*

45. Read, H. (1974), *A Concise History of Modern Painting* (new edition), London: Thames and Hudson. Read describes the influence of Japanese woodcut prints on European painters (pp. 22–25).

46. Eisner, E. W. (1989), The professional education of teachers of art (invited address), Daigaku Bijutsu Kyoiku Gatsukai [Society of University Art Education Conference], Wakayama, Japan, 21 November, 1989.

Index

D

E

F

G

H

T

U

V

W

Y

Z